THE QUEST FOR COMMUNITY

D1218330

THE QUEST FOR

COMMUNITY

A Study in the Ethics of Order & Freedom

Robert Nisbet

ICS PRESS

Institute for Contemporary Studies
San Francisco, California

This book, a new edition of a classic work, is a publication in the ICS Series in Self-Governance, dedicated to the study of self-governing institutions.

First published by Oxford University Press in 1953. Issued in 1962 under the new title, *Community and Power*. Reissued in 1969 under the original title, *The Quest for Community*. This edition published by ICS Press, 1990.

Inquiries, book orders, and catalogue requests should be addressed to ICS Press, Institute for Contemporary Studies, Latham Square, 1611 Telegraph Avenue, Suite 902, Oakland, CA 94612. (510) 238-5010. FAX (510) 238-8440.

The analyses, conclusions, and opinions expressed in ICS Press publications are those of the authors and not necessarily those of the Institute for Contemporary Studies, or of the Institute's officers, directors, or others associated with, or funding, its work.

Library of Congress Cataloging-in-Publication Data

The quest for community / Robert A. Nisbet.
    p.   cm.
    ISBN 1-55815-058-7
    1. Ethics.   2. Social ethics.   3. Social sciences and ethics.
    1. Title.

BJ51.N56   1990
320.5'09'04'—dc20   90-32568
                                                    CIP

Contents

WILLIAM A. SCHAMBRA   FOREWORD

In 1953, the year Robert Nisbet's *Quest for Community* was published, scholars were beginning to suggest that strong ideological currents would no longer roil the waters of American politics—that the great, passionate movements of old had been softened and dissolved by a new politics of petty, haggling economic interests. Communism, one of the most ominous of the twentieth century's ideological movements, remained a threat to American freedom, but primarily as an armed, distinctly alien, and conspicuously pernicious system of thought—clearly totalitarian and "un-American," embodied in the blockades around Berlin and the horrors of Korean battlefields.

The Quest for Community, however, warned that totalitarianism had a different, far more "humane," and therefore more insidious face. For totalitarianism did not always present itself as a brutal, irrational, mysterious "focus of evil," according to Nisbet. It was in fact deeply rooted in—and drew its strength from its ability to satisfy—one of the most potent, rational, and decent of human impulses: the yearning for community.

"The quest for community will not be denied," Nisbet maintained, "for it springs from some of the powerful needs of human nature—needs for a clear sense of cultural purpose, membership, status, and continuity." The essence of totalitarianism—indeed, "the single most impressive fact in the twentieth century in Western society," noted Nisbet—was "the fateful combination of widespread quest for community . . . and the apparatus of political power" wielded by the centralized, territorial state.

Throughout most of its history, Nisbet observed, mankind had satisfied the yearning for membership, status, and belonging through the small communities of the human experience—communities like the family, church, neighborhood, and local fraternal, ethnic, and voluntary associations. The previous two centuries, however, had witnessed their decline, as the state, propelled by the unitarian, centralizing, rationalistic political theories of the eighteenth century, had set about to consolidate its power by displacing and absorbing the functions and authority of intermediate associations.

Once those associations no longer performed functions vital to the individual—no longer figured symbolically or materially in the central human dramas of birth, marriage, and death, in the provision of jobs and obligations that have meaning for our lives—they began to wither away, and the individual potentially stood alone. Such a condition represented the ideal to eighteenth-century thinkers, who eagerly anticipated the emergence of the rugged, self-sufficient individual in the wake of the destruction of the repressive intermediate associations. By the twentieth century, however, it had become clear that the sense of community was very much an enduring and urgent human need. Individualism, Nisbet suggested, had come to mean only isolation, loneliness, disconnectedness, alienation, and despair.

This provided fertile ground for the growth of the state. Not only could it absorb—and perform more efficiently and "humanely"—the social functions of the traditional, smaller communities, it also promised to alleviate the isolation and loneliness of the individual. This it would do through the vision of the "absolute, the total political community," a tightly knit, all-encompassing organization within which individuals once again would be given clearly defined status and purpose, a sense of comradeship and belonging, a sense of oneness with fellow citizens. "In its promise of unity and belonging," Nisbet noted, "lies much of the magic of totalitarian mystery, appeal and authority."

Every symbolic, cultural, and rhetorical device would be employed by the state to coax the individual into this vast new national family or neighborhood, as it penetrated every recess of society and assumed every practical and ritualistic communitarian function formerly performed by intermediate associations. Some devices were particularly compelling as forgers of national, political community. One of them was war.

War—even rhetorical substitutes for war, so long as they generated the same invigorating moral and social atmosphere—could pull the masses together in common endeavor, and infuse them with a sense of purpose and unity. As Nisbet noted in *Quest*, war could generate an "intoxicating atmosphere of spiritual unity that arises out of the common consciousness of participating in a moral crusade"; society attains its "maximum sense of organization and community and its most exalted sense of moral purpose during the period of war."

Another useful community-forging device was the focus of political power and ritual on a single, articulate national leader who could embody, speak for, and bind more closely together the new national family. "Only the man who represented not sections, not localities, not partial interests, but the *whole* of the people, the people in their mystic political oneness, would be able to save the people from corruptions and oppressions," Nisbet wrote.

An all-encompassing, national political community, possessed of all the practical and symbolic attributes of intimate human associations, bound together by the intoxicating spirit of war and by the equally intoxicating rhetoric of a charismatic leader—this was the genuine face of the total political state in the twentieth century, according to Nisbet. The true horror of it, he insisted, was precisely that it did *not* generally manifest itself in the brutal repression or naked terror of Soviet or Nazi totalitarianism. The national community was, rather, more commonly a benevolent and humanitarian provider of the material needs of its citizens, and a potent furnisher of relief from their unbearable sense of isolation. As Alexis de Tocqueville described it in one of Nisbet's favorite passages, its power was "absolute, minute, regular, provident and mild." In spite of its good intentions—or rather, precisely because of its good intentions—the national political community remained, in its all-encompassing reach, the most profound threat to freedom in human history, Nisbet insisted.

The Progressive Vision

Equipped with the new perspective provided by *Quest*, virtually all significant American political thought and behavior throughout the twentieth century could be understood as an effort to create and vindicate the great, national community. It had been no secret, of course, that the national state had grown significantly over the century, as Theodore Roosevelt's New Nationalism, Woodrow Wilson's New Freedom, and Franklin D. Roosevelt's New Deal had absorbed more and more of the social and political responsibilities of the states and local communities. Nisbet enabled us to understand, however, that this growth was not the "inevitable" fruit of historical progress or of modernization and industrialization, as liberalism commonly explained it, nor a mysterious, evil manifestation of alien socialism, as some conservatives believed, but instead a result of the state's capacity to satisfy the powerful, deep-rooted passion for community.

Suddenly, the rhetoric of twentieth-century progressive liberalism took on a new, more significant—and more ominous—meaning. The early Progressives—Herbert Croly, Walter Lippmann, John Dewey, Theodore Roosevelt—argued for a stronger state apparatus as a way to build a sense of unity, loyalty, common sacrifice, and mutual belonging among the American people. They argued for it, in short, in the name of national community. Croly, for example, hoped that a powerful and compelling "national idea" would then be bound together by a "religion of human brotherhood," which could be "realized only through the loving-kindness which individuals feel . . . particularly toward their fellow countrymen."

According to Progressive thought, one of the chief devices for forging national community was a powerful, articulate president who could nurture the unity of the people. As Wilson described the president, "the voices of the nation . . . unite in his understanding in a single meaning and reveal to him a single vision, so that he can speak . . . the common meaning of the common voice." No one appreciated better than Theodore Roosevelt the power of the presidential "bully pulpit," from which the people could be summoned to duty, brotherhood, and self-sacrifice, in the name of national oneness. Americans, he insisted, should strive to "make this nation . . . a democracy of true brotherhood, which knows neither North nor South, East nor West, which recognizes services and not pleasure as the ideal . . . which stands for each individual's performance of his own duty towards others even more than his insistence on his rights."

The Progressives discovered in World War I the valuable community-forging properties of war. As Lippmann contentedly remarked, "the war has given Americans a new instinct for order, purpose, and discipline" and has served to "draw Americans out of their local, group, and ethnic loyalties into a greater American citizenship." Once having experienced what Dewey called the "social possibilities of war," liberalism would never stop searching for war's "moral equivalent," which would serve to produce its sense of national unity and common moral purpose without the actual spilling of blood.

The progressive vision of national community, marked by a strong sense of national oneness, mutual belonging, and common sacrifice, pulled together by a powerful president as well as by the unifying spirit of real or imagined war, went on to form the theoretical underpinning of Franklin Roosevelt's New Deal. As Roosevelt put it once, the goal of the New Deal was to "[extend] to our national life the old principle of the local community." He was a master of the bully pulpit and of the moral equivalent of war. In his first inaugural address he suggested that the Great Depression demanded the same degree of national unity and sacrifice required in times of war. America, he insisted, must "move as a trained and loyal army willing to sacrifice for the good of a common discipline" and understand that "larger purposes will bind upon us all as a sacred obligation with a unity of duty hitherto evoked only in time of armed strife." The presidency he likened to the "leadership of [a] great army of our people dedicated to a disciplined attack upon our common problems."

Behind the steady expansion of the central state throughout the first half of the twentieth century, then, lay precisely the vision of national community that Nisbet had described in *Quest*. That same vision would go on to inspire John F. Kennedy's New Frontier, which urged Americans to "ask not what your country can do for you," but what "you can do for your country." Above all, it fueled Lyndon Johnson's Great Society and its tremendous expansion of the reach of the national state throughout the mid-1960s. "I see America as a family," Johnson proclaimed, "bound together by common ties of confidence and affection, and common aspirations toward duty and purpose." To him, the presidency's "first role and first responsibility is to help perfect that unity of the people." The moral equivalent of war he found in the "war on poverty," deliberately so named because, he believed, war evokes "cooperation . . . [and a] sense of brotherhood and unity."

Through most of the twentieth century, American conservatism put up but feeble intellectual resistance to liberalism's vision of national community, in large part because it did not comprehend—or chose to ignore or disparage—the inescapable human yearning for community that explained its appeal. Conservative thought remained in the thrall of eighteenth-century individualism and so posited against the national community only the splendid, isolated, rugged individual, solitarily pursuing wealth through the impersonal, anonymous mechanisms of the free market. Conservatives failed to comprehend the lessons of *Quest:* that the yearning for community "cannot be denied," and that by the twentieth century, individualism for most meant not noble self-sufficiency, but loneliness and alienation. Indeed, Nisbet suggested, conservatism's emphasis on individualism was not only politically unpalatable, but would also serve to augment, rather than circumscribe, the state, by fueling the loneliness and disconnectedness that drove isolated individuals into the arms of the national community. Small wonder, then, that the conservatism of the Eisenhower years left no lasting imprint on American politics, proving rather to be merely a brief period of sobriety between two intoxicating episodes of the politics of national community.

In short, when *Quest* was published in 1953, liberalism had no use for its message because it was wedded precisely to the idea of national community, the dangers of which the volume had been written to describe and avert. Conservatism was equally unprepared to listen because it championed an individualism that, Nisbet insisted, was of no use as a counterweight to the total state. In 1953, Nisbet's was a relatively lonely voice speaking against the increasing dominance of national community. *The Quest for Community* was not all jeremiad, however. It pointed toward a way to satisfy the quest for community without resort to national community—a way that would thereby preserve freedom. If the total political state flourished as a consequence of the erosion of traditional intermediate associations, then, Nisbet suggested, friends of liberty should fight for the preservation and propagation of these institutions. If function and authority could be restored to family, neighborhood, church, and local association, individuals might once again find the sense of status and belonging they sought, without appeal to the central state. The multiplicity of reinvigorated, autonomous associations, in turn, would serve as breakwaters or barriers to the reach of the state. As Nisbet put it, "in the division of authority and the multiplication of its sources lie the most enduring conditions of freedom."

The New Vision

The Quest for Community, therefore, provided not only a crucial intellectual framework for understanding the most significant political development of the twentieth century, the rise of the national community, but also the groundwork for a future politics that might reflect once again the understanding that intermediate associations could satisfy both the quest for community and the yearning for freedom. The dim outlines of that future politics began to emerge in the turmoil and confusion of the late 1960s and the early 1970s. If there was a central theme to the diverse and seemingly mutually contradictory currents of unrest during that period, it was the loss of faith in the idea of national community. As Theodore White noted in *The Making of the President, 1968,* "alienation" became such a fashionable word in the politics of that time precisely because it captured this new skepticism: It was the "negative of the old words, the old faith that America was a community, and that government served the community." At the same time, America began groping its way toward a new (or rather, very old) way of satisfying the yearning for community, within intimate, participatory groups like the family, neighborhood, and ethnic and voluntary association. In other words, it began to open itself to the truths written in the pages of *The Quest for Community.*

The New Left, for instance, came together as a major political movement when college students around the country discovered that others were "quite as lonely as they are . . . quite as hungry for some kind of community as they are," in the words of Mario Savio. That community, however, was not to be found in the central state, which now seemed a distant, alienating, impersonal, bureaucratic monstrosity. Instead it was to be found in the devolution of authority to small, tightly knit "participatory democracies," which would, in the words of the Port Huron Statement, "bring people out of isolation and into community." Likewise, the Black Power movement rejected the idea of a national, integrated community, in the name of reinvigorated ethnic association, within which, as Stokely Carmichael and Charles Hamilton suggested, blacks would be able "to reassert their own definitions, to reclaim their history, their culture; to create their own sense of community and togetherness."

More generally, however, a mood of dissatisfaction with the national community idea gripped millions of average American citizens, who by and large had retained allegiance to and continued to value family, church, neighborhood, and local community. In their eyes, the state had gone too far in its absorption of authority and function from treasured local associations. The state's bureaucracies and courts disparaged and assailed the moral and cultural standards of local communities as they manifested themselves in local laws and customs, suggesting that they were parochial, narrow-minded, reactionary, and even unconstitutional. Thus local communities were told they could neither send their children to nor have them pray in the local school, nor erect religious displays in public places, nor ban forms of expression considered offensive and pornographic, nor enforce standards of sexual conduct, nor define the circumstances in which abortion might be proper, nor enforce the law in such a way that genuine justice was accorded criminals and victims.

The New Left and Black Power reactions against national community proved ephemeral, of course, but the same cannot be said of the widespread, deep-seated resentment evoked in the average citizen by the state's heavy-handed interference with the prerogatives of local community. In fact, it became the salient political fact of the later 1970s and 1980s and remains so today. No candidate of either party, for instance, has captured the presidency in the past twenty years without denouncing intrusive, insensitive, overcentralized, bureaucratic government and promising to return authority and function to states, local communities, neighborhoods, and private associations. The language of national community has become electoral poison, while that of local community and intermediate association has become the key to electoral success.

The Democratic party, loath to give up the idea of national community, has paid a heavy price. Walter Mondale was swamped in the 1984 election after basing his campaign on the futile effort to revive allegiance to national community. "My America is a community, a family, where we care for each other," he told the unappreciative voters, while it is the president's pre-eminent task to "make up a community and keep us a community." Similarly, Michael Dukakis in 1988 sought unsuccessfully to persuade the voters to return to "a simple but a very profound idea—an idea as powerful as any in history. It is the idea of community . . . the idea that we are in this together . . . regardless of who we are or where we come from."

The only Democrat to win the presidency in the past two decades did so precisely because he seemed to speak for and reflect the traditional, neighborly values of Plains, Georgia, rather than a commitment to national community. Jimmy Carter professed to believe during his 1976 campaign that "our neighborhoods and families can succeed in solving problems where governments will always fail" and noted that "the only way we will ever put the government back in its place is to restore the families and neighborhoods to their proper places." Later, Carter would fall away from these views, deciding instead that Americans suffered from a "malaise" that could be cured only by a new dose of national community. The immediate remedy was, of course, yet another moral equivalent of war—in this case, a rather far-fetched war on the energy crisis, which, he maintained, could "help us conquer the crisis of the spirit in our country. It can rekindle our sense of unity . . . and give our Nation and all of us individually a new sense of purpose." In the election of 1980, the voters once again demonstrated just how unpersuasive and stale that language had become.

According to the Democrats, meanwhile, the Republican party remains committed to self-interested, laissez-faire individualism and to the unbridled workings of a heartless, exploitative, anticommunitarian marketplace. "Let us end this selfishness, this greed, this new championship of caring only for yourself," Mondale pleaded in 1984, urging voters to turn the Republicans out. In fact, however, the Republican party and a broad segment of American conservatives have adopted a very different message over the past decade. They seem to have heeded Nisbet's suggestion that rugged individualism is a bankrupt notion, failing, as it does, to address the quest for community. Republican party doctrine through the Reagan and Bush years has come to reflect Nisbet's view that the yearning for community is most satisfactorily and safely accomplished through return of authority and function to intermediate associations.

President Reagan's political career, for instance, was based on sentiments captured nicely in a speech from his 1976 campaign, in which he called for "an end to giantism, for a return to the human scale—the scale that human beings can understand and cope with; the scale of the local fraternal lodge, the church organization, the block club, the farm bureau.

It is activity on a small, human scale that creates the fabric of community."
After becoming president, he continued to insist that "the renaissance of
the American community, a rebirth of neighborhood—that is the heart and
soul of rebuilding America."

Similarly, George Bush repudiated the idea of national community in
his vision of "a nation *of* communities, of thousands of ethnic, religious,
social, business, labor union, neighborhood, regional and other organizations, all of them varied, voluntary and unique . . . a brilliant diversity spread
like stars, like a thousand points of light in a broad and peaceful sky."

Propelled by these new beliefs—having discovered the political futility
of preaching an individualism that signified only loneliness and alienation—the Republican party has drawn into its column millions of those
voters repelled by the national community's attempt to absorb and displace
local communities. It has reaped the electoral benefits of a new politics
based on the return of authority and function to intermediate associations—based, that is, on *The Quest for Community*'s prescriptions.

If that volume's message seemed somewhat out of tune with the
intellectual climate of 1953, in other words, it has become essential for
understanding the climate of this decade. American politics is no longer
merely the party of the state versus the party of the individual. There is a
new politics, characterized by the reaction against the national community
idea and the intrusive, centralized state—and equally against raw, self-
interested individualism—on behalf of local communities and associations.
As Nisbet had urged, intermediate associations are increasingly viewed once
again as the prime source of membership, status, and belonging—as the
chief agents of community. And as he had reminded us, it is precisely the
diversity, autonomy, and strength of local associations—their resistance to
total absorption into the national community—that has forestalled the
emergence of the total state in America. They have, indeed, proved to be
the indispensable breakwaters of freedom.

It must not be thought, however, that politics is the only realm within
which intermediate associations have enjoyed a renaissance. We understand
today that many of our most pressing social problems can be solved only
by the resurrection of such institutions as the family, neighborhood, church,
and local community. We are now prepared to admit, for instance, that the
problem of poverty—the threat of a permanent underclass forever depen-

dent on welfare—cannot be solved simply by providing yet more welfare. The cycle of poverty can be broken only by a renewal of self-confidence, self-discipline, and belief in hard work within the individual—and those values are taught chiefly by strong, vibrant families, churches, and neighborhoods.

Those same values, and so those same institutions, are indispensable weapons in the battle against drug abuse because they alone provide young people the inner resources to "just say no." Furthermore, they alone forestall the sense of alienation that makes drug abuse such an appealing escape.

We know now that stronger neighborhoods, perhaps beginning with nothing more elaborate than a "crime watch" network, are the best means for driving out drug traffickers and suppressing street crime in general. Within criminal justice today, there is a new school of thought called "community-oriented policing," the essence of which is that the police are more likely to succeed in enforcing the law where they stimulate and anchor their efforts in strong, closely knit neighborhood organizations. Where urban areas can generate a strong sense of local community, not only is crime suppressed, but physical deterioration is arrested and even reversed, business is lured back, and once-hopeless slums become thriving urban neighborhoods once again. It has also been found that public housing units turned over to the management of vital community organizations begin to improve in appearance, collect more rent, and experience less welfare dependency and fewer births out of wedlock.

Finally, it is understood today that the business of educating the young cannot proceed in the value-free, loosely structured environment so popular with educational reformers in the 1960s and 1970s. Instead, the most successful schools—schools that still manage to teach, even in the toughest neighborhoods—are those that develop a community of learning, with firm, shared standards of conduct, high and rigorously enforced expectations, instruction in moral values, and the cooperation and involvement of families and neighborhood.

Social policy as well, then, has grasped the importance of the community to be found in intermediate associations, assuring us that the new language of local community is in truth something considerably more than political rhetoric. Indeed, the *social* practice of intermediate associations is far greater than the *political* practice. For no matter how devoted to intermediate associations political candidates profess to be during campaigns, as soon as they are in charge of the state apparatus they come under intense pressure from intellectual, political, and media elites to "do something" about the problems before the nation. And to do—or at least to be seen to do—something almost invariably means mobilizing the bureaucratic mechanisms of the state, in what turns out to be yet another futile attempt by Washington to solve problems that are best left to local communities. Indeed, the effort usually turns out to be worse than futile. As often as not, the problems become worse because the state once again commences to absorb functions and authority from the intermediate associations, thereby only weakening further the most natural mechanisms for dealing with social distress.

If *The Quest for Community* poses any challenge for American politics and social policy, it would be to develop some way to translate the political rhetoric of small community into policy. The still sizable and potent state apparatus must be brought to reinforce, rather than to displace, intermediate associations. In many areas, of course, reinforcement would require simply relaxing the smothering embrace of the state. Thus Nisbet suggests a "new philosophy of *laissez faire*," but this time, not to create "conditions within which autonomous individuals could flourish," but "conditions within which autonomous groups could flourish." Perhaps, however, it is possible to do more. Ways might be found for the state apparatus actively to shore up local communities or to rebuild them where they have failed. But given the inclination of the national community to absorb all it sets out merely to assist, the work of reinvigorating mediating institutions is a formidable challenge indeed.

Conversely, and equally important, we need to find a way to translate the social practice of intermediate associations—which are tackling some of the most intractable of our nation's problems—into suitable political rhetoric. Our political leaders must occasionally find words, and the courage, to say that many useful things are in fact "being done" about problems, even though no high-visibility, high-cost federal initiative is planned. Given the pressures on national leaders to be seen to be doing something in their own right, though, reforming our public rhetoric is a formidable challenge too.

If Robert Nisbet's *The Quest for Community* is a powerful tool for understanding the political and social developments of the past three decades, it has a timeless and deeply personal dimension as well. For it is an elegant, deeply insightful treatment of the enduring human condition. As Nisbet points out, although the quest for community is the grand, definitive political fact of the past several centuries, it is also something with which we all struggle, in our individual, daily existence, wherever and whenever we live. For all its political and social truths, then, perhaps *Quest's* most valuable and abiding quality is that it invites us to reflect on our own personal condition and yearnings, on the meaning in our own lives of alienation, disconnectedness, belonging, family, and community. *The Quest for Community* is therefore both a profoundly prescient work of political sociology and a remarkably revealing mirror held up to our own souls.

Washington, D.C.
January 1990

PREFACE, 1970

No changes have been made in the text of the book for this printing. I do not mean to suggest that there are not changes I would make were I writing the book today. Such changes are inevitable: the product of time and circumstance, but chiefly of one's own development of thought. Any effort to incorporate these in a book written nearly twenty years ago would surely, however, be abortive. Far better, it seems to me, to leave the book with its imperfections rather than to try vainly to recapture the setting, mind, and mood from which the book originally sprang.

The changes would not be, in any event, changes of central theme or conclusion. I believe today, as I believed throughout the 1940s, when this book was beginning to take form in my mind, that the single most impressive fact in the twentieth century in Western society is the fateful combination of widespread quest for community—in whatever form, moral, social, political and the apparatus of political power that has become so vast in contemporary democratic states. That combination of search for community and existing political power seems to me today, just as it did twenty years ago, a very dangerous combination. For, as I argue in this book, the expansion of power feeds on the quest for community. All too often, power comes to resemble community, especially in times of convulsive social change and of widespread preoccupation with personal identity, moral certainty, and social meaning. This is, as I try to make clear throughout the book, the essential tragedy of modern man's quest for community. Too often the quest has been through channels of power and revolution which have proved destructive of the prime sources of human community. The structure of political power which came into being three centuries ago on the basis of its eradication of medieval forms of community has remained—has indeed become ever more—destructive of the contexts of new forms of community.

No, the central argument of the book would remain the same, were I writing it today instead of twenty years ago. There would be, however, some changes of emphasis, if only as a means of making clearer the central argument of the book. Let me indicate briefly what these few changes would consist of.

In the first place, I would, to the best of my ability, preclude any possible supposition on the reader's part that there is in this book any lament for the old, any nostalgia for village, parish, or other type of now largely erased form of social community of the past. Rereading the book today, I am frank in saying that I cannot find a nostalgic note in the entire book. It is not the revival of old communities that the book in a sense pleads for; *it is the establishment of new forms:* forms which are relevant to contemporary life and thought. What I have tried very hard to do, however, is to show that a structure of power capable of obliterating traditional types of community is capable of choking off new types of community. Hence the appeal, in the final pages of the book, for what I call a new *laissez faire*, one within which groups, associations, and communities would prosper and which would be, by their very vitality, effective barriers to further spread of unitary, centralized, political power.

There is, second, the theme of alienation. I would, I think, give it even greater importance in the book today than I did when I wrote it twenty years ago, well before the contemporary deluge of books and articles on alienation had begun. For it has become steadily clearer to me that alienation is one of the determining realities of the contemporary age. It will not do to relegate it to the realm of the symbols which influence intellectuals and which do not, at first thought, seem to implicate the lives of others in society. In the first place, intellectuals' symbols, taken as a whole, widely and often deeply influence popular behavior. For we live in an age of rather high literacy. And in the second place the same currents of thought and feeling which have caught up intellectuals have also, in different ways, at different levels, caught up large numbers of persons who do not pretend to be intellectuals but who are responsive nonetheless to the urgencies of the time. For many of them, too, alienation is a conspicuous state of mind.

By alienation I mean the state of mind that can find a social order remote, incomprehensible, or fraudulent; beyond real hope or desire; inviting apathy, boredom, or even hostility. The individual not only does not feel a part of the social order; he has lost interest in being a part of it. For a constantly enlarging number of persons, including, significantly, young persons of high school and college age, this state of alienation has become profoundly influential in both behavior and thought. Not all the manufactured symbols of togetherness, the ever-ready programs of human relations, patio festivals in suburbia, and our quadrennial crusades for presidential candidates hide the fact that for millions of persons such institutions as state, political party, business, church, labor union, and even family have become remote and increasingly difficult to give any part of one's self to.

There is another way of noting this: through the prevailing reactions of intellectuals to social and economic issues; Schumpeter, in his great book *Capitalism, Socialism and Democracy,* wrote that one of the flaws of capitalism is its inexhaustible capacity for alienating the intellectuals. This is true, but it needs qualification. For a long time capitalism at least supplied the motive power for revolt among intellectuals. This was not only an important manifestation of social energy but also a subtle form of identification. (No one revolts against what he is totally alienated from.) I am thinking of such matters as the struggle for the rights of the underprivileged, labor unions, ethnic equality, and the like. But it is hard to miss the fact that today there is a kind of alienation even from the ideological issues of capitalism, leading one to wonder what is to supply the friction in the future for social change.

There are several common ways of describing, or specifying, alienation—all to be found in the literature of the West, at least since the Conservative revolt against rationalism at the beginning of the nineteenth century. Let me indicate them briefly. They should be noted even though I do not, as I shall explain, regard them as fundamental to our problem.

There is, first, alienation from the past. Man, it is said, is a time-binding creature; past and future are as important to his natural sense of identity as the present. Destroy his sense of the past, and you cut his spiritual roots, leaving momentary febrility but no viable prospect of the future. In our age, as we are frequently told, past and present are not merely separated categories but discontinuous ones in the lives of large numbers of persons, more than a few of whom have sought escape from their past. It is sometimes said that this detachment from past is an inevitable consequence of popular democracy; it is not easy for an equalitarian, status-based present to remain on terms of intelligibility with an inequalitarian, class-based past. Whatever the basis, loss of a sense of the past is an important matter, if only for its functional necessity to revolt. How can there be a creative spirit of youthful revolt when there is nothing for revolt to feed upon but itself?

Then, there is alienation from physical place and nature. In many societies, and for long periods of time, men identify themselves by where they are born and sink their roots. We still pretend interest in place of birth on job and school admission forms, but it has become at bottom a useless ritual and will probably disappear as have race and religion, identifying attributes which also were once deemed important as marks of identity. Given the slow erosion of regions and localities in present-day mass culture, under the twin impact of nationalism and economism, it doesn't really matter where one comes from—that is, in terms of business and politics. Psychologically it may be an important matter, for disruption of a sense of place is no venial matter in the human being's effort to identify himself—to himself as well as others. It is said that our spreading technological insulation from nature—from heat and cold, the changing seasons, the visible stellar bodies and the whole landscape—is also a factor in this type of alienation. Surely, no civilization, no group within a civilization, has ever removed itself as far from nature as we have.

Closely related is alienation from things. Here I mean property, hard property, the kind that one can touch, be identified with, become ennobled or debased by, be driven to defend against attack. One remembers the use Galsworthy made of property in *The Forsyte Saga*. And Schumpeter warned us that the transition from capitalism to socialism would not even be noticed by a population whose idea of property is not hard property but soft property—shares and equities in something distant, personally unmanaged, and impersonal. It is said that the passion for automobiles among American boys, a passion which can destroy or weaken educational aspiration, and account for much juvenile delinquency in this country, is a consequence, at least in part, of the deep-seated desire for hard property that is thwarted in so many areas of our society today.

All of these are indeed manifestations of alienation, but I do not regard them as fundamental types. Not, at least, as they are stated. For, in each of them, an important link is left out: the social bond; that is, community. I would suggest, for example, that man has never had a creative or sustaining relation to the past except through certain types of communal relationship that themselves bind past, present, and future. When we find a society or age rich and creative in its sense of the past, we are in the presence of something I can only think of as the telescoping of generations. In genuinely creative societies—the Athens of Aeschylus, the Florence of Michelangelo—there is a telescoping of the generations that is not hidden by all the more manifest facts of individual revolt. Past and present have a creative relationship not because of categories in men's minds but because of certain social bonds which themselves reach from past to future.

These are ties which have become, like many others, weak and rootless in the present day. And this, I suggest, is why alienation from the past so obviously affects youth, and helps make the problem of coming to adulthood so widely painful and baffling. How, apart from stable ties with preceding generations, can the image of adulthood be kept clear in a society? There are natural barriers between boyhood and manhood in all places and all times, but these become formidable only in a society where responsibility for making men has devolved almost exclusively upon the small and isolated conjugal family. Other ages had kindred, class, race, and similar "genetic" unities. Only the archaist would say these specific bonds are necessary, but it is difficult to see any new relationships in our fragmented and often atomized society that show signs of replacing the old ones.

Similarly, I think alienation from place and property turns out to be, at bottom, estrangement from close personal ties which give lasting identity to each. Native heath is hardly distinguishable from the human relationships within which landscape and animals and things become cherished and deeply implanted in one's soul. So far as love of, and affinity with, nature is concerned, we have to remember that we are dealing here with a state of mind that has itself cultural roots—chiefly in the romantic revival at the end of the eighteenth century. It is not easy to find love for natural elements in most of the world's literature. Nature was, and remained for our forefathers in this country down until two or three generations ago, a vast force to cope with, to attack, to be often defeated by, but seldom admired or loved. And I know sections of the world where dense communities of persons have been separated from nature for centuries, but where, whatever else may be wrong, alienation is hardly to be noticed. The same is true of property. It is not hardness or softness of property; it is the kind of relationship within which property exists that is crucial. If it is a close and significant relationship, the sense of ownership will be a vital one no matter what the form of property.

I believe, then, that community is the essential context within which modern alienation has to be considered. Here I have reference not so much to a state of mind—although that is inevitably involved—as I do to the more concrete matters of the individual's relation to *social function* and *social authority*. These, I would emphasize, are the two supports upon which alone community, in any reasonably precise sense, can exist and influence its members.

There are countless persons today for whom the massive changes of the past century have meant a dislocation of the contexts of function: the extended family, neighborhood, apprenticeship, social class, and parish. Historically, these relationships had both depth and inclusiveness in individual life because they themselves had functional significance; because, however informally, they had a significant relationship to that distribution of function and authority which is a society's organization. And because they had this, they had meaning in the lives of individuals. Having function, they could create a sense of individual function, which is one of the two prime requirements of community.

The other is authority. By authority, I do not mean power. Power, I conceive as something external and based upon force. Authority, on the other hand, is rooted in the statuses, functions, and allegiances which are the components of any association. Authority is indeed indistinguishable from organization, and perhaps the chief means by which organization, and a sense of organization, becomes a part of human personality. Authority, like power, is a form of constraint, but, unlike power, it is based ultimately upon the consent of those under it; that is, it is conditional. Power arises only when authority breaks down.

Apart from authority, as even the great anarchists have insisted, there can be no freedom, no individuality. What the anarchists said, and this is the splendid essence of anarchism and the link between it and such conservatives as Tocqueville and Acton, is, first, that there must be *many* authorities in society, and, second, that authority must be closely united to objectives and functions which command the response and talents of members. Freedom is to be found in the interstices of authority; it is nourished by competition among authorities.

It is well to emphasize this, for it is the essential context of treatment of the problem of freedom. We are prone to see the advance of power in the modern world as a consequence, or concomitant, of the diminution of individual freedom. But a more useful way would be to see it in terms of the retreat of authority in many of the areas of society within which human beings commonly find roots and a sense of the larger whole. The alleged disorganization of the modern family is, in fact, simply an erosion of its natural authority, the consequence, in considerable part, of the absorption of its functions by other bodies, chiefly the state.

The abandonment by a university faculty, a labor union, or a church, of authority over its membership and its essential functions and responsibilities will inevitably be accompanied by the expansion of external, administrative power, for a vacuum is intolerable. Unhappily, remote power, however omnipotent and encompassing, can oftentimes come to seem preferable to authority at close quarters, a fact that has much to do with the history of centralization and bureaucracy.

Authority and liberation, convention and revolt—these are the creative rhythms of civilization. They are as vivid in the history of politics as in the histories of art and poetry, science and technology, education and religion. If there is not a recognized authority or convention, how can there be the occasional eruption of revolt and liberation that both the creative process and the free mind require? Apart from authority there can be no really vital social relationship in society; this is as true in the family as it is in the university or the church. It is power, not authority, that seeks homogeneity, regimentation, and the manipulated articulation of parts by hierarchies of administrators. And it is the competition of authorities within society at large that, above most things I can think of, keeps a society mobile and free. "Multiply your associations and be free," wrote the great Proudhon.

It is the ideology of power, I believe, that has had the most to do in the history of modern society with the general reduction of social differences and conflicts, the leveling and blurring of social authorities, and the gradual filling of the interstices within which creativeness and freedom thrive. It is power of this type—not merely absolute but often bland, providential, minute, and sealing—that has reduced so many of the social and cultural frictions that cultural advancement has depended upon, historically; that even intellectual energy depends upon. And it is power in this same sense that has destroyed or weakened many of the established contexts of function and natural authority—and, by its existence, choked off the emergence of new contexts and thus created a great deal of the sense of alienation that dominates contemporary man.

Here I come to another point that I wish I had given stronger and clearer emphasis: the wide diffusion of the ideology of centralized power in contemporary society. Except for a few paragraphs in the final chapters, I have dealt with centralization as though it were confined to processes of formal political government. This is inadequate.

The ideology of power that I am concerned with is to be seen in other and frequently decisive areas of modern society—in city government and planning, business enterprises, public housing projects, churches, great universities, and school systems. It would be hard indeed to say that centralized power over human life and aspiration, and all the administrative techniques that go with it, is more dangerous in the larger areas of national government than it is in the relatively small institutional areas. ("Small" is perhaps not the word for some of the school systems, corporations, labor unions, churches, and cities of the present age.) For it is in the latter that we have our direct and day to day relation to society.

From the ideology of unified and total power has come all too often a conception of human organization not very different, at bottom, from a military post. No relationship must exist that is not contemplated by central command and assimilated into formal hierarchy of external administration. We see this in school systems today, especially in large cities (the danger of Federal assistance to public schools is not the source of the money but the predictable incorporation of such assistance in both established and emerging bureaucracies which, like all bureaucracies, especially at the lowest levels, will make fidelity to letter of the law a transcending objective, making it even more difficult to keep alive the spirit within which good teaching alone can thrive). We see it in our vast and choked cities where to talk of community is to talk nonsense. We see it in a great deal of the planning—both governmental and private—of housing.

Consider some of the tragedies perpetrated in the name of slum clearance. To be moved from a slum, which, after all, if it is old enough, has a culture and more or less natural gathering places, to an architecturally grim, administratively monolithic, housing project may indeed "clean up" the streets for a time and give surrounding areas higher economic value to absentee owners. But the ultimate consequence, a depressing amount of experience shows all too often, may be a new type of slum, one with little hope of culture or community, one in which gangs and violence as well as alienation will be the logical and predictable consequence.

There are countless other aggregates in modern society not very different, in terms of function and authority, from the public housing project. One thinks of the innumerable suburbs that have sprung up since the Second World War, particularly bedroom suburbs, where there is little more sense of community than there is in the housing project. How could there be? Community is the product of people working together on problems, of autonomous and collective fulfillment of internal objectives, and of the experience of living under codes of authority which have been set in large degree by the persons involved. But what we get in many sections of the country is a kind of suburban horde. There is no community because there are no common problems, functions, and authority. These are lacking because, under a kind of "rotten borough" system, effective control is vested elsewhere—in boards, councils, and offices of counties, districts, or adjacent cities.

It is not different, at bottom, in other types of association. Where power is external or centralized, where it relieves groups of persons of the trouble of making important decisions, where it is penetrating and minute, then, no matter how wise and good it may be in principle, it is difficult for a true community to develop. Community thrives on self-help (and also a little disorder), either corporate or individual, and everything that removes a group from the performance of or involvement in its own government can hardly help but weaken the sense of community. People do not come together in significant and lasting associations merely to be together. They come together to do something that cannot easily be done in individual isolation. But when external absorption of power and function threatens to remove the basis of community, leaving functionless and authorityless aggregates, what else but the social horde and alienation can be the result?

It will be said that the problems presented in this respect are difficult, perhaps impossible, given the orientation toward mass democracy that so much of our recent history shows, given an industrialism that seems to leap over communities and even regions, and given the craving for irreconcilable cultural and social ends that a great deal of popular behavior exemplifies in present-day America. They are indeed difficult problems, although I question whether the scale involved is any greater, really, than the transformations of society and landscape that we have seen taking place under other compulsions during the past thirty years.

The main, and perhaps insuperable difficulty is perspective. May I repeat here what I wrote in Chapter Eleven: "The modern facts of political mechanism, centralization, and collectivism are seen in the perspective of inevitable development in modern history. They seem to be the very direction of history itself." It is this view, I continue to think, that presents our greatest difficulty, for, as Martin Buber pointed out to us so brilliantly a decade ago in his *Paths in Utopia,* the intellectual's dread of utopianism, his pious desire to be historically "realistic," his premise of a track of historical development that somehow we must remain on, whatever the costs in regimentation, is, of all obstacles, the most decisive in the problem of social planning. This is one reason why, I think, so much social thought, until recently, has seemed sterile from the point of view of those whose business it is to make the basic decisions in organizational and community work.

More than anything else it is the massive transformation of the American social scene since the Second World War that has focused attention upon the relative poverty of resources in the social sciences. Vast industrial relocations, redevelopments of central cities, city and regional planning, community organization, serious efforts on the part of civic agencies to prevent, rather than merely punish, crime, the innumerable social and psychological problems involved in the administering of both governmental and private social security systems—all of these and other problems have led to an almost desperate turning to social scientists for help.

Of a sudden, a good deal of so-called social science was proved empty or irrelevant despite the public pretense to the contrary of some academic intellectuals. It became evident that more reliable knowledge—slim though it was—frequently lay in the experiences of social workers, businessmen, architects, city-managers, and politicians than in whole volumes of the social science journals. Several generations of social thought based upon determinism had produced very little of value to society. The familiar prescriptions of governmental ownership or management, by which liberals had for decades salved their social consciences, began to turn sour in the mouth when it became apparent that the real problem often was not *whether* the government shall render aid, but *how*. In any event, the prescriptions themselves have begun to pall, and this may be a healthy sign even if it does mean national elections with issues resembling epitaphs of the past rather than battle cries of present and future.

Happily there have been some major changes in the social sciences in recent decades. It seems to me that more knowledge concerning groups and communities—usable, relevant knowledge—has come forth in the last fifteen years than in the preceding fifty. There are, of course, many reasons for this, but high among them, I think the evidence shows clearly, is a widespread abandonment of deterministic premises concerning history. This done, it has not been really difficult to disengage moral and political predilections from research in a way that would have seemed inconceivable in the 1920s and 1930s when so-called social science was all too often a witches' brew of moralism, social work, and philosophy of history.

At first thought, utopianism and a genuine social science may seem to be incompatible. But they are not. Utopianism is compatible with every thing but determinism, and it can as easily be the over-all context of social science as can any other creative vision. I make no apology for the frankly utopian cast of the final pages of my book. I wish only that I had made it even more emphatic. Utopianism, after all, is social planning, and planning, as I have stressed in the final pages, is indispensable in the kind of world that technology, democracy, and high population bring. Conservatives who aimlessly oppose planning, whether national or local, are their own worst enemies.

What is needed, however, is planning that contents itself with the setting of human life, not human life itself. To plan for masses of individuals is not merely a hopeless exercise in human calculus; it is, of all ways I can think of, the one most likely to produce that combination of externally contrived goals and unconditional power in support of these goals that is the substance of tyranny and the path to annihilation of personality. It is in this light that I plead, at the end of the book, for a new *laissez faire*, one concerned, not with imaginary economic atoms in a supposed legal void, but with the groups and associations that we are given in experience, and the integrity and reasonable autonomy of which are the prime conditions of individual integrity and autonomy.

Robert A. Nisbet
Riverside, California
October 1961
Revised version, 1969

PREFACE TO THE FIRST EDITION

This book deals with political power—more specifically, with the impact of certain conceptions of political power upon social organization in modern Western society. It begins with what I have called the loss of community, for of all symptoms of the impact of power upon human personality in the contemporary Western world the most revealing seems to me to be the preoccupation, in so many spheres of thought and action, with community—community lost and community to be gained. I do not doubt that behind this preoccupation there lie many historical changes and dislocations—economic, religious, and moral. But I have chosen to deal with the *political* causes of the manifold alienations that lie behind the contemporary quest for community. Moral securities and allegiances always have a close and continuing connection with the centers and diffusions of authority in any age or culture. Fundamental changes in culture cannot help but be reflected in even the most primary of social relationships and psychological identifications. Put in these terms, we cannot possibly miss the revolutionary importance, in modern Western society, of the political State and of idea systems which have made the State pre-eminent. With all regard for the important social and psychological changes that have been induced by technological, economic, and religious forces in modern society, I believe that the greatest single influence upon social organization in the modern West has been the developing concentration of function and power of the sovereign political State. To regard the State as simply a legal relationship, as a mere superstructure of power, is profoundly delusive. The real significance of the modern State is inseparable from its successive penetrations of man's economic, religious, kinship, and local allegiances, and its revolutionary dislocations of established centers of function and authority. These, I believe, are the penetrations and dislocations that form the most illuminating perspective for the twentieth-century's obsessive quest for moral certainty and social community and that make so difficult present-day problems of freedom and democracy. These are the essential subject matter of this book.

Sections of this book have appeared in *The American Journal of Sociology, The Journal of Politics, The Journal of the History of Ideas,* and in the book, *Studies in Leadership,* edited by Alvin Gouldner and published by Harper and Brothers. Permission to republish these sections in slightly revised form is gratefully acknowledged.

References in the book have been held to a bare minimum, and they can do no more than suggest the extent of my indebtedness to the many minds that have dealt with various aspects of my subject. To all of them I gladly record here an appreciation not the less genuine for its necessary generality. There are certain individuals to whom I owe thanks of a special kind. The first is the late Frederick J. Teggart, for many years Professor of Social Institutions at the University of California at Berkeley. The second is George P. Adams, Mills Professor of Mental and Moral Philosophy and Civil Polity at the same university. It is unnecessary to attempt to indicate the precise nature of my debt to each; suffice it to say that apart from interests and insights gained originally from both of these men it is difficult for me to imagine any part of this book's coming into existence. I desire to express appreciation also to Robert M. MacIver whose learned and perceptive writings on the nature of association and authority were the beginnings of my own interest in the subject and have remained valued sources of enlightenment. It is a pleasure to acknowledge gratefully here the suggestions and encouragement of my friends Reinhard Bendix, Kingsley Davis, Robert Merton, and Maria Rogers, all of whom took time to read an early draft of the manuscript. Naturally, no one of them is to be held responsible for any shortcomings the book may have.

Finally, I must express deepest appreciation to the University of California, in part for leave and financial assistance which made possible much of the writing of the book, but chiefly for the privilege of membership in its distinguished company of teachers and scholars.

Robert A. Nisbet
Berkeley
December 1952

PART ONE

COMMUNITY AND THE
PROBLEM OF ORDER

THE LOSS OF COMMUNITY

One may paraphrase the famous words of Karl Marx and say that a specter is haunting the modern mind, the specter of insecurity. Surely the outstanding characteristic of contemporary thought on man and society is the preoccupation with personal alienation and cultural disintegration. The fears of the nineteenth-century conservatives in Western Europe, expressed against a background of increasing individualism, secularism, and social dislocation, have become, to an extraordinary degree, the insights and hypotheses of present-day students of man in society. The widening concern with insecurity and disintegration is accompanied by a profound regard for the values of status, membership, and community.

In every age there are certain key words which by their repetitive use and re-definition mark the distinctive channels of faith and thought. Such words have symbolic values which exert greater influence upon the nature and direction of men's thinking than the techniques used in the study or laboratory or the immediate empirical problems chosen for research. In the nineteenth century, the age of individualism and rationalism, such words as *individual, change, progress, reason,* and *freedom* were notable not merely for their wide use as linguistic tools in books, essays, and lectures but for their symbolic value in convictions of immense numbers of men. These words were both the outcome of thought and the elicitors of thought. Men were fascinated by their referents and properties.

All of these words reflected a temper of mind that found the essence of society to lie in the solid fact of the discrete individual—autonomous, self-sufficing, and stable—and the essence of history to lie in the progressive emancipation of the individual from the tyrannous and irrational statuses handed down from the past. Competition, individuation, dislocation of status and custom, impersonality, and moral anonymity were hailed by the rationalist because these were the forces that would be most instrumental in emancipating man from the dead hand of the past and because through them the naturally stable and rational individual would be given an environment in which he could develop illimitably his inherent potentialities. Man was the primary and solid fact; relationships were purely derivative. All that was necessary was a scene cleared of the debris of the past.

If there were some, like Taine, Ruskin, and William Morris, who called attention to the cultural and moral costs involved—the uprooting of family ties, the disintegration of villages, the displacement of craftsmen, and the atomization of ancient securities—the apostles of rationalism could reply that these were the inevitable costs of Progress. After all, it was argued — argued by liberals and radicals alike—in all great ages of achievement there is a degree of disorder, a snapping of the ties of tradition and security. How else can the creative individual find release for his pent-up powers of discovery and reason if the chains of tradition are not forcibly struck off?

This was the age of optimism, of faith in the abstract individual and in the harmonies of nature. In Mark Twain's *Huckleberry Finn,* what we are given, as Parrington points out in his great study of American thought, is the matchless picture of a child of nature revolting against the tyrannies of village, family, and conventional morality. It is a revolt characterized, not by apprehensiveness and insecurity, but by all the confidence of the frontier. In the felicities and equalities of nature Huck finds joyous release from the cloistering prejudices and conventions of old morality. Truth, justice, and happiness lie in man alone.

In many areas of thought and imagination we find like perspectives. The eradication of old restraints, together with the prospect of new and more natural relationships in society, relationships arising directly from the innate resources of individuals, prompted a glowing vision of society in which there would be forever abolished the parochialisms and animosities of a world founded upon kinship, village, and church. Reason, founded upon natural interest, would replace the wisdom Burke and his fellow conservatives had claimed to find in historical processes of use and wont, of habit and prejudice.

"The psychological process which social relations were undergoing," Ostrogorski has written of the nineteenth century, "led to the same conclusions as rationalism and by the same logical path-abstraction and generalization." Henceforth, man's social relations "were bound to be guided not so much by sentiment, which expressed the perception of the particular, as by general principles, less intense in their nature perhaps, but sufficiently comprehensive to take in the shifting multitudes of which the abstract social groups were henceforth composed, groups continually subject to expansion by reason of their continual motion."[1]

Between philosophers as far removed as Spencer and Marx there was a common faith in the organizational powers of history and in the self-sufficiency of the individual. All that was needed was calm recognition of the historically inevitable. In man and his natural affinities lay the bases of order and freedom. These were the affirmations that so largely dominated the thought, lay as well as scholarly, of the nineteenth and early twentieth century. All of the enmity of the French Enlightenment toward the social relationships that were the heritage of the Middle Ages became translated, during the nineteenth century, into a theoretical indifference to problems of the relation of individual security and motivation to contexts of association and cultural norm. Both freedom and order were envisaged generally in terms of the psychology and politics of individual release from the old.

We see this in the social sciences of the age. What was scientific psychology but the study of forces and states of mind within the natural individual, assumed always to be autonomous and stable? Political science and economics were, in their dominant forms, concerned with legal and economic atoms—abstract human beings—and with impersonal relationships supplied by the market or by limited general legislation. All social and cultural differences were resolved by the rationalist into differences of quantity and intensity of individual passions and desires. The stability of the individual was a function of his unalterable instincts and his sovereign reason; the stability of society was guaranteed by the laws of historical change. The two goals of scientific universality and moral emancipation from the past became largely indistinguishable in the philosophy and the social science of the age. Bentham's boast that he could legislate wisely for all of India from the recesses of his own study was hardly a piece of personal eccentricity. It sprang from a confidence both in reason and in the ineradicable sameness and stability of individuals everywhere.

Above everything towered the rationalist's monumental conviction of the *organizational* character of history—needing occasionally to be facilitated, perhaps, but never directed—and of the self-sufficing *stability* of the discrete individual.

Two

Today a different set of words and symbols dominates the intellectual and moral scene. It is impossible to overlook, in modern lexicons, the importance of such words as *disorganization, disintegration, decline, insecurity, breakdown, instability,* and the like. What the nineteenth-century rationalist took for granted about society and the nature of man's existence, as the result of an encompassing faith in the creative and organizational powers of history, the contemporary student of society makes the object of increasing apprehension and uncertainty.

At the present time there is in numerous areas of thought a profound reaction to the rationalist point of view. No longer are we convinced that basic organizational problems in human relations are automatically solved by readjustments of political or economic structures. There is a decided weakening of faith in the inherent stability of the individual and in the psychological and moral benefits of social impersonality. Impersonality, moral neutrality, individualism, and mechanism have become, in recent decades, terms to describe pathological conditions of society. Nearly gone is the sanguine confidence in the power of history itself to engender out of the soil of disorganization seeds of new and more successful forms of social and moral security.

A concern with cultural disorganization underlies almost every major philosophy of history in our time. The monumental historical synthesis of a Toynbee represents anew the effort of the prophetic historian to find in the casual forces of history meanings that will illuminate the darkness of the present age. Like St. Augustine's *City of God,* written to sustain the faith of fifth-century Christians, Toynbee's volumes, with all their magnificent learning and religious insight, are directed to the feelings of men who live beneath the pall of insecurity that overhangs the present age. One cannot resist the suspicion that for most of Toynbee's readers the governing interest is in the sections of *A Study of History* that deal not with genesis and development but with decline and disintegration. And it is hard to put aside the suspicion that Toynbee himself has reserved his greatest interpretative skill for the melancholy phenomena of death and decay, a circumstance which, like Milton's characterization of Satan, may bespeak an irresistible, if morally reluctant, love for his subject. Toynbee's cataloguing of historic stigmata of social dissolution—schism in society and the soul, archaism, futurism, and above all, the process of "deracination," the genesis of the proletariat—reads like a list of dominant themes in contemporary thought.

Are not the works of the major prophets of the age, Niebuhr, Bernanos, Berdyaev, Sorokin, Spengler, and others, based foremost upon the conviction that ours is a sick culture, marked by the pathologies of defeat and failure of regenerative processes? Is it not extraordinary how many of the major novelists and poets and playwrights of the present age have given imaginative expression to themes of dissolution and decay—of class, family, community, and morality? Not only are these themes to be seen among the Titans—Proust, Mann, Joyce, Kafka, Eliot—but among a large and increasing number of secondary or popular writers. It is hard to miss the centrality of themes of dissolution in contemporary religious and literary expressions and the fascination that is exerted by the terminology of failure and defeat. Disaster is seen as the consequence of process rather than event, of "whimper" rather than "bang," to use the words of T. S. Eliot.

How extraordinary, when compared with the optimism of half a century ago, is the present ideology of lament. There is now a sense of disorganization that ranges all the way from the sociologist's concern with disintegration of the family and small community to the religious prophet's intuition that moral decay is enveloping the whole of Western society. Premonitions of disaster have been present in all ages, along with millennial hopes for the termination of the mundane world. But the present sense of dissolution is of a radically different sort. It looks to no clear salvation and it is held to be the consequence neither of Divine decree nor of fortuitous catastrophe. It is a sense of disorganization that takes root in the very conditions which to earlier generations of rationalists appeared as the necessary circumstances of progress. Where the nineteenth-century rationalist saw progressively higher forms of order and freedom emerging from the destruction of the old, the contemporary sociologist is not so sanguine. He is likely to see not creative emancipation but sterile insecurity, not the framework of the new but the shell of the old.

There is a large and growing area of psychology and social science that emphasizes this contemporary preoccupation with disintegration and disorganization. Innumerable studies of community disorganization, family disorganization, personality disintegration, not to mention the myriad investigations of industrial strife and the dissolution of ethnic subcultures and "folk" areas, all serve to point up the idea of disorganization in present-day social science. The contemporary student of man is no more able to resist the lure of the evidences of social disorganization than his nineteenth-century predecessor could resist the manifest evidences of creative emancipation and reorganization. However empirical his studies of social relationships, however bravely he rearranges the semantic elements of his terminology to support belief in his own moral detachment, and however confidently he may sometimes look to the salvational possibilities of political legislation for moral relief, it is plain that the contemporary student of human relations is haunted by perceptions of disorganization and the possibility of endemic collapse.[2]

Three

A further manifestation of the collapse of the rationalist view of man, and even more revealing, is the conception of man's moral estrangement and spiritual isolation that pervades our age. Despite the influence and power of the contemporary State there is a true sense in which the present age is more individualistic than any other in European history. To examine the whole literature of lament of our time—in the social sciences, moral philosophy, theology, the novel, the theater—and to observe the frantic efforts of millions of individuals to find some kind of security of mind is to open our eyes to the perplexities and frustrations that have emerged from the widening gulf between the individual and those social relationships within which goals and purposes take on meaning. The sense of cultural disintegration is but the obverse side of the sense of individual isolation.

The historic triumph of secularism and individualism has presented a set of problems that looms large in contemporary thought. The modern release of the individual from traditional ties of class, religion, and kinship has made him free; but, on the testimony of innumerable works in our age, this freedom is accompanied not by the sense of creative release but by the sense of disenchantment and alienation. The alienation of man from historic moral certitudes has been followed by the sense of man's alienation from fellow man.

Where the lone individual was once held to contain within himself all the propensities of order and progress, he is now quite generally regarded as the very symbol of society's anxiety and insecurity. He is the consequence, we are now prone to say, not of moral progress but of social disintegration.

Frustration, anxiety, insecurity, as descriptive words, have achieved a degree of importance in present-day thought and writing that is astonishing. Common to all of them and their many synonyms is the basic conception of man's alienation from society's relationships and moral values. If in Renaissance thought it was the myth of reasonable man which predominated; if in the eighteenth century it was natural man; and, in the nineteenth century, economic or political man, it is by no means unlikely that for our own age it is alienated or maladjusted man who will appear to later historians as the key figure of twentieth-century thought. Inadequate man, insufficient man, disenchanted man, as terms, reflect a multitude of themes in contemporary writing. Thus Berdyaev sees before him in the modern world the "disintegration of the human image"; Toynbee sees the proletarian, he who has lost all sense of identity and belonging; for Ortega y Gasset it is mass man, the anonymous creature of the market place and the mass ballot; for John Dewey, it is the lost individual—bereft of the loyalties and values which once endowed life with meaning.

"The natural state of twentieth-century man," the protagonist of a recent novel declares, "is anxiety." At the very least, anxiety has become a major state of mind in contemporary imaginative writing. Underlying many works is the conception of man as lost, baffled, and obsessed. It is not strange that for so many intellectuals the novels and stories of Franz Kafka should be, or have been until recently, the basis of almost a cult. Whatever the complexity and many-sidedness of Kafka's themes, whatever the deepest roots of his inspiration, such novels as *The Trial* and *The Castle* are, as many critics have observed, allegories of alienation and receding certainty. The residual meaning of these novels may well be man's relation to God, a universal and timeless theme. But it is nearly impossible not to see them also as symbolizations of man's effort to achieve status, to uncover meaning in the society around him, and to discover guilts and innocences in a world where the boundaries between guilt and innocence become more and more obscured. The plight of Kafka's hero is the plight of many persons in the living world: isolation, estrangement, and the compulsive search for fortresses of certainty and the equities of judgment.

The theme of the individual uprooted, without status, struggling for revelations of meaning, seeking fellowship in some kind of moral community, is as recurrent in our age as was, in an earlier age, that of the individual's release from the pressure of certainty, of his triumph over tribal or communal laws of conformity. In a variety of ways this contemporary theme finds its way into popular writing, into the literature of adventure and the murder mystery. The notion of an impersonal, even hostile, society is common—a society in which all actions and motives seem to have equal values and to be perversely detached from human direction. Common too is the helplessness of the individual before alien forces—not the hero who does things but, as Wyndham Lewis has put it, the hero to whom things are done. The disenchanted, lonely figure, searching for ethical significance in the smallest of things, struggling for identification with race or class or group, incessantly striving to answer the question, "Who am I, What am I," has become, especially in Europe, almost the central literary type of the age.

Not even with Richard III's sense of bleak triumph does the modern protagonist cry out, "I am myself alone." Where in an earlier literature the release of the hero from society's folkways and moral injunctions and corporate protections was the basis of joyous, confident, assertive individualism, the same release in contemporary literature is more commonly the occasion for morbidity and obsession. Not the free individual but the lost individual; not independence but isolation; not self-discovery but self-obsession; not to conquer but to be conquered: these are major states of mind in contemporary imaginative literature.

They are not new ideas. A whole school of literary criticism has devoted itself in recent years to the reinterpretation of writers in other ages who, like Hawthorne, Melville, and Dostoevsky, portrayed the misery of estrangement, the horror of aloneness.[3] In Tolstoy's *Ivan Ilyich* and in almost all of Dostoevsky's novels we learn that the greatest of all vices is to claim spiritual and moral autonomy and to cast off the ties that bind man to his fellows. So too in the theological writings of Kierkegaard there is luminously revealed the dread reality of man, solitary and tormented, in a hostile universe. In the writings of the Philosophical Conservatives, at the very beginning of the nineteenth century, the vision was central of man's isolation and impotence once he had got loose from society's traditions and moral constraints. Far from being new ideas these are as old as moral prophecy itself.

What is now so distinctive about these ideas is their penetration into so many areas of thought which, until recently, stressed a totally different conception of the nature of man. For a long time in modern European thought the rationalist view of self-sufficing, self-stabilizing man was ascendant in moral philosophy, Protestant theology, and social science. Few were the works that did not take the integrity and self-sufficiency of man before God as almost axiomatic. But now in widening spheres of thought we find a different concept of man.

Thus the theologian Paul Tillich sees before him in the Western world today a culture compounded not of traditional faith and confidence, but one agitated by feelings of fear and anxiety, uncertainty, loneliness, and meaninglessness. So long as a strong cultural heritage existed, and with it a sense of membership, the modern ethic of individualism was tolerable. "But when the remnants of a common world broke down, the individual was thrown into complete loneliness and the despair connected with it."[4]

Historically, Protestantism has given its emphasis to the immediacy of the individual to God, and, in theory, has relied little on the corporate nature of ecclesiastical society or the principle of hierarchical intermediation. Popularly, religion was directed not to Kierkegaard's solitary, tormented individual, alone in a hostile universe, but to the confident, self-sufficing man who carried within himself the seeds not only of faith and righteousness but of spiritual stability as well.

But this faith in the spiritual integrity of the lone individual is perceptibly declining in much Protestant thought of the present time. Today there are many leaders of the Protestant churches who have come to realize the inadequacy and irrelevance of the historic emphasis upon the church invisible and the supposedly autonomous man of faith. "It is this autonomous individual who really ushers in modern civilization and who is completely annihilated in the final stages of that civilization," declares Reinhold Niebuhr.[5]

Behind the rising tide of alienation and spiritual insecurity in contemporary society, more and more theologians, Jewish, Catholic, and Protestant alike, find the long-celebrated Western tradition of secular individualism. The historic emphasis upon the individual has been at the expense of the associative and symbolic relationships that must in fact uphold the individual's own sense of integrity. Buber, Maritain, Brunner, Niebuhr, and Demant are but the major names in the group that has come to recognize the atomizing effects of the long tradition of Western individualism upon man's relation to both society and God. "When the relation between man and God is subjective, interior (as in Luther) or in timeless acts and logic (as in Calvin) man's utter dependence upon God is not mediated through the concrete facts of historical life," writes Canon Demant.[6] And when it is not so mediated, the relation with God becomes tenuous, amorphous, and insupportable.

For more and more theologians of today the solitary individual before God has his inevitable future in Jung's "modern man in search of a soul." Man's alienation from man must lead in time to man's alienation from God. The loss of the sense of visible community in Christ will be followed by the loss of the sense of the invisible. The decline of community in the modern world has as its inevitable religious consequence the creation of masses of helpless, bewildered individuals who are unable to find solace in Christianity regarded merely as creed. The stress upon the individual, at the expense of the churchly community, has led remorselessly to the isolation of the individual, to the shattering of the man-God relationship, and to the atomization of personality. This is the testimony of a large number of theologians in our day.

So too in the social sciences has the vision of the lost individual become central. It was the brilliant French sociologist Émile Durkheim who, at the beginning of the present century, called attention to the consequences of moral and economic individualism in modern life. Individualism has resulted in masses of normless, unattached, insecure individuals who lose even the capacity for independent, creative living. The highest rates of suicide and insanity, Durkheim discovered, are to be found in those areas of society in which moral and social individualism is greatest.

Suicide varies inversely with the degree of integration in society. Hence, as Durkheim pointed out in studies which have been confirmed by the researches of many others, there is a higher rate of suicide among Protestants, among urban dwellers, among industrial workers, among the unmarried, among, in short, all those whose lives are characterized by relative tenuousness of social ties.[7]

When the individual is thrown back upon his own inner resources, when he loses the sense of moral and social involvement with others, he becomes prey to sensations of anxiety and guilt. Self-destruction is frequently his only way out. Such sensations, Durkheim concluded from his studies of modern society, are on the increase in Western society. For, in the process of modern industrial and political development, established social contexts have become weak, and fewer individuals have the secure interpersonal relations which formerly gave meaning and stability to existence.

At the present time, in all the social sciences, the various synonyms of alienation have a foremost place in studies of human relations. Investigations of the "unattached," the "marginal," the "obsessive" the "normless," and the "isolated" individual all testify to the central place occupied by the hypothesis of alienation in contemporary social science.

In studies of the aged, the adolescent, and the infant; of marriage, the neighborhood, and the factory; of the worker, the unemployed, the intellectual, and the bureaucrat; of crime, insanity, alcoholism, and of mass movements in politics, the hypothesis of alienation has reached an extraordinary degree of importance. It has become nearly as prevalent as the doctrine of enlightened self-interest was two generations ago. It is more than a hypothesis; it is a perspective.

Thus Elton Mayo and his colleagues, in their pioneering studies of industrial organization in the Western Electric plant, found that increasingly modern industry tends to predispose workers to obsessive responses, and the number of unhappy individuals increases. "Forced back upon himself, with no immediate or real social duties, the individual becomes a prey to unhappy and obsessive personal preoccupations." There is something about the nature of modern industry that inevitably creates a sense of void and aloneness. The change from what Mayo calls an established to an adaptive society has resulted for the worker in a "profound loss of security and certainty in his actual living and in the background of his thinking. . . . Where groups change ceaselessly, as jobs and mechanical processes change, the individual experiences a sense of void, of emptiness, where his fathers knew the joy of comradeship and security."[8]

Similarly in innumerable studies of the community, especially the urban community, the process of alienation is emphasized. "The urban mode of life," we read, "tends to create solitary souls, to uproot the individual from his customs, to confront him with a social void, and to weaken traditional restraints on personal conduct. . . . Personal existence and social solidarity in the urban community appear to hang by a slender thread. The tenuous relations between men, based for the most part upon a pecuniary nexus, make urban existence seem very fragile and capable of being disturbed by a multitude of forces over which the individual has little or no control. This may lead some to evince the most fruitful ingenuity and heroic courage, while it overpowers others with a paralyzing sense of individual helplessness and despair."[9]

Perceptions of alienation are not confined to studies of Western urban culture. In recent years the attention of more and more anthropologists has been focused on the effects that Western culture has had upon the lives and thought of individuals in preliterate or folk societies. The phenomenon of detribalization has of course been long noted. But where most early students of native cultures were generally reassured by the preconceptions of rationalism, seeing in this detribalization the manifold opportunities of psychological release and cultural progress, recent students have come more and more to emphasize the characteristics of alienation which are the consequence of the destruction of traditional groups and values.

It has become apparent to many anthropologists that the loss of allegiance to caste, clan, tribe, or community—a common consequence of what Margaret Mead has called the West's "psychic imperialism"—coupled with the native's inability to find secure membership in the new modes of authority and responsibility, leads to the same kind of behavior observed by sociologists and psychologists in many Western areas. "The new individual," writes one anthropologist, himself a South African native, "is in a spiritual and moral void. Partial civilization means. . . a shattering of ancient beliefs and superstitions. They are shattered but not replaced by any new beliefs. Customs and traditions are despised and rejected, but no new customs and traditions are acquired, or can be acquired."[10] So too have the more recent observations and writings of such anthropologists as Malinowski, Thurnwald, and many others emphasized the rising incidence of personal alienation, of feelings of insecurity and abandonment, among individuals in native cultures throughout the world.

In no sphere of contemporary thought has the image of the lost individual become more dominant and directive than in the fields of psychiatry and social psychology. A large number of pathological states of mind which, even a short generation ago, were presumed to be manifestations of complexes embedded in the innate neurological structure of the individual, or to be the consequence of some early traumatic experience in childhood, are now widely regarded as the outcome of a disturbed relation between the individual patient and the culture around him. The older rationalist conception of stable, self-sufficing man has been replaced, in large measure, by a conception of man as unstable, inadequate, and insecure when he is cut off from the channels of social membership and clear belief. Changes and dislocations in the cultural environment will be followed by dislocations in personality itself.

From the writings of such psychiatrists as Karen Horney, Erich Fromm, and the late Harry Stack Sullivan we learn that in our culture, with its cherished values of individual self-reliance and self-sufficiency, surrounded by relationships which become ever more impersonal and by authorities which become ever more remote, there is a rising tendency, even among the "normal" elements of the population, toward increased feelings of aloneness and insecurity. Because the basic moral values of our culture come to seem more and more inaccessible, because the line between right and wrong, good and bad, just and unjust, becomes ever less distinct, there is produced a kind of cultural "set" toward unease and chronic disquiet.

From such "normal" conditions arise the typical neuroses of contemporary middle-class society. The neurotic is, quite generally, the human being in whom these sensations of disquiet and rootlessness become chronic and unmanageable. He is the victim of intensified feelings of insecurity and anxiety and intolerable aloneness. From his conviction of aloneness he tends to derive convictions of the hostility of society toward him. Many a psychiatrist has observed with Karen Horney that among neurotics there is, in striking degree, "the incapacity to be alone, varying from slight uneasiness and restlessness to a definite terror of solitude. . . . These persons have the feeling of drifting forlornly in the universe, and any human contact is a relief to them."[11]

What is of importance here is not so much the diagnoses of neurosis which are to be found in the writings of the new school of psychiatry but, rather, the implied diagnosis or evaluation of the society in which neurotics live. Two generations ago when the foundations of clinical psychiatry were being laid by Freud, there was, for all the keen interest in neurotic behavior, little doubt of the fundamental stability of society. Then, the tendency was to ascribe neurotic behavior to certain conflicts between the nature of man and the stern demands of a highly stable, even oppressive, society. This tendency has not, to be sure, disappeared. But it is now matched, and probably exceeded, by tendencies to ascribe the roots of neurosis to the structure of society itself. The human person has not been forgotten, but more and more psychiatrists are prone to follow Harry Stack Sullivan in regarding personality as but an aspect of interpersonal relations and personality disorders as but manifestations of social instability. And with these judgments there is the further, more drastic judgment, that contemporary society, especially middle-class society, tends by its very structure to produce the alienated, the disenchanted, the rootless, and the neurotic.

Four

Despite the matchless control of physical environment, the accumulations of material wealth, and the unprecedented diffusion of culture in the lives of the masses, all of which lend glory to the present age, there is much reason for supposing that we are already entering a new Age of Pessimism. More than one prophet of our day has discovered contemporary relevance in Sir Gilbert Murray's celebrated characterization of the ancient Athens that lay in the wake of the disastrous Peloponnesian Wars as suffering from a "failure of nerve." Ours also is an age, on the testimony of much writing, of amorphous, distracted multitudes and of solitary, inward-turning individuals. Gone is the widespread confidence in the automatic workings of history to provide cultural redemption, and gone, even more strikingly, is the rationalist faith in the individual. Whether in the novel, the morality play, or in the sociological treatise, what we are given to contemplate is, typically, an age of uncertainty, disintegration, and spiritual aloneness.

To be sure it is by no means certain how far the preoccupations of intellectuals, whether novelists or sociologists, may be safely regarded as an index to the conditions of a culture at large. It may be argued that in such themes of estrangement we are dealing with rootless shadowy apprehensions of the intellectual rather than with the empirical realities of the world around us. Extreme and habitual intellectualism may, it is sometimes said, produce tendencies of a somewhat morbid nature—inner tendencies that the intellectual is too frequently unable to resist endowing with external reality.

Doubtless there is something in this diagnosis. The prophet, whether he be theologian or social scientist, is necessarily detached in some degree from the common currents of his age. From this detachment may come illuminative imagination and insight. But from this same detachment may come also an unrepresentative sense of aloneness, of alienation. However brilliant the searchlight of imagination, the direction of its brilliance is inevitably selective and always subjective to some extent.

Nevertheless, making all allowance for the possibly unrepresentative nature of much of the literature of decline and alienation, we are still left with its astonishing diversity and almost massive clustering in our age. Were themes of isolation and disintegration confined to a coterie, to writers manifestly of the ivory tower, there would be more to support the view of the unrepresentative nature of the present literature of lament. But such themes extend beyond the area of imaginative literature and moral prophecy. They are incorporated in the works of those who are most closely and empirically concerned with the behavior of human beings.

Nor can we overlook the fact that between the mind of the intellectual and the interests and cravings of the public there is always a positive connection of some kind. We need not go as far as Toynbee, Mannheim, and T. S. Eliot in their conceptions of creative minorities, élites, and classes to recognize that in any society there is a close and continuing relation between the actual condition of a culture and the image of that culture which directs the minds of its intellectual leaders—its philosophers, artists, scientists, and theologians. In the nineteenth century and for a decade or two after, the intellectual's faith in the inevitability of progress and the self-sufficiency of man were matched by broad, popular convictions. And in the mid-twentieth century there is a good deal of evidence to suggest that philosophical intimations of alienation and dissolution are set in a context of analogous mass intimations.

There are of course prophets of optimism who find hope in the monumental technological achievements of the age and in the manifest capacity of our industrial machine to provide food and comfort for the many. Such minds see in present conditions of social and moral distress only an ephemeral lag between man's still incompletely evolved moral nature and his technological achievements. In the long run, it is argued, the material progress of society will not be denied, and with the diffusion of material goods and technical services there will be an ever constant lessening of present disquietudes.

But it has become obvious, surely, that technological progress and the relative satisfaction of material needs in a population offer no guarantee of the resolution of all deprivations and frustrations. Human needs seem to form a kind of hierarchy, ranging from those of a purely physical and self-preservative nature at the bottom to needs of a social and spiritual nature at the top. During a period when a population is concerned largely with achieving satisfaction of the lower order of needs—satisfaction in the form of production and distribution of material goods—the higher order of needs may scarcely be felt by the majority of persons. But with the satisfaction of the prime, material needs, those of a social and spiritual nature become ever more pressing and ever more decisive in the total scheme of things. Desires for cultural participation, social belonging, and personal status become irresistible and their frustrations galling. Material improvement that is unaccompanied by a sense of personal belonging may actually intensify social dislocation and personal frustration.

"The true hallmark of the proletarian," Toynbee warns us, "is neither poverty nor humble birth, but a consciousness—and the resentment which this consciousness inspires—of being disinherited from his ancestral place in society and being unwanted in a community which is his rightful home; and this subjective proletarianism is not incompatible with the possession of material assets."[12]

Whether or not it is the presence of the machine and its iron discipline that creates, as so many argue in our day, the conditions of depersonalization and alienation in modern mass culture, the fact is plain that the contemporary sense of anxiety and insecurity is associated with not merely an unparalleled mechanical control of environment but, more importantly, with widespread *faith* in such control. Fears of famine, pestilence, destruction, and death have been present in all ages and have been allayed by appropriate mechanisms of relief. What is so striking about the present sense of anxiety is that it has little determinable relation to these timeless afflictions and is rooted in an age when their control has reached unprecedented heights of success.

It is impossible to escape the melancholy conclusion that man's belief in himself has become weakest in the very age when his control of environment is greatest. This is the irony of ironies. Not the most saturnine inhabitant of Thomas Love Peacock's *Nightmare Abbey,* not even the author of that nineteenth-century dirge, *The City of Dreadful Night,* foresaw the Devil in the guise he has taken.

2   THE IMAGE OF COMMUNITY

Out of intimations of dissolution and insecurity has emerged an interest in the properties and values of community that is one of the most striking social facts of the present age. We see this interest in the actions of the market place, in the imaginative labors of the poet and the novelist, and in the most abstract speculations and researches of the sciences of human behavior. In many spheres of contemporary thought the imperatives of community are irresistible. Along with the pervasive vocabulary of alienation, noted in the preceding chapter, there is an equally influential vocabulary of community. *Integration, status, membership, hierarchy, symbol, norm, identification, group*—these are key words in the intellectual's lexicon at the present time.

There is much warrant for regarding the present wide-spread interest in community as a significant renewal of intellectual conservatism, as an efflorescence of ideas and values that first arose in systematic form as part of the conservative reaction to the French Revolution at the end of the eighteenth century. In the writings of such men as Edmund Burke, de Maistre, de Bonald, Chateaubriand, Hegel, and others we find premonitions and insights that bear an extraordinarily close relation to the contemporary ideology of community.[1] The French Revolution had something of the same impact upon men's minds in Western Europe at the very end of the eighteenth century that the Communist and Nazi revolutions have had in the twentieth century. In each instance the seizure of power, the expropriation of rulers, and the impact of new patterns of authority and freedom upon old institutions and moral certainties led to a re-examination of ideas on the nature of society.[2]

For the Philosophical Conservatives the greatest crimes of the Revolution in France were those committed not against individuals but against institutions, groups, and personal statuses. These philosophers saw in the Terror no merely fortuitous consequence of war and tyrannic ambition but the inevitable culmination of ideas contained in the rationalistic individualism of the Enlightenment. In their view, the combination of social atomism and political power, which the Revolution came to represent, proceeded ineluctably from a view of society that centered on the individual and his imaginary rights at the expense of the true memberships and relationships of society. Revolutionary legislation weakened or destroyed many of the traditional associations of the *ancien régime*—the gilds, the patriarchal family, class, religious association, and the ancient commune. In so doing, the Conservatives argued forcefully, the Revolution had opened the gates for forces which, if unchecked, would in time disorganize the whole moral order of Christian Europe and lead to control by the masses and to despotic power without precedent.

It was this view of the Revolution as the work primarily of disorganization and insecurity that separated conservatism from the dominant liberal and individualistic philosophies of the early nineteenth century. From this basic conception of the effects of the Revolution upon traditional society, the conservatives proceeded to a view of man and society that stressed not the abstract individual and impersonal relations of contract but personality inextricably bound to the small social group; relationships of ascribed status and tradition; the functional interdependence of all parts of a society, including its prejudices and superstitions; the role of the sacred in maintaining order and integration; and, above all, the primacy of society to the individual.

The family, religious association, and local community—these, the conservatives insisted, cannot be regarded as the external products of man's thought and behavior; they are essentially prior to the individual and are the indispensable supports of belief and conduct. Release man from the contexts of community and you get not freedom and rights but intolerable aloneness and subjection to demonic fears and passions. Society, Burke wrote in a celebrated line, is a partnership of the dead, the living, and the unborn. Mutilate the roots of society and tradition, and the result must inevitably be the isolation of a generation from its heritage, the isolation of individuals from their fellow men, and the creation of the sprawling, faceless masses.[3]

Two

The conservatism of our own age of thought is new only in context and intensity. Through the writings of such intermediate figures as Comte, Tocqueville, Taine, Maine, Arnold, and Ruskin, the root ideas and values of early nineteenth-century conservatism have found their way straight to our own generation and have become the materials of a fresh and infinitely diversified veneration for community. The present revolt against individualistic rationalism bears striking resemblance to the revolt produced by the French Revolution.

In many areas of contemporary thought lie evidences of a positive regard for community and status that contrasts sharply with the general emphasis upon release and individuation which so dominated Protestant theology, moral philosophy, imaginative literature, and the social sciences until quite recently. Always behind the major theoretical problems of an age lie the less tangible but no less potent moral aspirations which give meaning and relevance to theoretical preoccupations. And at the present time it is, plainly, the aspiration toward moral certainty and social community that gives relevance to so much of the theoretical and imaginative work of the age.

The same temper of mind that has led the imaginative writer, the novelist, the poet, and the dramatist to seize so tenaciously upon the lost individual as the characteristic figure of the century, and upon processes of disillusionment and defeat, has led him also to seek, through intuitive vision, the basis of redemptive community. This literary search may end, as it did typically in the nineteen-thirties, in the predestined proletariat. Or, it may end, as it does in certain more recent works, in the church—or in the monastery, in class, in the tranquil countryside, in party, or even in the army. Man's integration with fellow man, his identification with race, culture, religion, and family, as escapes from aloneness become intolerable—these are rich themes at the present time. Even where the vision of community lacks certainty and clarity, we still cannot overlook the almost complete collapse of that literary revolt against the village, church, class, and community so spectacular in American writing a generation or two ago. Who now can read with undistracted attention of the efforts of a Carol Kennicott to escape the tyrannies of Main Street when the efforts of so many people are seemingly directed toward a recapture of the small town with all its cohesions and constraints? It is hard not to conclude that the theme of community and status exerts upon the literary mind of today a fascination every bit as intense as that exerted a generation or more ago by the idols of release and revolt. Belonging, not escape, is the imperative moral value.

The same is to be seen in much of the literary criticism of the present time. The major idols of criticism are no longer, as they were in the earlier decades of the century, free expression, sheer individuality, and emancipation from the past. Tradition, authority, and formal discipline have to a very large extent replaced the earlier values. Problems of form, structure, and technique in literary criticism and philosophy have a suggestive analogy to theoretical problems of structure and integration in the social sciences and psychology. The profound concern with the technical aspects of structure and method, with standards and canons of literary morality, and with the innumerable problems of symbolism and imagery and roots, may be no more than a significant chapter in the history of critical taste. But, like some of the technical problems in moral philosophy and the social sciences at the present time, they have a wider context, a context that is created by the preoccupation with intellectual and moral community. The basic problem of the writer's relation to what Sir Osbert Sitwell has called "the strange proletarian cosmopolis of the twentieth century" has many manifestations, ranging from the most technical of formal analyses to the most stridently sermonistic. But none of these manifestations is very far away from the towering moral problem of the age, the problem of community lost and community regained.[4]

Similarly, in a great amount of contemporary theological writing we are struck by an analogous intensity of the ethic of community. The same perceptions that lead, as we have seen, to a theological recognition of multitudes of distracted, spiritually isolated individuals in modern society lead also to an ever profounder concern with such matters as religious symbolism, liturgy, hierarchy, and general problems of religious discipline and tradition. The historic tendency in Protestantism toward a general depreciation of the external symbolic and associative properties of religion has, in very considerable measure, been reversed. More and more Protestant leaders now turn with new respect to traditional doctrines that bear the mark of Catholic or Jewish orthodoxy. The power of a religion—one that is rich in ritual and symbolism—to inspire and to integrate, especially in mass industrial society, has not been missed by such Protestant leaders as Reinhold Niebuhr. Deeply Protestant as Niebuhr is, he is yet willing to agree with such non-Protestant theologians as Maritain, Buber, and Demant that a religion which neglects the external communal ties between man and man is a religion likely to offer nothing in support of the man-God relationship. Niebuhr is not alone. In many quarters the imperative of community has become as evocative as was, in former ages, the imperative of individual faith. "The language of the Kingdom," writes the Anglican Demant, "the language of the family, of sonship, and fatherhood and membership, and also the language of friendship, is the language of *status*."[5]

Nowhere, however, is the concern for community more striking at the present time than in the social sciences. It has a directive force in the choice of significant problems and in the formulation of hypotheses that is at least equal to that exerted by the idea of change in the nineteenth and early twentieth centuries.[6] Research projects tend to center increasingly on problems of individual assimilation within groups, classes, and cultures. The astonishing spread of the study of group structure, group dynamics, interpersonal relations, and of associative components in economic and political behavior bears rich testimony to the change that has taken place in recent decades in the type of problem regarded as significant. If, in the eighteenth and nineteenth centuries, economic and political problems were generally predominant, supplemented by problems of individual instinct and motive force, it is manifestly the *social* problem that now holds the field—social in the precise sense that it pertains to man's primary relations with man. The social group has replaced the individual as the key concept in a great deal of social science writing, and it is almost as apt to observe that social *order* has replaced social *change* as the key problem. Beyond count are the present speculations, theories, and projects focused on the mechanics of group cohesion, structure, function, and the varied processes of assimilation and adjustment.

The most significant intellectual revolt in the social sciences against rationalistic individualism is not the drive toward political collectivism that Dicey observed half a century ago. It is now a conservative revolt and is to be seen in those approaches to the study of man where the individual has been replaced by the social group as the central unit of theoretical inquiry and ameliorative action; where organicism and its offspring, functionalism, hold sway in the interpretation of behavior and belief; where there is a dominant interest in themes and patterns of cultural integration, in ritual, role, and tradition, and in the whole range of problems connected with social position and social role. Granted the personal detachment and the purely analytical objectives which characterize most of these studies, the conclusion is plain that the problems themselves, like analogous problems in other spheres of theory, reflect a set of deep moral urgencies. In the same way that older theoretical problems of change and mobility had behind them, historically and logically, moral aspirations to progress, so contemporary theoretical problems of social statics are given meaning and drive by moral aspirations toward community.

Three

The theorist seeks to discern patterns of thought, like patterns of culture, in modern society only at his peril. What I have here called the image of community in modern thought has, obviously, many exceptions. Individualism is far from dead. The often bitter controversies that characterize the contemporary interest in status and community and cohesion make this absolutely clear. If, today, it is the functional anthropologist or the industrial sociologist who is subjected to attack by latter-day individualists, tomorrow it will be the New Critic, and the day after the neo-orthodox Protestant theologian. Individualism dies slowly. What is left, often clamant, is the individualist conscience.

Despite this, I cannot help thinking that the concern for community, its values, properties, and means of access, is the major intellectual fact of the present age. Whatever evidence remains of the individualist conscience and the rationalist faith, it is hard to miss the fact that individualism and secularism are on the defensive. New imperatives are the order of the day. And these are not confined to the ranks of intellectuals.

Is not the most appealing popular religious literature of the day that which presents religion, not in its timeless role of sharpening man's awareness of the omnipresence of evil and the difficulties of salvation, but as a means of relief from anxiety and frustration? It enjoins not virtue but adjustment. Are not the popular areas of psychology and ethics those involving either the theoretical principles or the therapeutic techniques of status and adjustment for the disinherited and insecure? "In what other period of human existence," asks Isaiah Berlin, "has so much effort been devoted not to the painfully difficult task of looking for light, but to the protection . . . of individuals from the intellectual burden of facing problems that may be too deep or complex?"[7] Every age has its literature of regeneration. Our own, however, is directed not to the ancient desire of man for higher virtue but to the obsessive craving of men for tranquillity and belonging.

For an ever-increasing number of people the conditions now prevailing in Western society would appear to have a great deal in common with the unforgettable picture Sir Samuel Dill has given us of the last centuries of the Roman Empire: of enlarging masses of individuals detached from any sense of community, status, or function, turning with a kind of organized desperation to exotic escapes, to every sort of spokesman for salvation on earth, and to ready-made techniques of relief from nervous exhaustion. In our own time we are confronted by the spectacle of innumerable individuals seeking escape from the very processes of individualism and impersonality which the nineteenth-century rationalist hailed as the very condition of progress.

Nostalgia has become almost a central state of mind. In mass advertising, the magazine story, and in popular music we cannot fail to see the commercial appeal that seems to lie in cultural themes drawn from the near past. It is plainly a nostalgia, not for the greater adventurousness of earlier times but for the assertedly greater community and moral certainty of the generations preceding ours. If the distinguishing mark of the late nineteenth and early twentieth century was transgression, that of the mid-twentieth century would appear to be the search for the road back.

Increasingly, individuals seek escape from the freedom of impersonality, secularism, and individualism. They look for community in marriage, thus putting, often, an intolerable strain upon a tie already grown institutionally fragile. They look for it in easy religion, which leads frequently to a vulgarization of Christianity the like of which the world has not seen before. They look for it in the psychiatrist's office, in the cult, in functionless ritualizations of the past, and in all the other avocations of relief from nervous exhaustion.

There is a growing appeal of pseudo-intimacy with others, a kind of pathetic dependence on the superficial symbols of friendship and association. If Hollywood provides us, both in its own life and in its pictures, with the most familiar examples of this pseudo-intimacy, they are assuredly not lacking in other areas of our mass culture. The craving for affection and tangible evidences of accord, which psychiatrists have declared to be so central in contemporary neurotic behavior, has a broad base in popular behavior.

Remedial techniques for the insecure, rootless, apprehensive individual loom large in our mass culture. They are evidenced in the new demands of organized labor in industry, demands that tend now to center on long-term security rather than on the more familiar short-run improvements in wages and hours. They are patent in the growing popular conception of university education as a means less of illumination than as an avenue to social status and intellectual certainty. In less tangible but no less revealing ways the image of community is to be seen in all the fantasy avenues to social belonging—the movie, the radio serial, and popular fiction.

Not a little of that rage for order in industry, education, religion, and government, which seems at times so relentlessly bound to destroy the contexts of individuality in culture, is the product of the devouring search for the conditions of security and moral certainty.

The belief that all important goals of human life are realizable through political and economic planning for large aggregates of the population is as powerful today as it was in the age of the French Enlightenment. But what has been abandoned are the older intellectual *goals* of political rationalism. These were the socially free individual, moral impersonality, contract, and competition. Their place has been taken in contemporary aspiration by the imperatives of personal status, security, and community.

What gives the current interest in community and psychological adjustment its frequently ominous cast is the combination of increasing social and moral insecurity with the undiminished popularity of certain political techniques of centralization and collectivism. There is widespread belief that the termination of individual insecurity and moral disquietude can come about through a sterilization of social diversity and through an increased political and economic standardization. The undoubted necessity of unity *within* the individual leads too often to the supposition that this may be achieved only through uniformity of the culture and institutions which lie *outside* the individual. And external power, especially political power, comes to reveal itself to many minds as a fortress of security against not only institutional conflicts but conflicts of belief and value that are internal to the individual. A peculiar form of political mysticism is often the result.

Four

The image of community may be seen behind certain types of political action in present Western society. It is hard to overlook the fact that the State and politics have become suffused by qualities formerly inherent only in the family or the church. In an age of real or supposed disintegration, men will abandon all truths and values that do not contain the promise of communal belonging and secure moral status. Where there is widespread conviction that community has been lost, there will be a conscious quest for community in the form of association that seems to promise the greatest moral refuge.

In one age of society, for example in the early Middle Ages, this quest may end in the corporate church, or in the extended family or village community. But in the present age, for enlarging masses of people, this same quest terminates in the political party or action group. It is the image of community contained in the promise of the absolute, communal State that seems to have the greatest evocative power. Especially has this become manifest in Europe. And, above all other forms of political association, it is the totalitarian Communist party that most successfully exploits the craving for moral certainty and communal membership. In it we find states of mind and intensities of fanaticism heretofore known only in certain types of religious cult.

Contemporary prophets of the totalitarian community seek, with all the techniques of modern science at their disposal, to transmute popular cravings for community into a millennial sense of participation in heavenly power on earth. When suffused by popular spiritual devotions, the political party becomes more than a party. It becomes a moral community of almost religious intensity, a deeply evocative symbol of collective, redemptive purpose, a passion that implicates every element of belief and behavior in the individual's existence.

The dread spectacle of totalitarianism as an organized movement in every Western country at the present time cannot be divorced from its proffer of community to individuals for whom sensations of dissolution and alienation have become intolerable. "The most obvious symptom of the spiritual disease of our civilization," declares Robert Birley, "is the widespread feeling among men that they have lost all control of their destinies. . . . Hitler's answer to that frustration was one of the main secrets of his power."[8]

The almost eager acceptance of the fantastic doctrines of the Nazis by millions of otherwise intelligent Germans would be inexplicable were it not for the accompanying proffer of moral community to the disenchanted and alienated German worker, peasant, and intellectual. If moral community came with political conversion, the Nazi proselyte could agree perversely with Tertullian that intellectual impossibility may even be the crowning appearance of truth.

Marxism as a mass movement is no different. If we wish to understand the appeal of Marxism we should do well to pay less attention to its purely intellectual qualities than to the social and moral values that inhere in it. To a large number of human beings Marxism offers status, belonging, membership, and a coherent moral perspective. Of what matter and relevance are the empirical and logical refutations made by a host of critics as against the spiritual properties that Marx offers to millions. Have not all the world's great religious leaders pointed to a truth that is bigger than, and elusive of, all purely rational processes of thought?

The evidence is strong that the typical convert to communism is a person for whom the processes of ordinary existence are morally empty and spiritually insupportable. His own alienation is translated into the perceived alienation of the many. Consciously or unconsciously he is in quest of secure belief and solid membership in an associative order. Of what avail are proofs of the classroom, semantic analyses, and logical exhortations to this kind of human being? So long as he finds belief and membership in his Marxism he will no more be dissuaded by simple adjuration than would the primitive totemist.

Until we see that communism offers today, for many people, something of the inspired mixture of community and assertive individuality offered two thousand years ago, in the cities of the Roman Empire, by the tiny but potent Christian communities, we shall be powerless to combat it. It will not be exorcised by the incantations of individualism, for, paradoxical as it may seem, in the Communist party community, the individual is constantly supported by feelings of almost millennial personal freedom. Here the brilliant words of a recent English reviewer are pertinent and illuminating:

"It is easy—only too easy—to say that these people have sacrificed their individuality and become units in an undifferentiated and soulless mass—that the whole phenomenon is merely another outbreak of what used to be called the 'herd instinct,' or what Dr. Erich Fromm calls 'the flight from freedom,' the urge to huddle into a safe, warm crowd. A truer psychology may suggest that what has happened is the exact contrary, and that for the primitive millions it has seemed rather an assertion than a denial of individuality. . . . From the outside, the communist may look like an ant in an anthill, but to himself he may seem to be a comrade helping to carry out a great design—what in another context would be called the Will of God; and the official deterministic philosophy will only operate to inspire a deadly assurance of ultimate success—another of the strange paradoxes that lurk in the vague hinterland of the human mind."[9]

We may justly regard the world communist movement as vicious in its acts, as profoundly evil at its core. But let us not make the fatal mistake of underestimating its nature and appeal. We shall be grotesquely unprepared to combat communism if we persist in regarding it as the mere summation of all the lesser evils and irrationalities of modern society, and its members as undeviatingly criminal or treasonable in intent. I do not question the fact that communism, like any other mass movement, in time attracts to itself energies and dispositions which, in other circumstances, would be directed toward the usual outlets of crime and violence. Communism has its gangsters, its men of hard and ruthless intent. But, as a mass movement, it possesses the qualities of spiritual intensity and devotion that have ever gone into organizations and actions of purest intent.

It is worth quoting our English reviewer again. "If religion is something which gives a meaning to life, which makes it worth living, then communism certainly answers to the definition; and it would be a fatal mistake to ignore its emotional appeal. Multitudes, it is clear, have experiences something like a revelation. The Marxian thesis has duly evolved into its antithesis: materialism has given them souls; determinism has freed their wills. For the first time they 'belong to' something, to a 'cause'—good or bad as it may be, but something at any rate which transcends their narrow personal interests and opens up a world in which each has his part to play and all can 'pull together.'" [10]

What Ignazio Silone has written of his own early experiences in the Communist party is illuminating here. "The Party became family, school, church, barracks; the world that lay beyond it was to be destroyed and built anew. The psychological mechanism whereby each single militant becomes progressively identified with the collective organization is the same as that used in certain religious orders and military colleges, with almost identical results. Every sacrifice was welcomed as a personal contribution to the price of collective redemption, and it should be emphasized that the links which bound us to the Party grew steadily firmer, not in spite of the dangers and sacrifices involved, but because of them. This explains the attraction exercised by communism on certain categories of young men and women, on intellectuals and on the highly sensitive and generous people who suffer most from the wastefulness of bourgeois society. Anyone who thinks he can wean the best and most serious-minded young people away from communism by enticing them into a well-warmed hall to play billiards, starts from an extremely limited and unintelligent conception of mankind." [11]

The greatest appeal of the totalitarian party, Marxist or other, lies in its capacity to provide a sense of moral coherence and communal membership to those who have become, to one degree or another, victims of the sense of exclusion from the ordinary channels of belonging in society. To consider the facts of poverty and economic distress as causes of the growth of communism is deceptive. Such facts may be involved but only when they are set in the social and moral context of insecurity and alienation. To say that the well-fed worker will never succumb to the lure of communism is as absurd as to say that the well-fed intellectual will never succumb. The presence or absence of three meals a day, or even the simple possession of a job, is not the decisive factor. What is decisive is the frame of reference. If, for one reason or another, the individual's immediate society comes to seem remote, purposeless, and hostile, if a people come to sense that, together, they are victims of discrimination and exclusion, not all the food and jobs in the world will prevent them from looking for the kind of surcease that comes with membership in a social and moral order seemingly directed toward their very souls.

Marxism, like all other totalitarian movements in our century, must be seen as a kind of secular pattern of redemption, designed to bring hope and fulfillment to those who have come to feel alienated, frustrated, and excluded from what they regard as their rightful place in a community. In its promise of unity and belonging lies much of the magic of totalitarian mystery, miracle, and authority. Bertrand Russell has not exaggerated in summing up the present significance of Marxism somewhat as follows: dialectical materialism is God; Marx the Messiah; Lenin and Stalin the apostles; the proletariat the elect; the Communist party the Church; Moscow the seat of the Church; the Revolution the second coming; the punishment of capitalists hell; Trotsky the devil; and the communist commonwealth kingdom come.

Five

So, too, in the changing moral character and growing spiritual influence of mass war can we observe the contemporary image of community. It is hard not to conclude that modern populations depend increasingly on the symbolism of war for relief from civil conflicts and frustrations. War strikes instantly at the breast of modern man. It soothes even where it hurts.

The power of war to create a sense of moral meaning is one of the most frightening aspects of the twentieth century. In war, innumerable activities that normally seem onerous or empty of significance take on new and vital meaning. Function and meaning tend to become dramatically fused in time of war.

One of the most extraordinary features of the gigantic atomic bomb project during the Second World War was the spectacle of tens of thousands of workers and scientists working for a period of years on a product the nature of which few of them knew or were permitted to discover. Life was almost wholly circumscribed by security regulations, formal organizational patterns, technical instructions, and complicated machines, all pointing toward a goal that was undiscoverable by the individual worker or lesser scientist. Even to look too closely into the identity of fellow workers was not encouraged. The ordinary channels of personal and professional organization were restricted, and the whole endeavor was insulated from popular contact as perfectly as security officers could contrive. Secrecy, individual separation from knowledge of actual function and purpose—these have probably never reached the heights elsewhere that they reached in this extraordinary war project.

What gave the Manhattan Project the possibility of success, not to mention the possibility of existing at all, with its many restrictions upon normal communication, with all its impersonality and enforced anonymity, was the deep moral compulsion of war, of participation in a spiritual crusade against the enemy. When the end of the war came, many of the demands of secrecy and depersonalization became nearly intolerable, leading in turn to disaffection and, if we may believe the testimony of some well-informed scientists, to a serious reduction in efficiency and achievement.

Such an organization is extreme, but it may with fairness be regarded as a kind of dramatic intensification of the position in which more and more industrial and professional people find themselves in the vast, impersonal spaces of modern industrial society. The anonymity and emptiness of so many factory and office existences in peace time become doubly oppressive after they have been temporarily relieved by the experience of a mass moral crusade in which the most routine duties are suffused by the sense of participation in a creative cause.

One of the most impressive aspects of contemporary war is the intoxicating atmosphere of spiritual unity that arises out of the common consciousness of participating in a moral crusade. War is no longer simply an affair of military establishments and matériel and soldiers. It is now something more nearly akin to the Crusades of medieval Europe, but in the name of the nation rather than of the Church.

The clear tendency of modern wars is to become ever more closely identified with broad, popular, moral aspirations: freedom, self-determination of peoples, democracy, rights, and justice. Because war, in the twentieth century, has become rooted to such an extent in the aspirations of peoples and in broad moral convictions, its intensity and range have vastly increased. When the goals and values of a war are *popular,* both in the sense of mass participation and spiritual devotion, the historic, institutional *limits* of war tend to recede further and further into the void. The enemy becomes not only a ready scapegoat for all ordinary dislikes and frustrations; he becomes the symbol of total evil against which the forces of good may mobilize themselves into a militant community.

This community-making property of war cannot be separated from certain tangible benefits of a social and economic nature. It is a commonplace that nationalism is nourished by the emotions of organized war. We are less likely to notice that many of the historic goals of secular humanitarianism are similarly nourished. More than one historian has observed that it is in time of war that many of the reforms, first advocated by socialists, have been accepted by capitalist governments and made parts of the structures of their societies. Equalization of wealth, progressive taxation, nationalization of industries, the raising of wages and improvements in working conditions, worker-management councils, housing ventures, death taxes, unemployment insurance plans, pension systems, and the enfranchisement of formerly voteless elements of the population have all been, in one country or another, achieved or advanced under the impress of war. The tremendous urge toward unity and the resolution of group differences, which is a part of modern war, carries with it certain leveling and humanitarian measures not to be omitted from the full history of modern warfare. For all the horrors of contemporary war and the genuine abhorrence of war which still exists among populations, its incidental benefits in the realm of social reform cannot be overlooked.

It is the moral element of war, as William James saw so clearly, that makes for the curious dualism in the response of the average person to war. We are all repelled by the horrors of the battlefield; we chafe under the economic sacrifices demanded and the interference with freedom of movement. But there is, undeniably, a spiritual fascination exerted by war in the present century that increasingly rises above the distasteful moments and sacrifices.

Society attains its maximum sense of organization and community and its most exalted sense of moral purpose during the period of war. Since it is always, now, identified with a set of essentially nonmilitary values—democracy, freedom, hatred of fascism, et cetera—there is an inevitable tendency for the nature of war itself to become more spiritualized and to seem more moral. Something of the millennial excitement and moral intoxication that the civil war in Spain produced in the minds of intellectuals in the nineteen-thirties is, when the purposes are more vivid and widespread and the personal stakes greater, communicated to a whole population in time of great war.

With the outbreak of war there is a termination of many of the factionalisms and sectarian animosities which ordinarily reflect the moral perplexities of modern politics. In their place comes what the English philosopher L. P. Jacks has so aptly called "the spiritual peace that war brings." To remark cynically that such tranquillity is artificial, that it rests upon an unmoral basis, misses the more important point that tranquillity is a foremost goal of modern man and that he is prone to accept it as he finds it. We should be blind indeed if we did not recognize in the war state, in the war economy, and in war morality qualities that stand in the most attractive contrast to the instability and the sense of meaninglessness of modern industrial and political life.

Millions of men and women learned during the recent World War something of the sharp contrast that exists between a society founded seemingly upon economic caprice, political impersonality, and general moral indifference, and a society that suddenly becomes infused with the moral intensity of a crusade and the spirituality of devotion to common ends. The effect of the war was to endow with meaning and excitement activities that ordinarily seemed without meaning or even knowable function. The pressure of mass numbers was lightened, the impersonality of existence was transfigured and, even if a large amount of personal anonymity remained, it was, in a curious and paradoxical way, an *identified* anonymity.

The centralization and bureaucratic regimentation which have always been native to organized warfare are, in the twentieth century, extended to widening areas of social and cultural life. War symbolism and the practical techniques of war administration have come to penetrate more and more of the minor areas of social function and allegiance. More and more of the incentives of science, education, and industry are made to rest upon contributions to the war effort. Increasingly, humanitarians find themselves defending cherished goals of equality and justice in terms of the strengthening influence these have to the nation preparing for war.

The line between civil and military administration becomes thinner and thinner. It is an easy matter to pass by imperceptible degrees from the primacy of real needs for the war effort to the primacy and dominance of pretended needs for war. Moreover, the traditional austerity, discipline, and unity of military command, together with all its reputed efficiencies, comes to have increasing appeal to large elements of the population. Mere tactical excellences of military officers become converted, through the alchemy of popular adulation, into imagined moral and political wisdom without limit. The military man succeeds in prestige the scholar, the scientist, the businessman, and the clergyman. Inevitably there is a tendency to magnify the importance of civil and moral pursuits by clothing them in military garments, by replacing normal hierarchies of leadership and prestige with the hierarchy of military rank and command. The discipline of war becomes community itself.

So too in the direct experience of war and military organization many millions of men learned even more certainly during the two world wars the contrast between life charged with moral meaning and life that is morally empty. Military society is closely associative. The pressure of numbers may seem at first unbearable to the more sensitive individuals, but in an astonishingly short time such pressure becomes not only tolerable but desirable. Equally unbearable at first may seem the disconcertingly clear and emphatic regulations and customs of the military, but here too, in a manner surprising to many, early misgivings are succeeded by a certain contentment in being in the presence of moral regulations whose very clarity and preciseness of coverage makes more pleasant the "free" areas not covered by the regulations and customs.

One of the most notable capacities of military life is to inspire in the individual soldier a feeling for the warmth of comradeship. Something of that spirit which, during an earlier age of European history, unfolded itself in a great profusion of fellowships and associations, reaching all spheres of social life, permeates the soldier's consciousness. There is an almost medieval hierarchy in military society with the individual's identity passing through the concentric rings of platoon, company, regiment, up to the field army itself. His identification with each of these units, especially the smaller ones, can become intense and morally exhilarating. Add to the institutionalized relationships the organic growing together of individuals who have shared common experiénces, rewards, and dangers, who, by the very nature of army life, are thrown together constantly in the performance of duties that have perceptible meaning and function, and the sense of communal belonging becomes perhaps the most cherished of all the soldier's values.

The loss of the sense of belonging, whether in the civilian intellectual whose moral participation has been no less intense for its vicariousness, or in the common soldier for whom it has been immediate and direct, leads not infrequently to deeply disquieting states of nostalgia and vague longing. These may transform themselves into innumerable emotions ranging from simple discontent to bitter alienation. It is not merely that an orderly, predictable world of values has been replaced by the unpredictabilities and moral voids of civil life. Fundamentally it is the loss of a sense of belonging, of a close identification with other human beings. [12]

The tragedy of contemporary war does not lie in its progressive destructive efficiency, its total mobilization of human beings and ideas, or even in its weakening or brutalization of cultural standards. It lies rather in the fact that the stifling regimentation and bureaucratic centralization of military organization is becoming more and more the model of associative and leadership relationships in time of peace and in nonmilitary organizations. It lies in the fact that military bureaucracy and regimentation tend increasingly to become invested with the attributes of moral community—a sense of identification, of security, and of membership. The result is to endow war with moral satisfactions ordinarily denied to the individual. However deeply man may continue to hate the devastation and killing and mutilation of war, he cannot, being human, forget altogether the superior sense of status, the achievement of humanitarian goals, and, above all, the warming sense of community that comes with war.

Six

In the burning words of the Grand Inquisitor, Dostoevsky has given us insight into the appeal of the absolute community.

"So long as man remains free he strives for nothing so incessantly and painfully as to find someone to worship. But man seeks to worship what is established beyond dispute, so that all men will agree at once to worship it.

For these pitiful creatures are concerned not only to find what one or the other can worship, but find something that all will believe in and worship; what is essential is that all may be *together* in it. This craving for *community* of worship is the chief misery of every man individually and of all humanity from the beginning of time."

In the nineteenth century, when these words were written, they could have been regarded by most Western intellectuals only with incredulity or indifference. After all, were not men everywhere progressively escaping this tribalistic togetherness? Was not this escape from community the very essence of modern civilization? But in the present age, few will doubt that the words of the Grand Inquisitor, baleful as they are, have a relevance that is disquieting and ominous.

3   THE PROBLEM OF COMMUNITY

This is an age of economic interdependence and welfare States, but it is also an age of spiritual insecurity and preoccupation with moral certainty. Why is this? Why has the quest for community become the dominant social tendency of the twentieth century? What are the forces that have conspired, at the very peak of three centuries of economic and political advancement, to make the problem of community more urgent in the minds of men than it has been since the last days of the Roman Empire?

The answer is of course complex. Any effort to resolve the conflicting imperatives of an age into a simple set of institutional dislocations is both vapid and illusory. The conflicts of any age are compounded of immediate cultural frustrations and of timeless spiritual cravings. Attempts to reduce the latter to facile sociological and psychological categories are absurd and pathetic. Whatever else the brilliant literature of political disillusionment of our day has demonstrated, it has made clear that efforts to translate all spiritual problems into secular terms are fraught with stultification as well as tyranny.

The problem before us is in one sense moral. It is moral in that it is closely connected with the values and ends that have traditionally guided and united men but that have in so many instances become remote and inaccessible. We do not have to read deeply in the philosophy and literature of today to sense the degree to which our age has come to seem a period of moral and spiritual chaos, of certainties abandoned, of creeds outworn, and of values devalued. The disenchantment of the world, foreseen by certain nineteenth-century conservatives as the end result of social and spiritual tendencies then becoming dominant, is very much with us. The humane skepticism of the early twentieth century has already been succeeded in many quarters by a new Pyrrhonism that strikes at the very roots of thought itself. Present disenchantment would be no misfortune were it set in an atmosphere of confident attack upon the old and search for the new. But it is not confident, only melancholy and guilty. Along with it are to be seen the drives to absolute skepticism and absolute certainty that are the invariable conditions of rigid despotism.

The problem is also intellectual. It cannot be separated from tendencies in Western thought that are as old as civilization itself, tendencies luminously revealed in the writings of Plato, Seneca, Augustine, and all their intellectual children. These are profound tendencies. We cannot avoid, any of us, seeing the world in ways determined by the very words we have inherited from other ages. Not a little of the terminology of alienation and community in our day comes directly from the writings of the philosophical and religious conservatives of other centuries. The problem constituted by the present quest for community is composed of elements as old as mankind, elements of faith and agonizing search which are vivid in all the great prophetic literatures. In large degree, the quest for community is timeless and universal.

Nevertheless, the shape and intensity of the quest for community varies from age to age. For generations, even centuries, it may lie mute, covered over and given gratification by the securities found in such institutions as family, village, class, or some other type of association. In other ages, ages of sudden change and dislocation, the quest for community becomes conscious and even clamant. It is this in our own age. To dismiss the present quest for community with vague references to the revival of tribalism, to man's still incomplete emancipation from conditions supposedly "primitive," is to employ substitutes for genuine analysis, substitutes drawn from the nineteenth century philosophy of unilinear progress. Moral imperatives, our own included, always hold a significant relation to *present* institutional conditions. They cannot be relegated to the past.

It is the argument of this book that the ominous preoccupation with community revealed by modern thought and mass behavior is a manifestation of certain profound dislocations in the primary associative areas of society, dislocations that have been created to a great extent by the structure of the Western political State. As it is treated here, the problem is social—social in that it pertains to the statuses and social memberships which men hold, or seek to hold. But the problem is also political—political in that it is a reflection of the present location and distribution of power in society.

The two aspects, the social and the political, are inseparable. For, the allegiances and memberships of men, even the least significant, cannot be isolated from the larger systems of authority that prevail in a society or in any of its large social structures. Whether the dominant system of power is primarily religious, economic, or political in the usual sense is of less importance sociologically than the *way* in which the power reveals itself in practical operation and determines the smaller contexts of culture and association. Here we have reference to the degree of centralization, the remoteness, the impersonality of power, and to the concrete ways in which it becomes involved in human life.

We must begin with the role of the social group in present-day Western society, for it is in the basic associations of men that the real consequences of political power reveal themselves. But the present treatment of the group cannot really be divorced from political considerations, which will be dealt with in later chapters.

Two

It has become commonplace, as we have seen, to refer to social disorganization and moral isolation in the present age. These terms are usually made to cover a diversity of conditions. But in a society as complex as ours it is unlikely that all aspects are undergoing a similar change. Thus it can scarcely be said that the State, as a distinguishable relationship among men, is today undergoing disorganization, for in most countries, including the United States, it is the political relationship that has been and is being enhanced above all other forms of connection among individuals. The contemporary State, with all its apparatus of bureaucracy, has become more powerful, more cohesive, and is endowed with more functions than at any time in its history.

Nor can the great impersonal relationships of the many private and semi-public organizations—educational, charitable, economic—be said to be experiencing any noticeable decline or disintegration. Large-scale labor organizations, political parties, welfare organizations, and corporate associations based upon property and exchange show a continued and even increasing prosperity, at least when measured in terms of institutional significance. It may be true that these organizations do not offer the degree of individual identification that makes for a deep sense of social cohesion, but disorganization is hardly the word for these immense and influential associations which govern the lives of tens of millions of people.

We must be no less wary of such terms as the "lost," "isolated," or "unattached" individual. However widespread the contemporary ideology of alienation may be, it would be blindness to miss the fact that it flourishes amid an extraordinary variety of custodial and redemptive agencies. Probably never in all history have so many organizations, public and private, made the individual the center of bureaucratic and institutionalized regard. Quite apart from the innumerable agencies of private welfare, the whole tendency of modern political development has been to enhance the role of the political State as a direct relationship among individuals, and to bring both its powers and its services ever more intimately into the lives of human beings.

Where, then, are the dislocations and the deprivations that have driven so many men, in this age of economic abundance and political welfare, to the quest for community, to narcotic relief from the sense of isolation and anxiety? They lie in the realm of the small, primary, personal relationships of society—the relationships that mediate directly between man and his larger world of economic, moral, and political and religious values. Our problem may be ultimately concerned with all of these values and their greater or lesser accessibility to man, but it is, I think, primarily social: social in the exact sense of pertaining to the small areas of membership and association in which these values are ordinarily made meaningful and directive to men.

Behind the growing sense of isolation in society, behind the whole quest for community which infuses so many theoretical and practical areas of contemporary life and thought, lies the growing realization that the traditional primary relationships of men have become functionally irrelevant to our State and economy and meaningless to the moral aspirations of individuals. We are forced to the conclusion that a great deal of the peculiar character of contemporary social action comes from the efforts of men to find in large-scale organizations the values of status and security which were formerly gained in the primary associations of family, neighborhood, and church. This is the fact, I believe, that is as revealing of the source of many of our contemporary discontents as it is ominous when the related problems of political freedom and order are considered.

The problem, as I shall emphasize later in this chapter, is by no means restricted to the position of the traditional groups, nor is its solution in any way compatible with antiquarian revivals of groups and values no longer in accord with the requirements of the industrial and democratic age in which we live and to which we are unalterably committed. But the dislocation of the traditional groups must form our point of departure.

Historically, our problem must be seen in terms of the decline in functional and psychological significance of such groups as the family, the small local community, and the various other traditional relationships that have immemorially mediated between the individual and his society. These are the groups that have been morally decisive in the concrete lives of individuals. Other and more powerful forms of association have existed, but the major moral and psychological influences on the individual's life have emanated from the family and local community and the church. Within such groups have been engendered the primary types of identification: affection, friendship, prestige, recognition. And within them also have been engendered or intensified the principal incentives of work, love, prayer, and devotion to freedom and order.

This is the area of association from which the individual commonly gains his concept of the outer world and his sense of position in it. His concrete feelings of status and role, of protection and freedom, his differentiation between good and bad, between order and disorder and guilt and innocence, arise and are shaped largely by his relations within this realm of primary association. What was once called instinct or the social nature of man is but the product of this sphere of interpersonal relationships. It contains and cherishes not only the formal moral precept but what Whitehead has called "our vast system of inherited symbolism."

It can be seen that most contemporary themes of alienation have as their referents disruptions of attachment and states of mind which derive from this area of interpersonal relations. Feelings of moral estrangement, of the hostility of the world, the fear of freedom, of irrational aggressiveness, and of helplessness before the simplest of problems have to do commonly—as both the novelist and the psychiatrist testify—with the individual's sense of the inaccessibility of this area of relationship. In the child, or in the adult, the roots of a coherent, logical sense of the outer world are sunk deeply in the soil of close, meaningful interpersonal relations.

It is to this area of relations that the adjective "disorganized" is most often flung by contemporary social scientists and moralists, and it is unquestionably in this area that most contemporary sensations of cultural dissolution arise. Yet the term disorganization is not an appropriate one and tends to divert attention from the basic problem of the social group in our culture. It has done much to fix attention on those largely irrelevant manifestations of delinquent behavior which are fairly constant in all ages and have little to do with our real problem.

The conception of social disorganization arose with the conservatives in France, who applied it empirically enough to the destruction of the gilds, the aristocracy, and the monasteries. But to Bonald and Comte the most fundamental sense of the term was moral. The Revolution signified to them the destruction of a vast moral order, and in their eyes the common manifestations of individual delinquency became suddenly invested with a new significance, the significance of social disorganization, itself the product of the Revolution. The term disorganization has been a persistent one in social science, and there is even now a deplorable tendency to use such terms as disintegration and disorganization where there is no demonstrable breakdown of a structure and no clear norm from which to calculate supposed deviations of conduct. The family and the community have been treated as disintegrating entities with no clear insight into what relationships are actually disintegrating. A vast amount of attention has been given to such phenomena as marital unhappiness, prostitution, juvenile misbehavior, and the sexual life of the unmarried, on the curious assumption that these are "pathological" and derive clearly from the breakdown of the family.[1]

But in any intelligible sense of the word it is not disorganization that is crucial to the problem of the family or of any other significant social group in our society. The most fundamental problem has to do with the *organized* associations of men. It has to do with the role of the primary social group in an economy and political order whose principal ends have come to be structured in such a way that the primary social relationships are increasingly functionless, almost irrelevant, with respect to these ends. What is involved most deeply in our problem is the diminishing capacity of organized, traditional relationships for holding a position of moral and psychological centrality in the individual's life.

Three

Interpersonal relationships doubtless exist as abundantly in our age as in any other. But it is becoming apparent that for more and more people such relationships are morally empty and psychologically baffling. It is not simply that old relationships have waned in psychological influence; it is that new forms of primary relationships show, with rare exceptions, little evidence of offering even as much psychological and moral meaning for the individual as do the old ones. For more and more individuals the primary social relationships have lost much of their historic function of mediation between man and the larger ends of our civilization.

But the decline of effective meaning is itself a part of a more fundamental change in the role of such groups as the family and local community. At bottom social organization is a pattern of institutional functions into which are woven numerous psychological threads of meaning, loyalty, and inter-dependence. The contemporary sense of alienation is most directly perhaps a problem in symbols and meanings, but it is also a problem in the institutional functions of the relationships that ordinarily communicate integration and purpose to individuals.

In any society the concrete loyalties and devotions of individuals tend to become directed toward the associations and patterns of leadership that in the long run have the greatest perceptible significance in the maintenance of life. It is never a crude relationship; intervening strata of ritual and other forms of crystallized meaning will exert a distinguishable influence on human thought. But, at bottom, there is a close and vital connection between the effectiveness of the symbols that provide meaning in the individual's life and the institutional value of the social structures that are the immediate source of the symbols. The immediacy of the integrative meaning of the basic values contained in and communicated by the kinship or religious group will vary with the greater or less institutional value of the group to the individual *and to the other institutions in society.*

In earlier times, and even today in diminishing localities, there was an intimate relation between the local, kinship, and religious groups within which individuals consciously lived and the major economic, charitable, and protective functions which are indispensable to human existence. There was an intimate conjunction of larger institutional goals and the social groups small enough to infuse the individual's life with a sense of membership in society and the meaning of the basic moral values. For the overwhelming majority of people, until quite recently the structure of economic and political life rested upon, and even presupposed, the existence of the small social and local groups within which the cravings for psychological security and identification could be satisfied.

Family, church, local community drew and held the allegiances of individuals in earlier times not because of any superior impulses to love and protect, or because of any greater natural harmony of intellectual and spiritual values, or even because of any superior internal organization, but because these groups possessed a virtually indispensable relation to the economic and political order. The social problems of birth and death, courtship and marriage, employment and unemployment, infirmity and old age were met, however inadequately at times, through the associative means of these social groups. In consequence, a whole ideology, reflected in popular literature, custom, and morality, testified to the centrality of kinship and localism.

Our present crisis lies in the fact that whereas the small traditional associations, founded upon kinship, faith, or locality, are still expected to communicate to individuals the principal moral ends and psychological gratifications of society, they have manifestly become detached from positions of functional relevance to the larger economic and political decisions of our society. Family, local community, church, and the whole network of informal interpersonal relationships have ceased to play a determining role in our institutional systems of mutual aid, welfare, education, recreation, and economic production and distribution. Yet despite the loss of these manifest institutional functions, and the failure of most of these groups to develop any new institutional functions, we continue to expect them to perform adequately the implicit psychological or symbolic functions in the life of the individual.

Four

The general condition I am describing in Western society can be compared usefully with social changes taking place in many of the native cultures that have come under the impact of Western civilization. A large volume of anthropological work testifies to the incidence, in such areas as East Africa, India, China, and Burma, of processes of social dislocation and moral insecurity. A conflict of moral values is apparent. More particularly, it is a conflict, as J. S. Furnivall has said, "between the eastern system resting on religion, personal authority, and customary obligation, and the western system resting on reason, impersonal law, and individual rights."[2]

This conflict of principles and moral values is not an abstract thing, existing only in philosophical contemplation. It may indeed be a crisis of symbolism, of patterns of moral meaning, but more fundamentally it is a crisis of allegiances. It is a result, in very large part, of the increasing separation of traditional groups from the crucial ends and decisions in economic and political spheres. The wresting of economic significance from native clans, villages, and castes by new systems of industry, and the weakening of their effective social control through the establishment of new systems of administrative authority has had demonstrable moral effects. The revolutionary intellectual and moral ferment of the modern East is closely connected with the dislocation of traditional centers of authority and responsibility from the lives of the people.

The present position of caste in India is a striking case in point. During the past twenty-five or more centuries various efforts have been made by political and religious leaders to abolish or weaken this powerful association through techniques of force, political decree, or religious persuasion. Whether carried out by ancient religious prophets or by modern Christian missionaries, the majority of such efforts have been designed to change the religious or moral *meaning* of caste in the minds of its followers. But such efforts generally have been fruitless. Even attempts to convert the untouchables to Christianity, to wean them away from the caste system of which they have been so horribly the victims, have been for the most part without success. The conversion of many millions to the Muslim creed led only to the creation of new castes.

But at the present time in widening areas of India there is a conspicuous weakening of the whole caste system, among the prosperous as well as among the poverty-stricken. Why, after many centuries of tenacious persistence, has the massive system of caste suddenly begun to dissolve in many areas of India?

The answer comes from the fact of the increasing dislocation of caste *functions*—in law, charity, authority, education, and economic production. The creation of civil courts for the adjudication of disputes traditionally handled by caste *panchayats;* the growing assumption by the State and by many private agencies of mutual-aid activities formerly resident in the caste or subcaste; the rising popularity of the idea that the proper structure of education is the formal school or university, organized in Western terms; and the intrusion of the new systems of constraint and function in the factory and trade union—all of these represent new and competing values, and they represent, more significantly, new systems of *function* and *allegiance.*

When the major institutional functions have disappeared from a local village government or from a subcaste, the conditions are laid for the decline of the individual's allegiance to the older forms of organization. Failing to find any institutional substance in the old unities of social life, he is prone to withdraw, consciously or unconsciously, his loyalty to them. They no longer represent the prime moral experiences of his life. He finds himself, mentally, looking in new directions.

Some of the most extreme instances of insecurity and conflict of values in native cultures have resulted not from the nakedly ruthless forces of economic exploitation but from most commendable (by Western standards) acts of humanitarian reform. Thus the introduction of so physically salutary a measure as an irrigation district or medical service may be attended by all the promised gains in abundance and health, but such innovations can also bring about the most complex disruptions of social relationships and allegiances. Why? Because such systems, by the very *humaneness* of their functions, assume values that no purely exploitative agency can, and having become values they more easily serve to alienate the native from his devotion to the meanings associated with obsolete functional structures. The new technology means the creation of new centers of administrative authority which not infrequently nullify the prestige of village or caste groups, leading in time to a growing conflict between the moral meaning of the old areas of authority and the values associated with the new.

The beginnings of the welfare State in India, for example, along with the creation of new private agencies of educational, charitable, and religious activity, have led inevitably to the pre-emption of functions formerly resident (in however meager or debased manner) in the kinship and caste groups. It is irrelevant, for present purposes, that many of these pre-emptions have been responsible for physical improvement in the life of the people. What must be emphasized here are the social and moral effects irrespective of intent—whether accomplished by predatory mining and factory interests or by the liberal humanitarian. What is crucial is the invasion of the area of traditional function by new and often more efficient functional agencies—in charity, law, education, and economics. The consequence is a profound crisis in meanings and loyalties.

It is no part of my intent to offer these observations in any spirit of lament for the old. It is an evident conclusion that for technical as well as moral reasons much of the old order is inadequate to the demand constituted by population density and other factors. It is important to insist, however, that the solution by new administrative measures of technical and material problems does not carry with it any automatic answer to the social and moral difficulties created by the invasion of ancient areas of function. For all their humanitarian sentiments, a large number of native reformers, as well as Western, have been singularly insensitive to the moral problems created in such countries as China and India by the advent of Western techniques. The displacement of function must lead in the long run to the diminution of moral significance in the old; and this means the loss of accustomed centers of allegiance, belief, and incentive. Hence the widely observed spectacle of masses of "marginal" personalities in native cultures, of individuals adrift, encompassed by, but not belonging to, either the old or the new. New associations have arisen and continue to arise, but their functional value is still but dimly manifest for the greater number of people, and their moral and psychological appeal is correspondingly weak. Hence the profound appeal of what the great Indian philosopher, Tagore, called "the powerful anesthetic of nationalism." Hence also the appeal, among a significant minority of intellectuals, of communism, which makes central the ethos of organization and combines it with therapeutic properties of concerted action.

What is to be observed so vividly in many areas of the East is also, and has been, for some time, a notable characteristic of Western society. The process is less striking, less dramatic, for we are directly involved in it. But it is nonetheless a profoundly significant aspect of modern Western history and it arises from some of the same elements in Western culture which, when exported, have caused such dislocation and ferment in foreign areas. We too have suffered a decline in the institutional function of groups and associations upon which we have long depended for moral and psychological stability. We too are in a state that can, most optimistically, be called transition—of change from associative contexts that have become in so many places irrelevant and anachronistic to newer associative contexts that are still psychologically and morally dim to the perceptions of individuals. As a result of the sharp reduction in meaning formerly inherent in membership, the problems of status, adjustment, and moral direction have assumed tremendous importance in the East as well as the West.

Five

Nowhere is the concern with the problem of community in Western society more intense than with respect to the family.[3] The contemporary family, as countless books, articles, college courses, and marital clinics make plain, has become an obsessive problem. The family inspires a curious dualism of thought. We tend to regard it uneasily as a final manifestation of tribal society, somehow inappropriate to a democratic, industrial age, but, at the same time, we have become ever more aware of its possibilities as an instrument of social reconstruction.

The intensity of theoretical interest in the family has curiously enough risen in direct proportion to the decline of the family's basic institutional importance to our culture. The present "problem" of the family is dramatized by the fact that its abstract importance to the moralist or psychologist has grown all the while that its tangible institutional significance to the layman and its functional importance to economy and State have diminished.

It is doubtless one more manifestation of the contemporary quest for security that students of the family increasingly see its main "function" to be that of conferring "adjustment" upon the individual, and, for the most part, they find no difficulty at all in supposing that this psychological function can be carried on by the family in what is otherwise a functional vacuum. Contemporary social psychology has become so single-mindedly aware of the psychological gratification provided by the group for individual needs of security and recognition that there is an increasing tendency to suppose that such a function is primary and can maintain itself autonomously, impervious to changes in *institutional* functions which normally give a group importance in culture. For many reasons the contemporary family is made to carry a conscious symbolic importance that is greater than ever, but it must do this with a structure much smaller in size and of manifestly diminishing relevance to the larger economic, religious, and political ends of contemporary society.

Historically the family's importance has come from the fact of intimate social cohesion united with institutional significance in society, not from its sex or blood relationships. In earlier ages, kinship was inextricably involved in the processes of getting a living, providing education, supporting the infirm, caring for the aged, and maintaining religious values. In vast rural areas, until quite recently, the family was the actual agency of economic production, distribution, and consumption. Even in towns and cities, the family long retained its close relation to these obviously crucial activities. Organized living was simply inconceivable, for the most part, outside of the context provided by kinship. Few individuals were either too young or too old to find a place of importance within the group, a fact which enhanced immeasurably the family's capacity for winning allegiance and providing symbolic integration for the individual.

The interpersonal and psychological aspects of kinship were never made to rest upon personal romance alone or even upon pure standards of individual rectitude. Doubtless, deviations from the moral code and disillusionment with romance were as common then as now. But they did not interfere with the cultural significance of the family simply because the family was far more than an interpersonal relationship based upon affection and moral probity. It was an indispensable institution.

But in ever enlarging areas of population in modern times, the economic, legal, educational, religious, and recreational functions of the family have declined or diminished. Politically, membership in the family is superfluous; economically, it is regarded by many as an outright hindrance to success. The family, as someone has put it, is now the accident of the worker rather than his essence. His competitive position may be more favorable without it. Our systems of law and education and all the manifold recreational activities of individuals engaged in their pursuit of happiness have come to rest upon, and to be directed to, the individual, not the family. On all sides we continue to celebrate from pulpit and rostrum the indispensability to economy and the State of the family. But, in plain fact, the family is indispensable to neither of these at the present time. The major processes of economy and political administration have become increasingly independent of the symbolism and integrative activities of kinship.

There is an optimistic apologetics that sees in this waning of the family's institutional importance only the beneficent hand of Progress. We are told by certain psychologists and sociologists that, with its loss of economic and legal functions, the family has been freed of all that is basically irrelevant to its "real" nature; that the true function of the family—the cultivation of affection, the shaping of personality, above all, the manufacture of "adjustment"—is now in a position to flourish illimitably, to the greater glory of man and society. In a highly popular statement, we are told that the family has progressed from institution to companionship.

But, as Ortega y Gasset has written, "people do not live together merely to be together. They live together to do something together." To suppose that the present family, or any other group, can perpetually vitalize itself through some indwelling affectional tie, in the absence of concrete, perceived functions, is like supposing that the comradely ties of mutual aid which grow up incidentally in a military unit will long outlast a condition in which war is plainly and irrevocably banished. Applied to the family, the argument suggests that affection and personality cultivation can somehow exist in a social vacuum, unsupported by the determining goals and ideals of economic and political society. But in hard fact no social group will long survive the disappearance of its chief reasons for being, and these reasons are not, primarily, biological but institutional. Unless new institutional functions are performed by a group—family, trade union, or church—its psychological influence will become minimal.

No amount of veneration for the psychological functions of a social group, for the capacity of the group to gratify cravings for security and recognition, will offset the fact that, however important these functions may be in any given individual's life, he does not join the group essentially for them. He joins the group if and when its larger institutional or intellectual functions have relevance both to his own life organization and to what he can see of the group's relation to the larger society. The individual may indeed derive vast psychic support and integration from the pure fact of group membership, but he will not long derive this when he becomes in some way aware of the gulf between the moral claims of a group and its actual institutional importance in the social order.

All of this has special relevance to the family, with its major function now generally reduced by psychologists to that of conferring adjustment upon individuals. Yet in any objective view the family is probably now less effective in this regard than it has ever been. It is plain that the family is no longer the main object of personal loyalty in ever larger sections of our population, and it is an overstrain on the imagination to suppose that it will regain a position of psychological importance through pamphlets, clinics, and high-school courses on courtship and marriage. How quaint now seems that whole literature on sexual adjustment in marriage with its implicit argument that sexual incompatibility is the basic cause of the reduced significance of marriage. Some of the solemn preoccupations with "family tensions" which now hold the field of clinical practice will one day no doubt seem equally quaint.

The current problem of the family, like the problem of any social group, cannot be reduced to simple sets of psychological complexes which exist universally in man's nature, or to an ignorance of sexual techniques, or to a lack of Christian morality. The family is a major problem in our culture simply because we are attempting to make it perform psychological and symbolic functions with a structure that has become fragile and an institutional importance that is almost totally unrelated to the economic and political realities of our society. Moreover, the growing impersonality and the accumulating demands of ever larger sections of our world of business and government tend to throw an extraordinary psychological strain upon the family. In this now small and fragile group we seek the security and affection denied everywhere else. It is hardly strange that timeless incompatibilities and emotional strains should, in the present age, assume an unwonted importance—their meaning has changed with respect to the larger context of men's lives. We thus find ourselves increasingly in the position of attempting to correct, through psychiatric or spiritual techniques, problems which, although assuredly emotional, derive basically from a set of historically given institutional circumstances.

Personal crises, underlying emotional dissatisfactions, individual deviations from strict rectitude—these have presumably been constant in all ages of history. Only our own age tends to blow up these tensions into reasons for a clinical approach to happiness. Such tensions appear more critical and painful, more intolerable to contemporary man, simply because the containing social structures of such tensions have become less vital to his existence. The social structures are expendable so far as the broad economic and political processes of our society are concerned and, consequently, they offer less support for particular emotional states. Not a few of the problems that give special concern to our present society—sex role, courtship and marriage, old age, the position of the child—do so because of the modified functional and psychological position of the family in our culture.

The widely publicized problems of the modern middle-class woman do not result, as certain Freudians have seemed to suggest, from a disharmony between her innate psychological character and the present values of feminism. Whatever may be the neurological nature of the female, as compared with that of the male, the special and distinctive problem of the woman in our culture arises from certain changes in social function and conceptualized role. What has been called women's emancipation from patriarchalism is, in a highly relevant sense, an emancipation from clear, socially approved function and role within the institutionalized family group. To put it in these terms does not lessen the intensity of the problem in many quarters, but it takes it out of the vague realm of supposed innate complexes and places it within the determinable context of historical changes in social position. It puts the psychological problems of women in exactly the same context in which lie contemporary problems of the role of the father and the child. The former problems may be more intense, more explicit, but they do not differ in kind from those besetting the existences of other members of the family.

The oftentimes absurd worship of the female, especially the mother, in contemporary American society, has frequently been interpreted by ardent feminists as a reflection of her recent rise to eminence after centuries of subordination to the male. But it reflects rather an unconscious overcompensation for the historical fact of her release from any clear and indispensable *social role* within the family.[4] And this is a part of the historical change in the function to society of the whole family group.

The sharp discrepancy between the family's actual contributions to present political and economic order and the set of spiritual images inherited from the past intensifies the problem of definition of sex role. From this basic discrepancy proceed all the elaborate, and frequently self-defeating, techniques of the "rational" cultivation of the family tie, the stunting dosages of scientific mother—love for the child, and the staggering number of clinics, conferences, lectures, pamphlets, and books on the subject of relations between parent and child, between husband and wife. It is this riot of rational techniques that has led to the bland and unexamined assumption that the family is today a more "affectionate" organization than it was a century ago.

In our society most of the period of storm and stress that is adolescence has little to do with the biological changes the child is undergoing. It has almost everything to do with the problem of role in the family and the clarity of the family's relation to society. In all past ages, and in many contemporary societies today, the development of the child into manhood or womanhood is attended, if not by actual lengthy and intense ceremonial rites, by relatively clear communications of value and purpose. And these have been possible only when there have been concrete institutional functions to symbolize and hence communicate. Today adolescence is the period, we are justified in saying, when the appalling discrepancy between shadow and substance in contemporary kinship first becomes evident to the child. It is then, in a profound if largely unconscious way, that he becomes aware of the gulf between inherited authority patterns and the actual functional contribution of the family. For in any group it is only the latter that can give effective meaning to the former.

Far more tragic in our culture is the position in which more and more of the aged find themselves. To interpret the present problem of old age as the consequence of living in a "youth-dominated" society is somewhat deceptive. All periods of culture have been characterized by great rewards for the young military leader, statesman, merchant, and writer. The age of some of the most distinguished members in the long history of Parliament in England is a case in point, and we may suppose that the brilliant young Pitt would find it far more difficult today to lead the House of Representatives in supposedly youth-dominated America than he did Parliament in eighteenth-century England. Conversely there is no clear evidence to indicate that the proportion of the aged who are now prominent in business, professions, and government is any smaller than in earlier times.

Since Cicero's *De Senectute* there has probably never been a period in which men have not faced the onset of old age with the feeling that its consolations must be compensatorily set down in writing in order to lessen the pathos of their enforced separation from previous activities. Today it is not the separation from wonted activities that is so painfully manifested in thought and behavior but the widening sense of alienation from family and society, a sense of alienation that is reflected not only in the staggering increase of the so-called senile neuroses and psychoses but in the old-age political movements.

In many instances the root causes are plainly economic, but the contemporary incidence of economic problems of the aged must itself be seen in relation to changes in social structure. To leave out of present consideration those whose position is purely the result of financial strain, there is obviously a growing number of elderly people whose estrangement comes from the altered social status and psychological role in which they find themselves. It is not always that they find themselves physically outside of a family group. In the most pathetic manifestations of this problem it is that such people find themselves in but not of the group. The change in the structure of the family has led to a change in the significance of individual members, especially of the aged.

The fantastic romanticism that now surrounds courtship and marriage in our culture is drawn in part no doubt from larger contexts of romanticism in modern history and is efficiently supported by the discovery of modern retail business that the mass-advertised fact of romance is good for sales. But the lushness of such advertising obviously depends on a previously fertilized soil, and this soil may be seen in large part as the consequence of changes in the relation of the family to the other aspects of the social order. The diminution in the functional significance of the family has been attended by efforts to compensate in the affectional realm of intensified romance. Probably no other age in history has so completely identified (confused, some might say) marriage and romance as has our own. The claim that cultivation of affection is the one remaining serious function of the family is ironically supported by the stupefying amount of effort put into the calculated cultivation of romance, both direct and vicarious. Whether this has made contemporary marriage a more affectionate and devoted relationship is a controversy we need not enter here.

The social roles of adolescence, old age, and affection have been profoundly altered by changes in the functional positions of the members of the family. Such states are *perceived* differently, both by the individuals immediately concerned and by others around them. So are the recurrent "crises" of personal life—birth, marriage, and death—regarded differently as a consequence of changes in the structure and functions of the family. Except from the point of view of the biologist, death, for example, is not the same phenomenon from one society to another, from one age to another. Death also has its social role, and this role is inseparable from the organization of values and relationships within which the physical fact of death takes place. Death almost everywhere is ritualized, ritualized for the sake of the deceased, if we like, but far more importantly for the sake of those who are left behind. Such ritualization has immensely important psychological functions in the direction of emotional release for the individuals most closely related to the dead person and in the direction, too, of the whole social group. But these death rites are not disembodied acts of obeisance or succor; they are manifestations of group life and function. They are closely related, that is, to other aspects of the family which have no immediate connection with the fact of death.

In our society we find ourselves increasingly baffled and psychologically unprepared for the incidence of death among loved ones. It is not that grief is greater or that the incomprehensibility of death is increased. It is in considerable part perhaps because the smaller structure of the family gives inevitably a greater emotional value to each of the members. But, more than this, it is the result, I believe, of the decline in significance of the traditional means of ritual *completion* of the fact of death. Death leaves a kind of moral suspense that is terminated psychologically only with greater and greater difficulty. The social *meaning* of death has changed with the social *position* of death.

Six

The problems arising from the diminished institutional and psychological importance of the family in our society also extend into wider areas of social and economic behavior. We find ourselves dealing increasingly with difficulties that seem to resolve themselves into matters of human motivation and incentives. An older economics and politics and educational theory took it for granted that all the root impulses to buying and selling and saving, to voting, and to learning lay, in prepotent form, in the individual himself. The relation between crucial economic motivations and the social groups in which individuals actually lived was seldom if ever heeded by the classical economists.

The late Harvard economist, Joseph Schumpeter, wrote tellingly on this point. "In order to realize what all this means for the efficiency of the capitalist engine of production we need only recall that the family and the family home used to be the mainspring of the typically bourgeois kind of profit motive. Economists have not always given due weight to this fact. When we look more closely at their idea of the self-interest of entrepreneurs and capitalists we cannot fail to discover that the results it was supposed to produce are really not at all what one would expect from the rational self-interest of the detached individual or the childless couple who no longer look at the world through the windows of a family home. Consciously or unconsciously, they analyzed the behavior of the man whose motives are shaped by such a home and who means to work and save primarily for wife and children. As soon as these fade out from the moral vision of the business man, we have a different kind of *homo economicus* before us who cares for different things and acts in different ways."[5]

Much of the predictability of human response, which the classical economists made the basis of their faith in the automatic workings is of the free market, came not from fixed instincts but from the vast conservatism and stability of a society that remained deeply rooted in kinship long after the advent of the capitalist age. Had it not been for the profound incentives supplied by the family and, equally important, the capacity of the extended family to supply a degree, however minimal, of mutual aid in time of distress, it is a fair guess that capitalism would have failed before it was well under way. The extraordinary rate of capital accumulation in the nineteenth century was dependent, to some extent at least, on a low-wage structure that was in turn dependent on the continuation of the ethic of family aid, even when this involved child labor in the factories.[6]

The same point may be made with respect to the relation of kinship symbolism and population increase. What Malthus and his followers regarded as embedded in the biological nature of man, the almost limitless urge to procreate, has turned out to be inseparable from the cultural fact of kinship, with its inherited incentives and values. As long as the family had institutional importance in society, it tended to maintain moral and psychological devotions which resulted in high birth rates—rates that invited the alarm of a good many sociologists. But with the decline in both the functional and psychological importance of kinship, and with the emergence of a culture based increasingly on the abstract individual rather than the family, there has resulted a quite different birth rate and a quite different set of population problems.

To be sure we are dealing here, in this matter of motivations and incentives, not merely with the effects of the changed significance of the family but with those of the changed significance of other social cohesions upon which our economy and political order depended for a long period of time. What has happened to the family has happened also to neighborhood and local community. As Robert S. Lynd has written: "Neighborhood and community ties are not only optional but generally growing less strong; and along with them is disappearing the important network of intimate, informal, social controls traditionally associated with living closely with others."[7] Within all of these lay not merely controls but the incentives that supplied the motive force for such pursuits as education and religion and recreation.

The point is that with the decline in the significance of kinship and locality, and the failure of new social relationships to assume influences of equivalent evocative intensity, a profound change has occurred in the very psychological structure of society. And this is a change that has produced a great deal of the present problem of incentives in so many areas of our society. Most of our ideas and practices in the major institutional areas of society developed during an age when the residual psychological elements of social organization seemed imperishable. No less imperishable seemed the structure of personality itself.

Educational goals and political objectives were fashioned accordingly, as were theories of economic behavior and population increase.

But we are learning that many of the motivations and incentives which an older generation of rationalists believed were inherent in the individual are actually supplied by social groups—social groups with both functional and moral relevance to the lives of individuals.

Modern planners thus frequently find themselves dealing, not simply with the upper stratum of decisions, which their forebears assumed would be the sole demand of a planned society, but with often baffling problems which reach down into the very recesses of human personality.[8]

Seven

Basically, however, it is not the position of the family or of any other single group, old or new, that is crucial to the welfare of a social order. Associations may come and go under the impact of historical changes and cultural needs. There is no single type of family, any more than there is a single type of religion, that is essential to personal security and collective prosperity. It would be wrong to assume that the present problem of community in Western society arises inexorably from the modifications which have taken place in old groups, however cherished these may be. But irrespective of particular groups, there must be in any stable culture, in any civilization that prizes its integrity, functionally significant and psychologically meaningful groups and associations lying intermediate to the individual and the larger values and purposes of his society. For these are the small areas of association within which alone such values and purposes can take on clear meaning in personal life and become the vital roots of the large culture. It is, I believe, the problem of intermediate association that is fundamental at the present time.

Under the lulling influence of the idea of Progress we have generally assumed until recently that history automatically provides its own solution to the basic problems of organization in society. We have further assumed that man is ineradicably gregarious and that from this gregariousness must come ever new and relevant forms of intermediate association.

It is tempting to believe this as we survey the innumerable formal organizations of modern life, the proliferation of which has been one of the signal facts in American history, or as we observe the incredible number of personal contacts which take place daily in the congested areas of modern urban life.

But there is a profound difference between the casual, informal relationships which abound in such areas and the kind of social groups which create a sense of belonging, which supply incentive, and which confer upon the individual a sense of status. Moreover, from some highly suggestive evidence supplied by such sociologists as Warner, Lazarsfeld, and especially Mirra Komarovsky, we can justly doubt that all sections of modern populations are as rich in identifiable social groups and associations as we have heretofore taken for granted.

The common assumption that, as the older associations of kinship and neighborhood have become weakened, they are replaced by new voluntary associations filling the same role is not above sharp question. That traditional groups have weakened in significance is apparently true enough but, on the evidence, their place has not been taken to any appreciable extent by new forms of association. Despite the appeal of the older sociological stereotype of the urban dweller who belongs to various voluntary associations, all of which have progressively replaced the older social unities, the facts so far gathered suggest the contrary: that a rising number of individuals belong to no organized association at all, and that, in the large cities, the unaffiliated persons may even constitute a majority of the population.[9]

As for the psychological functions of the great formal associations in modern life—industrial corporations, governmental agencies, large-scale labor and charitable organizations—it is plain that not many of these answer adequately the contemporary quest for community. Such organizations, as Max Weber pointed out, are generally organized not around personal loyalties but around loyalty to an office or machine. The administration of charity, hospitalization, unemployment assistance, like the administration of the huge manufacturing corporation, may be more efficient and less given to material inequities, but the possible gains in technical efficiency do not minimize their underlying impersonality in the life of the individual.

Much of the contemporary sense of the impersonality of society comes from the rational impersonality of these great organizations. The widespread reaction against technology, the city, and political freedom, not to mention the nostalgia that pervades so many of the discussions of rural-urban differences, comes from the diminished functional relationship between existent social groups in industry or the community and the remote efficiency of the larger organizations created by modern planners. The derivative loss of meaning for the individual frequently becomes the moral background of vague and impotent reactions against technology and science, and of aggressive states of mind against the culture as a whole. In spatial terms the individual is obviously less isolated from his fellows in the large-scale housing project or in the factory than was his grandfather. What he has become isolated from is the sense of meaningful proximity to the major ends and purposes of his culture. With the relatively complete satisfaction of needs concerned with food, employment, and housing, a different order of needs begins to assert itself imperiously; and these have to do with spiritual belief and social status.

"The uneasiness, the malaise of our time," writes C. Wright Mills, "is due to this root fact: in our politics and economy, in family life and religion—in practically every sphere of our existence—the certainties of the eighteenth and nineteenth centuries have disintegrated or been destroyed and, at the same time, no new sanctions or justifications for the new routines we live, and must live, have taken hold. Among white-collar people, the malaise is deep-rooted; for the absence of any order of belief has left them morally defenseless as individuals and politically impotent as a group. Newly created in a harsh time of creation, white-collar man has no culture to lean upon except the contents of a mass society that has shaped him and seeks to manipulate him to its alien ends. For security's sake he must attach himself somewhere, but no communities or organizations seem to be thoroughly his."[10]

The quest for community will not be denied, for it springs from some of the powerful needs of human nature—needs for a clear sense of cultural purpose, membership, status, and continuity. Without these, no amount of mere material welfare will serve to arrest the developing sense of alienation in our society, and the mounting preoccupation with the imperatives of community. To appeal to technological progress is futile. For what we discover is that rising standards of living, together with increases in leisure, actually intensify the disquietude and frustration that arise when cherished and proffered goals are without available means of fulfillment. "Secular improvement that is taken for granted," wrote Joseph Schumpeter, "and coupled with individual insecurity that is acutely resented is of course the best recipe for breeding social unrest."[11]

The loss of old moral certainties and accustomed statuses is, however, only the setting of our problem. For, despite the enormous influence of nostalgia in human thinking, it is never the recovery of the institutionally old that is desired by most people. In any event, the quest for the past is as futile as is that of the future.

The real problem is not, then, the loss of old contexts but rather the failure of our present democratic and industrial scene to create new contexts of association and moral cohesion within which the smaller allegiances of men will assume both functional and psychological significance. It is almost as if the forces that weakened the old have remained to obstruct the new channels of association.

What is the source of this failure? The blame is usually laid to technology, science, and the city. These, it is said, have left a vacuum. But the attack on these elements of modern culture is ill-founded, for no one of these is either logically or psychologically essential to the problem at hand. Neither science, nor technology, nor the city is inherently incompatible with the existence of moral values and social relationships which will do for modern man what the extended family, the parish, and the village did for earlier man.

Here, our problem becomes inevitably historical. For the present position of the social group in political and industrial society cannot be understood apart from certain historical tendencies concerned with the location of authority and function in society and with certain momentous conflicts of authority and function which have been fundamental in the development of the modern State.

PART TWO

THE STATE AND
COMMUNITY

4   History as the Decline of Community

The history of a society can be considered in many aspects. It can be seen in terms of the rise of democracy, the fall of aristocracy, the advance of technology, the recession of religion. It can be conceived, as Tocqueville conceived it, as the work of equality; as Acton considered it, as the work of freedom; or, in Bertrand Russell's terms, as the story of power. There is no limit to the ways of profitably regarding the history of any given society. Each mode of consideration is, as Whitehead has reminded us, "a sort of searchlight elucidating some of the facts, and retreating the remainder into an omitted background."[1]

History, the late F. J. Teggart insisted, is plural. It is plural in sequence of event and plural in result. There is no one general statement that can remain meaningful before the diversity of historical materials. For a long time the idea of progress was held capable of assimilating and making intelligible the diverse experiences of man's past. Today it is no longer so held. If there is any single general idea that has replaced it, it is the idea of decline. But the idea of decline is no more, no less, correct than the idea of progress. History is neither progress nor decline alone. It is both. What is determinative in the historian's judgment is simply that aspect of the present he chooses to illuminate.

Thus, if we value the emergence of the individual from ancient confinements of patriarchal kinship, class, gild, and village community, the outcome of modern European history must appear progressive in large degree. For, plainly, the major toll of modern social change has been exacted from such communal entities as these. From the point of view of the individual—the autonomous, rational individual—the whole sequence of events embodied in Renaissance, Reformation, and Revolution must appear as the work of progressive liberation. There is nothing wrong with this appraisal of history. It is undeniably illuminative. But it is inescapably selective.

If, on the other hand, we value coherent moral belief, clear social status, cultural roots, and a strong sense of interdependence with others, the same major events and changes of modern history can be placed in a somewhat different light. The processes that have led to the release of the individual from old customs and solidarities have led also to a loss of moral certainties, a confusion of cultural meanings, and a disruption of established social contexts. We cannot, in sum, deal with the progressive emancipation of individuals without recognizing also the decline of those structures from which the individual has been emancipated. Judgments of progress must always be specific and selective; they cannot be disengaged from opposing judgments of decline and disruption.

A preference for the emancipation of the individual and for the advancement of secularism, mobility, and moral freedom may well be sovereign in our total moral appraisal. We may regard these developments in modern history as worth whatever has been exacted from moral certainty and social interdependence. But such preference, understandable though it be, is no warrant for omitting from consideration the historical facts of decline and disintegration. No approach to history and—to the problems of the present is valid that does not regard the present as the outcome, in varying proportions, of both advancement and decline.

Two

If we are to understand the conditions that lie behind the quest for community in our society, we must look not merely to contemporary social and psychological dislocations but to the historical sequences of change which have led up to them. There is a quickly reached limit to the value of diagnoses that dispense with the historical record and that seek, like those of the anthropologist, to explain the present solely in terms of present processes. The historical past has a persistent and penetrating influence upon the behavior and ideas of any generation. Perhaps the greatest contribution of Marx to nineteenth-century economics and psychology was his insistence that all economic and psychic relationships are historically determined. If we would diagnose our own age we had better do so historically, for history is the essence of human culture and thought.

The dislocations and tensions of our own age can be clarified only by reference to certain massive changes that have taken place in modern history in the larger contexts of human association. These are changes in allegiance to institutions, in the location of social functions, in the relationship of men and the norms of culture, and, above all, in the source and diffusion of political power. The present problem of intermediate association in State, industry, and community has its roots in certain conflicts of authority and function that have been notable aspects of the social history of modern Europe.

The historical changes to which I refer have been remarked variously. In the nineteenth century the English conservative, Sir Henry Maine, on the basis of studies in comparative law, was led to see in modern history a continuous movement away from the centrality of the social group, with its attributes of status and membership, to the primacy of the legally autonomous individual and impersonal relations of contract. "Throughout all its course [the movement of progressive societies] has been distinguished by the gradual dissolution of family dependency and the growth of individual obligation in its place. The Individual is steadily substituted for the Family as the unit of which civil laws take account."[2]

Karl Marx was also struck by this drift of social relationships, and, characteristically, he attributed it to the revolutionary influence of the bourgeoisie. "The bourgeoisie, wherever it has got the upper hand, has put an end to all feudal, idyllic relations. It has pitilessly torn asunder the motley feudal ties that bound man to his 'natural superiors,' and has left remaining no other nexus between man and man than naked self-interest, than callous 'cash payment.' It has drowned the most heavenly ecstasies of religious fervor, of chivalrous enthusiasm, of philistine sentimentalism, in the icy waters of egotistical calculation. . . . It has converted the physician, the lawyer, the priest, the man of science, into its paid wage-laborers. The bourgeoisie has torn away from the family its sentimental veil, and has reduced the family relation to a mere money relation."[3]

Similarly, some of the German sociologists of the late nineteenth century called attention to the processes of modern history that have led to an atomization or mechanization of the primary social relationships. Tönnies expressed this as a continuous weakening of the ties of *Gemeinschaft*—the communal ties of family, gild, and village—and a constant maximization in modern times of the more impersonal, atomistic, and mechanical relationships of what he called *Gesellschaft*.[4] Simmel, following insights of Marx and Engels, dealt extensively with the depersonalizing influence upon traditional moral and social patterns of the modern spread of money as a dominant means of exchange. Because of the easy convertibility of all qualitative values and status relationships into fluid relationships of contract, based upon money, modern capitalism has had a leveling and fragmenting effect upon the contexts of status and membership.[5] In somewhat the same way, the great Max Weber pointed out the incidence of powerful processes of rationalization and bureaucratization upon systems of authority, patterns of culture, and the location of social function. These processes have led, Weber declared, to a supremacy in modern times of the impersonal office and of mechanical systems of administration within which the primary unities of social life have become indistinct and tenuous.[6]

The French sociologists Le Play and Durkheim, in their monumental studies of society, were also led to point out the atomizing effects upon society of such forces as technology, individualism, and the division of labor. "What is in fact characteristic of our development," wrote Durkheim, "is that it has successively destroyed all the established social contexts; one after another they have been banished either by the slow usury of time or by violent revolution, and in such fashion that nothing has been developed to replace them."[7]

So too have such scholars as von Gierke, Duguit, Maitland, Tawney, the Hammonds, and many others called attention to the contrast that exists between contemporary society, organized increasingly in impersonal terms and resting on the legally separate individual, and an earlier form of society characterized by the primacy of custom and community. On the basis of this perceived contrast innumerable specific studies of law, education, kinship, town, and religion have rested.

So far as Western society is concerned, the frame of reference for all of these contrasts is the transition from medieval to modern Europe. It is the social structure of the Middle Ages, real or imagined, that has provided a common point of departure for interpretations as different as those of the socialist Marx and the conservative Maine. It must be our point of departure also.

"Modern history," declared Lord Acton, "tells how the last four hundred years have modified the medieval conditions of life and thought." There is wisdom in this generalization. The essence of modern social and cultural history has been the almost incessant preoccupation with principles and structures which are, in substance, medieval. Modern systems of political representation, religious structure, kinship, class, and law cannot be understood except as institutional continuities, modified and readjusted by historical event, arising out of the Middle Ages. And a large number of distinctively modern social movements are made intelligible only when they are seen as responses to economic and intellectual conditions left by the changes or disruptions in medieval institutions and moral certainties.

Three

Amid all the interpretations and judgments of historians regarding medieval society, ranging from the idealizations of a Belloc or Cram to the incisive realism of a Coulton, there is agreement upon certain social characteristics of the Middle Ages, irrespective of the moral inferences to be drawn from them. The first is the pre-eminence in medieval society—in its economy, religion, and morality—of the small social group. From such organizations as family, gild, village community, and monastery flowed most of the cultural life of the age. The second fact, deriving from the first, is the centrality of personal status, of membership, in society. In the Middle Ages, Jacob Burckhardt has written, "Man was conscious of himself only as a member of a race, people, party, family, or corporation—only through some general category." [8] The reality of the separate, autonomous individual was as indistinct as that of centralized political power. Both were subordinated to the immense range of association that lay intermediate to individual and ruler and that included such groups as the patriarchal family, the gild, the church, feudal class, and the village community. And, as we shall see, the epic of modern European history is composed in very large part of the successive extrications of both individual and State from the fetters of medieval group life.

"All who are included in a community," wrote Aquinas, "stand in relation to that community as parts to the whole." The immense influence of the whole philosophy of organism and that of the related doctrine of the great chain of being, which saw every element as an infinitesimal gradation of ascent to God, supported and gave reason for the deeply held philosophy of community. Whether it was the divine Kingdom itself or some component mundane association like the family or gild, the whole weight of medieval learning was placed in support of the reality of social wholes, of communities. To be sure there were sharp challenges to this metaphysical realism, from William of Occam on, and one of the most fascinating aspects of the development of modern philosophy is the succession of metaphysical and epistemological disengagements of the individual and his will from the organismic unities of medieval thought. But, in general, the philosophy of community was dominant in medieval thought.

The centrality of community was much more than a philosophical principle however. Whether we are dealing with the family, the village, or the gild, we are in the presence of systems of authority and allegiance which were widely held to precede the individual in both origin and right. "It was a distinctive trait of medieval doctrine," Otto von Gierke writes in his great study of medieval groups, "that within every human group it decisively recognized an aboriginal and active right of the group taken as a whole."[9] As many an institutional historian has discovered, medieval economy and law are simply unintelligible if we try to proceed from modern conceptions of individualism and contract. The group was primary; it was the irreducible unit of the social system at large.

The family, patriarchal and corporate in essence, was more than a set of interpersonal relations. It was a fixed institutional system within which innumerable, indispensable functions were performed. Upon it, rather than upon the individual, were levied taxes and fines; to it, rather than the individual, went the honors of achievement. In its corporate solidarity lay the ground of almost all decision affecting the individual—his occupation, welfare, marriage, and the rearing of his children. Property belonged to the family, not the individual, and it could not easily be alienated from the family. Law began with the inviolable rights of the family over its members, and public law, such as it was, could not generally cross the threshold of the family. Beyond the immediate, conjugal family stretched the extended family numbering sometimes hundreds of persons in close association, tightly knit together by custom and function. And beyond the domain of tangible kinship, the immense symbolic influence of the family reached into scores of organizations which adopted the nomenclature and spirit of kinship.

So, too, the prevailing system of agriculture was, as Vinogradoff has emphasized, "communal in its very essence. Every trait that makes it strange and inconvenient from the point of individualistic interests renders it highly appropriate to a state of things ruled by communal conceptions."[10] To be sure there were variations in the intensity of this communality from one area to another, but wherever open-field husbandry was practiced the sheer technical demands of the system, with its complicated network of strips, enjoined upon the peasant a degree of solidarity with his fellows that the later enclosure acts and reform programs found difficult to break. The villager had little alternative, in such surroundings, but to subordinate himself and his desires to those of the village group. And, given the nucleus of households with families in enforced close association, given also the system of communal apportionment of the shares in the arable, the communal decisions about times and places of cultivation, the existence of the all-important commons, and the individual functionaries who served the village as a whole under the watchful eyes of the manorial lord, it is not strange that medieval agriculture should have been pervaded by an ethic of group solidarity, which the agricultural reformers of the eighteenth century found strange to the point of unreason. In the Middle Ages, Maitland has somewhere written, villagers sacrificed efficiency upon the altar of communal equality. "A village formed what we call a community," Homans has written, "not only because all its members were submitted to the same set of customs—because the land of every villager lay in the form of strips intermingled with those of his neighbors, because every villager followed the same traditional rotation of crops and sent his cattle to run in a common herd. A village formed a community chiefly because all its members were brought up to consent and act together as a group."[11]

Even in the towns, where there was a freer air, where there was inevitably a greater amount of individual autonomy, we cannot miss the decisive role of corporate association. What were the towns—at least those which were not survivals of the Roman Empire—but, in origin, associations of merchants and tradesmen. The walls surrounding so many of these towns were no thicker than the protective framework of corporate rights which lay in the charters of the towns. A town was more than a simple place of residence and occupation; it was itself a close association, and its members—*citizens, in the medieval sense*—were bound to live up to its articles and customs almost as rigorously as the peasants on a manor.[12] Within the town were innumerable small associations, the gilds—organizations based first upon occupation, to be sure, but also upon sacred obligations of mutual-aid, religious faith, and political responsibility. Here, too, in these urban social organizations we are dealing with structures of authority and function which long resisted the later efforts of businessmen and political rulers to subjugate or destroy them. And from such studies as those of Rashdall[13] we can observe the dominance of the principle of corporate association even in the realm of higher education. The university (a word applied indiscriminately in the twelfth and thirteenth centuries to almost any form of fellowship that served a definite function) was basically a gild of masters and students, the prime object of which was the stabilization of learning and the protection of its votaries.

Finally, in the vast empire of religion we see, perhaps at its height, the principle of corporate association with its corollaries of communal obligation and faith mediated by membership in a visible community. It would be absurd to exaggerate either the religious devotion of medieval man or the extent of his associative obligations. It will suffice to say that there were both Pharisees and Protestants in the medieval Church. Yet, we cannot miss the profusion of religious fellowships, frith-gilds, monasteries, and ecclesiastical courts; the emphasis on the communion of saints, on supererogatory works, auricular confession; or the innumerable penetrations of religion into the market place—which seventeenth- and eighteenth-century businessmen were to find so insufferable. In the Middle Ages, allowing for all obliquities and transgressions, the ethic of religion and the ethic of community were one. It was indeed this oneness, so often repressive of individual faith, so often corrupting to the purity of devotion, that the religious reformers like Wyclif, Hus, Calvin, and others were to seek strenuously to dissolve. And so, for quite different reasons, were later political rulers to seek to dissolve this unity. The affinity between extreme religious individualism and allegiance to central national power which Shaw emphasizes in his play *St. Joan* is an actual historical affinity. Each element was dangerous to the corporate Church. Together, as later events proved, they were irresistible.

Further elaboration upon the centrality of the social group and its attributes of status is unnecessary. Despite the mobility, greater than many earlier historians were wont to realize, reflected in medieval commerce, in the great fairs, in the wanderings of scholars, in the administration of the Church, not to mention the innumerable holy quests, the literature of the age reveals a mentality dominated by matters of allegiance, membership, tradition, and group solidarity. Law and custom were virtually indistinguishable, and both were hardly more than the inner order of associations.

Two points only are in need of stress here. The first is the derivation of group solidarity from the core of the indispensable functions each group performed in the lives of its members. The larger philosophy of community unquestionably had its influence, but the major reason for the profound hold of the family and the local community and gild upon human lives was simply the fact that, apart from membership in these and other groups, life was impossible for the vast majority of human beings. The second point to stress is that the solidarity of each functional group was possible only in an environment of authority where central power was weak and fluctuating. As Ernest Barker has written, the medieval State "abounded in groups and in the practice of what we may call communal self-help because it was not yet itself a fully organized group. When it became such it asserted itself and curtailed the rights of groups with no little vigor."[14] It is indeed this curtailment of group rights by the rising power of the central political government that forms one of the most revolutionary movements of modern history.

Four

Terms of aggregation like the word "medieval" are peculiarly liable, in historical discussion, to arbitrary and distorted usage. As a word, medieval is more commonly made to represent an artificially limited period of time in European history than it is to describe a set of intellectual principles and social institutions which can scarcely be dated at all. Neither the fifteenth nor the sixteenth century ended medieval society if, by medieval, we have reference to types of kinship, property, education, religion, and class. It would be more accurate to see such centuries as a kind of watershed of history, and even then we have to be very careful of the areas and spheres we are referring to. For, measured in institutional terms, large sections of European society remained medieval until well into the nineteenth century.

Nevertheless, it is possible to see that by the sixteenth century, many of the communalisms of the Middle Ages had declined sharply. Even earlier, as early as the thirteenth and fourteenth centuries, there were those who endeavored resolutely to reduce the significance of the whole sphere of association that lay intermediate to the individual and Pope, the individual and emperor, or the individual and king. Such endeavors are to be seen in a great variety of papal edicts, monarchical decrees, and imperial proposals. Making all allowance for the centrality of the social group in medieval life, we should be shortsighted if we missed the often sharp conflicts of principle and practice in the realm of function and authority. Still, it remains true that on the whole these conflicts were absorbed by medieval structures.

It is a different story when we come to the sixteenth century. We are now at the beginning of a world in which the individual—the artist, scientist, the man of business, the politician, and the religious devotee— becomes steadily more detached, in area after area, from the close confinements of kinship, church, and association. This is preeminently the century of the beginnings of secularism, religious dissent, economic individualism, and of political centralization. And in these massive institutional changes we cannot miss the decline of much of the communalism that flourished in the twelfth and thirteenth centuries.

It is necessary, however, to look more closely into this asserted process of decline. Decline, like progress, is a word that frequently obscures the concrete manifestations of change. Because of organismic conceptions of change, it has long been assumed that there is a kind of indwelling tendency toward change in all social institutions and relationships. Because the realities of fixity and persistence are commonly overlooked, under the spell of automatic change, the actual conditions of change are also overlooked. Similarly, it has been assumed that there is a kind of organic continuity and unity of social change which leads necessarily toward a resolution of all conflicts in society to homogeneity and adjustment. To vindicate the principles of continuity and homogeneity has been, in a real sense, the major effort, since Aristotle, of students of social change. Even when, as in recent times, the non-native elements of the idea of Progress have been sharply challenged, the more fundamental conception of the continuity of change has largely been retained.

This assumption has been made the more feasible by the equally widespread conception of institutions as more or less independently structured entities, each capable of being viewed separately, each supposedly endowed with some kind of indwelling tendency toward form and development. The result has been not only to deal with the history of institutions in an essentially unhistorical manner, that is by separating them from determinable historical processes, but, what is equally serious, in an essentially unpsychological manner. The presumed exteriority of institutions to human beings has led to an unreal differentiation between institutions and the concrete purposive strivings of individuals who live in terms of intellectual goals and moral ends. Such institutions as kinship, community, and religion have been dealt with in something of the same manner in which a biologist deals with development in an organism. A tendency to growth is assumed, and this growth is envisaged in the perspectives of homogeneity and continuity.

But any analysis of institutions as purposive systems of individual ideas, as systems, above all, of individual allegiance, makes plain the reality of conflict and crisis in the history of such institutions as family, community, and property. We cannot understand the dynamic element in institutions by searching for supposedly universal tensions in human relationships, any more than we can understand it by positing at the outset a timeless principle of development in society. Social change is never continuous development. It is not development at all in any tangible sense of that word. Neither is it the simple consequence of the mechanical impact of events upon passive institutions and groups. The latter may come closer to the conditions of change, but what is important is to see that social change is fundamentally the intellectual and emotional *reaction of individuals* to intrusions or alterations of their environment. Social change appears only when the results of such intrusions are incorporated, however confusedly or reluctantly, in the life organizations of individuals and thus come to exert a demonstrable influence upon the purposive and meaningful nature of their consciousness. The conflict between established habits and environmental compulsions to change can be a drastic one.

Change is always, at bottom, the reaction of individuals to new circumstances and the consequent effort of individuals to comprehend these new circumstances, to make them meaningful, and to build them into new values and new systems of allegiance. It is thus a matter of conflict frequently *within* a social system—family, or community, or church—and it is, more significantly, a matter of frequent conflict *among* institutions. For, since each institution is a pattern of functions and meanings in the lives of individuals, and hence demanding of individual loyalties, the change in one institution— the loss or addition of functions and meanings that are vital—must frequently react upon the structure of some other institution and thus awaken conflicting responses in the mind of the individual.[15]

Of all conflicts in European history, the most fundamental have been those relating to the location of social function and the administration of authority in human lives. From these have arisen the intense, often agonizing, conflicts of allegiance which we see in the spiritual history of a society. It is not necessary to invoke Hegelian or Marxian teleologies to see these conflicts. They are embedded in the empirical materials of institutional history—in the struggle of Church with clan in the early Middle Ages, of Church and State in the later Middle Ages, and in the incessant conflicts of State and gild, State and village community, State and feudal class in still later periods. Such conflicts arise from the very nature of institutions regarded as structures of function, authority, and allegiance.

When Marx, largely under the suggestive influence of the early interpreters of the French Revolution, made class conflict the central fact in historical interpretation, he was not wrong in seizing upon the reality of conflict, and it is not wholly his fault if followers as well as enemies have chosen to interpret this conflict in the picturesque terms of the barricades. Where Marx was grievously in error was in singling out the ill-defined category of class—the institution in capitalist society with the least possible claim to being regarded as a significant structure of personal allegiance and functions—and in investing conflict with a teleological essence that must make it culminate in a new Golden Age of tranquillity. He was wrong in overlooking the far more momentous conflicts in social history between such institutions as kinship, religion, gild, and State. But Marx was profoundly right in stressing the centrality of conflict in institutional change.

In the orthodox rationalist tradition little attention was paid to periods and spheres of crisis in society and to persistent conflicts of values among coterminous institutions. The gospel of homogeneity and adjustment held the field. Attention was fixed on what was believed to be the natural provision of nature for the smooth and orderly change of society as a whole. That a plurality of institutions could exert upon individuals powerful and possibly irreconcilable conflicts of allegiance was seldom considered by the progressive rationalist.

Nevertheless the conflict is there, and it is a fact of the highest significance in history. Sometimes this conflict is passive, awakening only vague sensations of tension. Elements of persistence and conformity in the individual may reduce the effects of the conflict on his allegiances. At other times it may be fierce and overt, reflected in widespread mass upheaval and in the central problems of the major social theorists. Such conflicts, small and large, do not, as the progressive rationalist has thought, resolve themselves inevitably into systems of new coherence and order—either in the individual consciousness or in the overt relationships of the major institutions. Where they are matters of crucial allegiance—as with respect to family, church, and State—they may remain for centuries, now relatively passive, now evocative and fiercely antagonistic.

If we are more commonly struck by these conflicts in some of the dramatic revolutions of modern Europe—1789, 1848, 1917—the fact remains that they are revealed throughout the course of modern political and social history. Whether in the writings of Luther and Calvin, in the pages of the French Encyclopedia, the economic essays of Hume or Smith, or in the works of Rousseau, Marx, and Mazzini, we cannot miss the implied conflicts of allegiance and authority. They are the very stuff of both intellectual and institutional history.

Five

These observations may be stated more concretely with reference to the institutions of religion and property in modern European history. In both institutions there has occurred a conspicuous decline in the communal conceptions that surrounded them in the medieval world. But behind this decline of religious and economic communalism lie certain momentous conflicts of authority and function, conflicts which become mirrored in the conflicting allegiances and altered statuses of innumerable human beings.

Thus, in the rise of Protestantism in the sixteenth century, we cannot help but see the sharp challenge that was given to the medieval Catholic concept of religion as being essentially an affair of hierarchical organization, sacrament, and liturgy. For an increasing number of human beings, after the sixteenth century, the corporate Church ceases to be the sole avenue of approach to God. In the devotions of Protestants, ritual, symbolism, hierarchy, in short all the appurtenances of the church visible, wane or disappear in religious life. Out of this atomization of religious corporatism emerges the new man of God, intent upon salvation through unassisted faith and unmediated personal effort.

At the back of this decline of religious communalism are certain decisive conflicts of authority and allegiance. These are conflicts, if we like, between the individual and Rome, dramatized by Luther's nailing of the theses to the church door. But, more fundamentally, they are conflicts between Church and sect, between Church and family, between State and Church, and between businessman and canon law. The Reformation becomes a vast arena of conflict of authority among institutions for the loyalty of individuals in such matters as marriage, education, control of economic activity, welfare, and salvation. Basically we are dealing with two momentous conceptions of religion: on the one hand, a conception that vests in the Church alone control of man's spiritual, moral, and economic existence; on the other, a conception that insists upon restricting the sphere of religion to matters of individual faith and transferring to other institutions, notably the State, responsibilities of a secular sort. This is a conflict that goes on even at the present time, and, although the high-water mark of the conflict is to be seen in the sixteenth and seventeenth centuries, it was apparent as early as the fourteenth century in the activities of Wyclif.

In Wyclif we find an almost modern devotion to the individuality of conscience and faith and a devotion also to a political environment capable of reducing the powers of the religious and economic institutions in society. He was opposed to ecclesiastical courts, to monasteries, to hierarchy within the Church, to all of those aspects of Christianity that hemmed in, as it seemed, the right of individual judgment. Not without cause has Wyclif been called the morning star of the Reformation.

Unfortunately for Wyclif, in the fourteenth century the doctrines of religious corporatism were too strong for his ideas of the primacy of the individual in matters of faith and of the State in all secular matters. But by the sixteenth century conflicts between Rome and many of the principalities and kingdoms of Western Europe had become so sharp that a more favorable environment for religious dissent was constituted. It is doubtful whether any of the major ideas of Luther and Calvin were new. But conditions had reached the point where age-old controversies within the Church could no longer be contained within its authority. New areas of authority, both economic and political, had arisen and become strong, and within some of these it was possible for the ideas of a Luther to achieve the revolutionary significance that had been denied those of Wyclif.

The great aim of such men as Luther and Calvin was the purification of doctrine and belief, but, like many before them, they knew that the advancement of these aims was dependent upon a radical change in the structure of religious authority and in the functional relationship of the Church to other institutions. If religion was to be purified, it had to be divorced from the corrupting influence of its social and economic functions in the life of man. And the religious faith of individuals bad to be protected from the noxious effects of external trappings of religion.

For Luther and Calvin the essence of religion lay not in external activities or relationships but in the power of individual faith. "As the soul needs the word alone for life and justification," wrote Luther, "so it is justified by faith alone, and not by any works. . . . Therefore the first care of every Christian ought to be to lay aside all reliance on works, and to strengthen his faith alone more and more." For Calvin, too, the primacy of individual faith was indubitable. He writes bitterly of the medieval school-men who "have deprived us of justification by faith, which lies at the root of all Godliness. . . . They, by the praise of good works transfer to man what they steal from God."

In Protestantism there has been a persistent belief that to externalize religion is to degrade it. Only in the privacy of the individual soul can religion remain pure. There has been little sympathy for the communal, sacramental, and disciplinary aspects of religion. Protestant condemnation of the monasteries and ecclesiastical courts sprang from a temper of mind that could also look with favor on the separation of marriage from the Church, that could prohibit ecclesiastical celibacy, reduce the number of feast days, and ban relics, scapularies, images, and holy pictures. The gilds were suspect, and even the bonds of wider kinship could often be regarded with disfavor on the ground that they represented a distraction from the direct relation of the individual to God. Works, liturgy, sacrament, and polity might be desirable, but only individual faith was crucial. Three principal elements of Christianity were left in Protestant theology: the lone individual, an omnipotent, distant God, and divine grace. All else was expunged by reformers whose distaste for Roman corruption led by imperceptible degrees to a forswearance of all those institutional and ceremonial aspects regarded as the channels of corruption.

What the literary historian, Edward Dowden, has written of Bunyan's *Pilgrim's Progress* is illuminating as a description of Protestantism. "All that is best and most characteristic in Bunyan proceeds from that inward drama in which the actors were three—God, Satan, and solitary human soul. If external influences from events or men affected his spirit, they came as nuncios or messengers from God or the Evil One. Institutions, Churches, ordinances, rites, ceremonies, could help him little or not at all. The journey from the City of Destruction to the Celestial City must be undertaken on a special summons by each man for himself alone; if a companion join him on the way, it lightens the trials of the road; but, of the companions, each one is an individual pilgrim, who has started on a great personal adventure, and who, as he enters the dark river, must undergo his particular experiences of hope or fear."[16]

At times, to be sure, as in the Geneva of Calvin, the organizational side of the new religion could be almost as stiff as, and perhaps more tyrannical than, anything in the Roman Church. There is indeed a frequent tendency among historians to overlook the sociological side of early Protestantism, manifested in the solidarity of many of its sects and movements. Yet, from almost the beginning, the spread of Protestantism is to be seen in terms of the revolt against, and the emancipation from, those strongly hierarchical and sacramental aspects of religion which reinforced the idea of religion as community. This is an aspect of religious history which, as we observed earlier, has come to plague the minds of many contemporary Protestant theologians, leading in the present day to a renewed interest in the communal properties of religion. The drive toward individualism and the attack upon corporatism remains the most luminous aspect of the religious revolution that began in the fifteenth and sixteenth centuries.

"The difference," Tawney has written, "between loving men as a result of first loving God and learning to love God through a growing love for men may not at first sight seem profound. To Luther it seemed an abyss, and Luther was right. It was, in a sense, nothing less than the Reformation itself. For, carried, as it was not carried by Luther, to its logical result, the argument made not only good works, but sacraments and the Church itself unnecessary."[17]

Six

In the history of modern capitalism we can see essentially the same diminution of communal conceptions of effort and the same tendency toward the release of increasing numbers of individuals from the confinements of gild and village community. As Protestantism sought to reassimilate men in the invisible community of God, capitalism sought to reassimilate them in the impersonal and rational framework of the free market. As in Protestantism, the individual, rather than the group, becomes the central unit. But instead of pure faith, individual profit becomes the mainspring of activity. In both spheres there is a manifest decline of custom and tradition and a general disengagement of purpose from the contexts of community.

It is impossible to miss the similarity between Calvin's man of God, supported only by inner faith and conscience, and the economists' man of industry—economic man—supported assertedly by innate drives toward self-gain and competitive endeavor. Both of these personages have been truly revolutionary elements in the modern world, and they must be seen as centers of new systems of authority and right. The rise of economic man, like the rise of the Protestant, must be seen in the context of struggles for assertion of initiative, but also in the context of conflicts in systems of authority.

Inevitably in this process of forming new centers of power and right there occurred, as Franz Oppenheimer has described it, "a breach in all those naturally developed relations in which the individual has found protection. . . . The community bonds were loosened. The individual found himself unprotected, compelled to rely on his own efforts and on his own reason in the seething sea of competition which followed."[18] Philosophically, what is new in capitalism is not the pursuit of gain. This is a timeless pursuit. Rather it is the supposition that society's well-being is best served by allowing the individual the largest possible area of moral and social autonomy. It was this moral and social autonomy that the surviving medieval corporations tended to block; through both force and principle the new middle class sought to exterminate or check at least the traditional communal authorities.

As in the history of Protestantism, the set of beliefs stressing the impersonal nature of justice, the individual root of success, and the abstraction of virtuous incentives from traditional morality has triumphed on the whole in the modern history of property. It has not always been a clear triumph. The actual nature of the contemporary corporation is perhaps as different from early capitalist enterprise and the free market as the latter were from the medieval gild. The individualistic aspects of capitalism, however, have maintained intellectual supremacy in much modern thought. A whole succession of philosophers, beginning with the Physiocrats and Adam Smith, have sought to discover in these aspects the bases of harmony and self-perpetuating progress. Even if the actual horrors of early capitalism seem to be the result less of genuine individualism than of an exploitative, highly disciplined conglomerate of collective associations— the workshops and factories—the fact remains that ownership of property and its "right of use and abuse" was in the hands of the individual entrepreneur. It is this side of capitalism, stemming so largely from the decline of custom and the atomization of traditional communities and associations, that is of greatest interest.

Innumerable historians, beginning with Marx and Engels, have described the impact of the new systems of commerce and manufacture upon social groups and customs that had been central in the medieval system. The Hammonds[19] have written memorable passages about the disintegrative effects of the factory on town and village community; they have pointed to the individualizing effects upon traditional morality of separating persons from the context of family and community, and to the rise of the new system of mechanical discipline, the factory. Behind the new discipline, represented by the factory bell and the overseer, the precise division of the day into units of wages-time, the mechanical modes of machine-driven precision, and the long series of minute regulations, there was "the great, impersonal system," within which human beings existed for the work day, not as members of society but as individual units of energy and production.

The impersonality of capitalism was rooted in the same exclusion of ritual, ceremony, and community from the new factory that characterized so many of the Protestant declarations of religious purpose. As Ostrogorski has written,[20] capitalism was an isolating and separating process that stripped off the historically grown layers of custom and social membership, leaving only leveled masses of individuals. Having aided in the destruction of the older unities, it strove to found a new kind of subordination and a new hierarchy to replace the older forms.

It is capitalism, above all other movements in modern history, that is most generally charged with responsibility for the modern leveling and proletarianization of cultures, for the creation of atomized masses of insecure individuals. Capitalism, it is said, has substituted quantity for quality, process for function, bigness for smallness, impersonality for personality, competitive tensions for the psychological harmonies of co-operation. It has transformed intense communities of purpose into the sprawling relationships of the market place.

Yet with all respect to the influence of capitalism, I do not think it can be called the primary agent in the transmutation of social groups and communities. I do not question the economic context in which many of the specific manifestations of social dislocation and transfer of allegiances took place in the eighteenth and nineteenth centuries. What I question is the ascription of either logical or historical primacy to the economic facts of the pursuit of wealth and the development of technology and the so-called middle class.

That incentives to wealth and financial gain are operative in virtually every area or sphere of life is beside the point here. It is the structure or context of these incentives that is of crucial importance. The economic determinist has argued that the basic influences in modern history have been those exerted, first, by changes in technology, and, second, by the rise and expansion of a middle class that set to work consciously or unconsciously to redesign the fabric of society in accord with its residual economic interests. From these interests, it is said, have come the tendencies of rationalization, impersonality, mechanism, and leveling which have so powerfully affected the cultural and social nature of modern European society.

It is this proposition that I find untenable. For, with all recognition of the influences of factory, technology, the free market, and the middle class, the operation of each of these has been given force only by a revolutionary system of power and rights that cannot be contained within the philosophy of economic determinism. This system is the political State.

5   THE STATE AS REVOLUTION

The argument of this book is that the single most decisive influence upon Western social organization has been the rise and development of the centralized territorial State. There is every reason to regard the State in history as, to use a phrase von Gierke applied to Rousseau's doctrine of the General Will, "a process of permanent revolution." The conflict between the central power of the political State and the whole set of functions and authorities contained in church, family, gild, and local community has been, I believe, the main source of those dislocations of social structure and uprootings of status which lie behind the problem of community in our age.

To refer categorically to the State is to risk a degree of abstraction and empirical unreality that leaves in view none of the concrete manifestations of political behavior in modern history. Such abstraction leads too often to personifications of the State, to visions of objective will, and to a false sense of the exteriority of the State to human aspirations and conduct.

On the other hand, not to deal with the State categorically is to risk losing, in the varied sequences of diplomatic, military, and political events the essential unity of the State as an idea system in the modern West and, more important, the powerful and cohesive nature of the State as an institution, as a system of human allegiances and motivations. In the next two chapters we shall be concerned with some of the more concrete aspects of the State and its historical relation to social organization. Here it is important to call attention in more general terms to the qualities that have made the Western State so revolutionary an idea system.

Like the family, or like capitalism, the State is a complex of ideas, symbols, and relationships. Unlike either kinship or capitalism, the State has become, in the contemporary world, the supreme allegiance of men and, in most recent times, the greatest refuge from the insecurities and frustrations of other spheres of life. Where capitalism has become enveloped throughout the Western world, and the East as well, in a thickening cloud of distrust and renunciation, and where kinship, like religion, has become increasingly devoid of institutional significance and symbolic appeal, the State has risen as the dominant institutional force in our society and the most evocative symbol of cultural unity and purpose.

If we are to understand the historical importance of the State in the Western world, we must be clear in our appreciation of certain general characteristics of the State as an historical entity.

In the first place, State and society must be sharply distinguished. Despite the considerable number of writers who make State and society synonymous, there is actually no more warrant for making the State a generic term to include all types of association than there is for so making religion or kinship. Historically, the State presents as distinctive a pattern of power and rights as either religion or the family. The usual reason advanced for disregarding the differences and making the State and society one is that the State is basically a system of authority and, since some kind of authority exists in every human association, all manifestations of society may legitimately be described as aspects of the State. But this is a piece of semantic juggling that cannot be tolerated unless we close our eyes to the historical record. The fact that almost no sphere of life in the contemporary world is removed from the processes of political behavior is no more of a justification for the historical blurring of distinction between State and society than is the fact that, in the medieval world, no sphere of life was wholly removed from the authority of the Church. From the point of view of any useful historical examination, the State must be regarded as but one form of relationship, existing, in varying degrees of prominence, among many other forms.

In the second place, and following closely from the first, the State is not the direct outgrowth of family, tribe, or local community. The belief in the kinship origin of the State has been among the most deeply rooted manifestations of the Western faith in developmental continuity. The popularity of the belief owes much to Aristotle's celebrated triadic scheme of evolution—from family to community to State—and has been nourished in modern times by frequent appeals to irrelevant and historically unconnected ethnographic materials. As is true in so many other alleged instances of developmental continuity, the fact of *logical* continuity has been converted into the supposition of *historical* continuity within a specific area or chronology. But, if we look not to imaginary beginnings in the never-never land of ethnological reconstruction but to historically connected sequences of change in such specific areas as ancient Athens, Rome, or modern England and France, we discover that the rise and aggrandizement of political States took place in circumstances of powerful opposition to kinship and other traditional authorities.

If there is any single origin of the institutional State, it is in the circumstances and relationships of war. The connection between kinship and family, between religion and Church, is no closer than that between war and the State in history. "The war chief and his band," writes Edward Jenks, "of whom we have such abundant evidence in early Teutonic history, are the earliest form of the State. . . . By its very nature it becomes an aggressor upon the province of the Clan."[1] In the beginning, in France, England, and elsewhere, the State is no more than a limited tie between military lord and his men. The earliest distinct function of the king is that of leadership in war. But to the military function is added, in time, other functions of a legal, judicial, economic, and even religious nature, and, over a long period, we can see the passage of the State from an exclusively military association to one incorporating almost every aspect of human life. The process of change is intermittent, given spasmodic impetus by new forces, with long periods of inertia, but it is one of the clearest and most relentless of all tendencies in Western history. And it is in light of this development of the military State into the legal and the economic State, a development involving ever greater territorial centralization of function and authority, that we may best see the revolutionary impact of the State upon other institutions and groups in society.

Finally, it is inadequate to regard the State, especially in its later phases of development, as a mere superstructure of power. In the beginning, to be sure, State and government were the same thing. The State was hardly more than the king himself, at most a limited *vertical* relation between king and subject. The powerful competing allegiances of Church, class, and economic association rendered the political tie, for a long time, a relatively tenuous one in the lives of most people in a national area. But the revolutionary quality of modern political history is to be seen in the gradual extrication of the political power from the fetters laid upon it by these earlier authorities, and in the increasing functional importance of political relationship in the lives of many human beings. The State begins to reach its most revolutionary influence when, as in France at the end of the eighteenth century, it ceases to be merely a vertical relation of power between king and subject and becomes a kind of *horizontal* relationship among individuals, with power made immanent in the Nation, with rights and duties made dependent upon the Nation. Since the eighteenth century, in most parts of Western Europe, the State has been, literally, to use Hobbes's earlier prophetic words, the people as a unity ruling over the people as a multitude. The contemporary State cannot be limited to a mere superstructure of power. It is an increasingly popular and ever more cohesive *mass relationship.*

Two

To be sure the State is power. What Walter Lippmann has written on this aspect of the State is illuminating. "It is of no importance in this connection whether the absolute power of the State is exercised by a king, a landed aristocracy, bankers and manufacturers, professional politicians, soldiers, or a random majority of voters. It does not matter whether the right to govern is hereditary or obtained with the consent of the governed. A State is absolute in the sense which I have in mind when it claims the right to a monopoly of all the force within the community, to make war, to make peace, to conscript life, to tax, to establish and disestablish property, to define crime, to punish disobedience, to control education, to supervise the family, to regulate personal habits, and to censor opinions. The modern State claims all of these powers, and, in the matter of theory, there is no real difference in the size of the claim between communists, fascists, and democrats. There are lingering traces in the American constitutional system of the older theory that there are inalienable rights which government may not absorb. But these rights are really not inalienable for they can be taken away by constitutional amendment. There is no theoretical limit upon the power of ultimate majorities which create civil government. There are only practical limits. They are restrained by inertia, and by prudence and even by good will. But ultimately and theoretically they claim absolute authority as against all churches, associations, and persons within their jurisdiction."[2]

The modern State is monistic; its authority extends directly to *all* individuals within its boundaries. So-called diplomatic immunities are but the last manifestation of a larger complex of immunities which once involved a large number of internal religious, economic, and kinship authorities. For administrative purposes the State may deploy into provinces, departments, districts, or "states," just as the army divides into regiments and battalions. But like the army, the modern State is based upon a residual unity of power. The State may occasionally delegate or place, as it were, in trusteeship certain powers, but anyone familiar with the processes of modern government, democratic or totalitarian, knows that it does this rarely and reluctantly. The extraordinary unity of relationship in the contemporary State, together with its massive accumulation of effective functions, makes the control of the State the greatest single goal, or prize, in modern struggles for power. Increasingly the objectives of economic and other interest associations become not so much the preservation of favored *immunities* from the State as the capturing or directing of the political power itself.

But the State has arrived at this eminence only over a long period of time in modern history. We refer often to the "absolute" State of early centuries in Western European history, but, in truth, the early State was too fragile and functionally insignificant a tie among individuals, even in England where the forces of centralization operated the earliest, to warrant applying the term without qualification. The king may have ruled at times with a degree of irresponsibility that few modern governmental officials can enjoy, but it is doubtful whether, in terms of effective powers and services, any king of even the seventeenth-century "absolute monarchies" wielded the kind of authority that now inheres in the office of many a high-ranking official in the democracies. There were then too many social barriers between the claimed power of the monarch and the effective execution of this power over individuals. The very prestige and functional importance of church, family, gild, and local community as allegiances limited the absoluteness of the State's power.

The expansion of the State in European history has been both territorial and functional. It is the latter that is more significant here. The history of the Western State has been characterized by the gradual absorption of powers and responsibilities formerly resident in other associations and by an increasing directness of relation between the sovereign authority of the State and the individual citizen. Present-day debates on the proper limits of governmental intervention in society sometimes overlook the fact that the whole history of the State in Europe has been characterized by innumerable "interventions" in the economic and moral life of people.

We may see this in the establishment of the King's Peace and in the beginnings of the common law in England, in the increasing utilization of Roman law principles for the centralization and consolidation of royal power on the Continent, in the growing conception of the State as the source of prescriptive law, in the invasions by the State into matters of property disposition, inheritance, and alienation of shares, in control of kinship activities formerly vested in the family alone, and in the increasing transfer to civil power of functions and authorities traditionally resident in the Church.[3] In innumerable places we may see the almost incessant historical intervention by the State in matters of decision and function which earlier belonged to other institutions. It is a historical process that began centuries ago and continues at the present time. Even the histories of capitalism and Protestantism fall within this political process.

Thus, with respect to the rise of capitalism, we may give full credit to internal conflicts of a purely economic sort in the gild system and to the influence of the middle class, but it is a fair generalization that, apart from the massive changes that were taking place in the structure of political power during the fifteenth and sixteenth centuries, capitalism would never have come into existence. The State's development of a single system of law, sanctioned by military power, to replace the innumerable competing laws of gild, Church, and feudal principality; its deliberate cultivation of trade in the hinterland; its standardized systems of coinage, weights, and measures; its positive subsidies and protections to those new businessmen who were seeking to operate outside the framework of gild and Church; its creation of disciplined State workhouses—all provided a powerful political stimulus to the rise of capitalism. Above everything else, the State offered, through its efforts at territorial consolidation of law, a scene increasingly impersonal and calculable—a scene within which businessmen might operate as individuals rather than as members of a traditional group. It is in these terms, indeed, that one historian has been led to wonder how far capitalism was the work of the businessman at all, and how far it was the consequence of the overthrow of the medieval system by the military might of the absolute State.[4]

Similarly in the rise of Protestantism the State provided, in many areas, an environment of protection for those individuals who were seeking to liberate themselves from the Roman Church. The political rulers may have been less interested in the theological elements of either Catholicism or Protestantism than they were in breaking the secular power of the Catholic Church, but the consequence was nevertheless a favorable one to such men as Luther. What is more important is the fact that as the State began to assume some of the social functions formerly placed in the Catholic Church, it provided, inevitably, valuable assistance to those religious reformers who were seeking to divest religion of its corrupting social trappings. The liaison between Luther and the German princes was more than a relation of temporary expediency. It was very nearly indispensable to the rise of a reformed Christianity which made the individual the prime unit.[5]

It is this maximization of political power, this penetration of the State into institutional areas formerly autonomous, that lies behind so much of the modern political interest in problems of individual freedom, individual rights, and social equality. The significance of the State in Western Europe cannot be limited to matters merely of power and rule. Its revolutionary influence has come from the fact that it has been, also, a complex of individual rights, freedoms, and equalities, and perhaps most important of all, a sphere of growing popular participation in the workings of society.

Military force and arbitrary decree may explain temporary conditions of servitude and dependence, but they will not explain the acceptance of the State as a positive, popular area of participation. Force alone will not explain the psychology of allegiance, or the growing moral dependence upon political action. The early distrust of the political sovereign in Western Europe and the traditional reliance upon religious and social systems for protection and security have been dissolved only by a growing conviction that a type of "freedom" comes from political power.

It is this aspect of the State, as we shall see later, that was to be so brilliantly emphasized by Rousseau in the eighteenth century. To Rousseau the real oppressions in life were those of traditional society—class, church, school, and patriarchal family. How much greater the realm of individual freedom if the constraints of these bodies could but be transmuted into the single, impersonal structure of the General Will arising out of the consciousness of all persons in the State. This, however, is a later conception of political freedom, one that attained its greatest influence in the nineteenth century. Behind it in time lies another that has a good deal of hard historical fact to support it: the visible emancipation, by the State and its law, of innumerable individuals from the often oppressive structures of gild, monastery, class, and village community. The proffer of, first, the personal power of the monarch and, then, the power of the seventeenth-century legal State in support of those eager to be freed of medieval group restrictions must be seen as one of the most powerful causes of modern, Western individualism in all spheres of life.[6] Between the State and the individual there arose a genuine affinity that was not obscured by later, often intense, conflicts between the public law and asserted private rights.

In the medieval world there was relatively little concern with positive, discrete rights of individuals, largely because of the diffuseness of political power and the reality of innumerable group authorities. But when the consolidation of national political power brought with it a destruction of many of the social bodies within which individuals had immemorially lived and taken refuge, when, in sum, law became a more centralized and impersonal structure, with the individual as its unit, the concern for positive, constitutionally guaranteed rights of individuals became urgent. European governments may have sought often, and successfully for long periods, to resist claims of individual right, but it is hard to miss the fact that the States (England, for example) which became the most successful, economically as well as politically, had the earliest constitutional recognition of individual rights, especially of property. In retrospect, however, we see that it was the sheer impact of State upon medieval custom and tradition, with the consequent atomizing and liberating effects, that, more than anything else, precipitated the modern concern with positive individual rights.

Similarly, with respect to political and social equality among individuals, the profound influence of the State is unmistakably apparent. Here again, the very centralization of monarchical and State power could not help but create the conditions for a growing interest in personal equality. For, in the interests of its own aggrandizement, the State was forced to restrict sharply the authorities of medieval classes and estates. In so doing it could not help but partially level these ranks and, by its growing stress upon the impersonality and equality of law, to create a scene in which many traditional medieval inequalities had to be diminished. As in other aspects of political history, this process is a slow and intermittent one in history. New inequalities of both a political and economic sort were being created, and the old ones were slow to dissolve. But the net effect of the State in history, as such students as Tocqueville and Halévy have emphasized, is nevertheless leveling.[7]

It is in the profoundly important concept of *citizenship* that we see the summation of so many of these combined authoritarian and libertarian qualities of the modern European State. In the Middle Ages, the citizen was literally the inhabitant of a free town. His status under the king, however, was that of *subject*. The two statuses were sharply distinguished then, and even at the end of the sixteenth century, in the writings of Bodin, we may see the continuation of this distinction. But in the modern history of politics, especially since the Age of Revolutions, the clear tendency has been for the terms citizen and subject to become virtually synonymous. The frame of reference has changed from the town to the nation as a whole, and the citizen is the atom-unit of the political association of the State. But in the modern concept of citizenship there inheres not merely the medieval idea of free status but also the idea of subjection to sovereign political power. The condition of subjection to rules and the condition of freedom have, in a sense, emerged from their medieval dualism and become fused into one concept and symbol.[8]

Three

It would be impossible to exaggerate the role of conflict between political power and the social group in the development of modern ideas of sovereignty, freedom, rights, and equality which together form the idea system of the Western State. All that was noted in the preceding chapter on the importance of conflict among institutional authorities in history has increased relevance when we deal with the State.

The real conflict in modern political history has not been, as is so often stated, between State and individual, but between State and social group. What Maitland once called the "pulverizing and macadamizing tendency of modern history" has been one of the most vivid aspects of the social history of the modern West, and it has been inseparable from the momentous conflicts of jurisdiction between the political State and the social associations lying intermediate to it and the individual. The conflict between central political government and the authorities of gild, village community, class, and religious body has been, of all the conflicts in history, the most fateful. From this conflict have arisen most of the relocations of authority and function which have formed the contexts of decline of medieval communalism and the emergence of both individual and central political power.

In the same way that the modern army has resulted historically from the breaking down of clan and communal immunities to service, and from the formation of new aggregates of individuals united directly by military command from a single center, so the development of the Western State, with all the qualities of power, freedom, rights, and citizenship referred to above, has been part of the general process of subordination and destruction of such groups as village, gild, and feudal class. The individual and State have been brought into ever closer legal relationship. To compare the position of the political power of the State in the thirteenth century with that power today is to realize that fundamental among all the "emancipations" of modern history has been the emancipation of the State from the restrictive network of religious, economic, and moral authorities that bound it at an earlier time.

In the preceding chapter we observed the social importance in medieval society of the smaller groups based upon kinship and function. This importance cannot be separated from the larger system of authority within which they existed. Organism, medieval society may have seemed to the Schoolmen, and Unity it may appear in retrospect to all those who, like Henry Adams, seek escape from the flux and diversity of the modern world. But, in fact, medieval society, from the point of view of formal authority, was one of the most loosely organized societies in history. Despite the occasional pretensions of centralizing popes, emperors, and kings, the authority that stretched theoretically from each of them was constantly hampered by the existence of jealously guarded "liberties" of town, gild, monastery, and village.[9]

"Such autocracy as existed in the Middle Ages," Pollard writes in his study of Wolsey, "was because of the absence of centralization. It was dilute, not because it was distributed in many hands, but because it was derived from many independent sources. There were the liberties of the church, based on law superior to that of the King; there was the law of nature, graven in the hearts of men and not to be erased by royal writs; and there was the prescription of immemorial local and feudal custom stereotyping a variety of jurisdictions and impeding the operation of a single will. There was no sovereignty capable of eradicating bondage by royal edict or act of parliament, regulating borough franchises, reducing to uniformity the various uses of the church, or enacting a principle of succession to the throne. The laws which ruled men's lives were the customs of their trade, locality, or estate and not the positive law of a legislator; and the whole sum of English parliamentary legislation for the whole Middle Ages is less in bulk than that of the single reign of Henry VIII."[10]

To be sure the corporate liberties of Church and gild and university could themselves become often more restrictive of the life of the individual than was easily tolerable, and not a little of the appeal of political government to such men as Wyclif arose from the protection it could occasionally offer from the "liberties" of other associations in society. But what is significant here is the immense range of legal autonomy possessed by the intermediate associations. The king, as Bracton and many another jurist of the Middle Ages declared, was *under* the law; he did not make it.[11] Neither did parliament, for it was an essentially judicial, not legislative, body until relatively late in history.[12] The real law of the Middle Ages lay in immemorial custom, in the rule of seigneur, gild master, or churchman. Such customs and rules were simply the inner order of associations, and the autonomy of these associations was, as we have seen, jealously prized. In the early Middle Ages, the right of an association to come into existence was commonly a free one, not contingent upon royal permission. "The borough, the gild merchant, the ordinary social or religious gild, all came into existence," Rashdall tells us, "held corporate property, and exercised other attributes of corporate responsibility without any charter or legal incorporation."[13]

It is the *particularism,* then, rather than the asserted unity of the Middle Ages that stands as the most significant fact in the understanding of its structure of authority.[14] Apart from the legal facts of diversity and decentralization ("anarchy" later legal rationalists were to call them), the pre-eminence of the medieval social group is unintelligible. This is the point that has so often been overlooked by modern reformers of an orthodox or scholastic set of mind who have endeavored to re-establish some variant of medieval moral or educational practice. The claims of kinship, gild, and university lay then in a framework of authority that has largely disappeared in the modern world. Such terms as *corpus morale, corpus mysticum,* and their many synonyms had deep roots in the legal particularism of the Middle Ages, and it is worthy of notice that the mystic unity of a given group was never so clamantly upheld as when the environing legal conditions were threatened.

Now, it is precisely among the conflicts between this whole area of intermediate authorities and the rising military power of the king that we may observe the legal foundations of the modern national State emerging. If it was characteristic of medieval society, as the Carlyles have emphasized, "that local and personal attachments were strong, while relations to the central authorities were comparatively weak and fluctuating,"[15] it has been equally characteristic of the modern world that central authorities have become increasingly powerful and the local and personal ones weak and fluctuating. And it is in terms of this massive rearrangement that we may see not merely the developing influence of the State but, also, the momentous shift of the referent of the word liberty from the group to the individual. State and individual become the key terms of modern political discussion just as surely as the group was the key term of medieval thought.

Lord Acton stated this superbly in his *History of Freedom:* "The modern theory, which has swept away every authority except that of the State, and has made the sovereign power irresistible by multiplying those who share it . . . condemns as a State within a State every inner group and community, class or corporation, administering its own affairs; and, by proclaiming the abolition of privileges, it emancipates the subjects of every such authority in order to transfer them exclusively to its own. . . . It recognizes liberty only in the individual, because it is only in the individual that liberty can be separated from authority, and the right of conditional obedience deprived of the security of limited command."[16]

Increasingly, then, within the contexts provided by struggle between State and medieval association, doctrines of right, duty, interest, and allegiance come to rest upon the claimed reality of society, regarded not as a *communitas communitatum* (the true origin of the word commons) but as a vast aggregate of socially free individuals. "After the associations into which individuals have been placed as members of society have been dissolved and destroyed," Ehrlich suggests, "the only connecting links that remain between the individual and society are ownership, contract, and the State."[17]

In all this the revived doctrines of Roman law performed a major function. The source of monarchical aspirations toward centralized power may have been in military necessity and the desire for increased revenue, but the rationalization of such aspirations was commonly drawn from the texts of Roman law. Maitland has rightly declared that "at the end of the Middle Ages a great change in men's thoughts about groups of men was taking place, and the main agent in the transmutation was Roman Law."[18] In Roman law, principles were to be found as atomizing in their theoretical consequences as military centralization was in a practical way. It is not correct to say, as von Gierke did, that Roman law, with its general emphasis on State and individual, "had nothing to say of the groups that mediated between the State and the individual." It had a great deal to say in its theory of corporations. But what it said was destructive of associative autonomy. The Roman doctrine of concession asserted in effect that all groups were dependent upon the will of the State for the exercise of their functions and authorities. Groups existed, so to speak, only in the legal contemplation of the sovereign. This was a revolutionary doctrine indeed. And to the doctrine of concession was added one that sprang from philosophical nominalism, the powerful principle that declared all corporate groups to be mere fictions, that declared individuals alone to be the real units of society. It is one of the ironies of history that this nominalist doctrine, first used by Innocent IV against some of the component groups of the Church, should have been turned later with such deadly effect upon the whole of the Catholic Church.[19] The Roman law stress upon the prince, who alone is *legibus solutus,* and upon individuals united only by the sovereignty of the State and by precarious relations of contract within the State, together with the rising influence of nominalism, sounded the death knell of the corporate pluralism and legal decentralization that had characterized medieval society.

Four

Our concern in this book is with modern Europe, but it both illuminates and reinforces the argument stated to observe, in two other notable ages, similar processes of conflict and change in the relation among group, individual, and State. We may see these in Greece and Rome.

In ancient Athens, as Zimmern has pointed out, "what we have to watch is the gradual snapping of the lesser loyalties which form the intermediate links between the State and the individual, till the citizen stands, free and independent, face to face with the City."[20] The conflict between the central government and the historic loyalties to clan and tribe was one of the decisive processes of Athenian history. This conflict was apparent in the circumstances leading up to the reforms of Solon, but it was a major factor determining the reforms of the great Cleisthenes. In his desire to centralize political power and to create a scene more favorable to military and economic demands, Cleisthenes was led, toward the end of the sixth century B.C., to the abolishment of dominant kinship structures as significant legal entities. His ingenious creation of the deme was an act designed to destroy any resurgence of old kinship loyalties by concentrating in it all crucial legal and political processes. In the deme the individual achieved political status, not, thereafter, in family. From the territorial unit of deme arose the structure of legal authority which encompassed all citizens of Attica. Both State and individual were freed.[21]

From Cleisthenes's reforms flowed both the democracy and the political individualism of the great fifth century. We may look to these conditions for much of the explanation of the great flowering of culture which took place in the fifth century. It was an age of creative individuality in many spheres. The individual became more and more conscious of himself as a discrete, rational being, and less and less conscious of himself as a member of a binding community of kinship and religion. Out of such circumstances came the intense preoccupation with change, the nature of the individual, the role of pure reason, that is to be found in the philosophy of Socrates and his contemporaries.

But out of these conditions came also reflections and actions of a different sort. To Thucydides, in the late fifth century B.C., individualism could appear increasingly symptomatic of a fatal disease, *stasis*, internal fragmentation and disruption. To him and others it constituted a threat both to the stability of society and to the integrity of the individual. Above all, to Plato at the very end of the fifth century B.C. the conflict of allegiances in Athens and the increasing alienation of individuals from morality seemed intolerable. What Plato saw in the society about him was disorganization and conflict, alienation and frustration. The bases of the old society were gone; internal strife and political misrule had replaced the religious and communal supports of the old order in Athens. The individual was left ever more precariously exposed to moral uncertainty and conflict of allegiances. What was necessary, as Plato saw the problem, was the radical completion of the process of politicization which had begun with the reforms of Cleisthenes. Man could not bear the spiritual consequences of intellectual and cultural diversity. The State must therefore become itself a community, unified and absolute, capable of resolving both the external and internal conflicts of man.

Despite the severity of Plato's ideal State, one must beware of labeling Plato an anti-individualist, for there is clearly a sense in which the Republic may be regarded as a profound plea for the individual—his justice, his security, and his freedom from want, uncertainty, and ignorance. It is impossible to read Plato's political writings without feeling the clear honest devotion to the individual as well as the State. The problem for Plato, as it was to be the problem for Rousseau two thousand years later, was that of discovering the conditions within which the absolute freedom of the individual could be combined with the absolute justice of the State.[22]

Plato's solution of the problem was radical. It was nothing less than the extermination of all forms of social and spiritual loyalty which would, by their mere existence, constitute distractive influences upon individuals and divisive allegiances within the total community of the State itself. "The zeal of the State had come upon Plato," Barker has written, "and had come as a fire to consume whatever was not of the State. A fire will not stop at exceptions; and these exceptions to the organic unity of the State he could not brook. . . . The whole system of Platonic communism is meant to set the individual free of everything which prevents him from taking his right place in the scheme of the State: it is designed to secure those conditions— in other words, to guarantee those 'rights'—which are necessary to the positive discharge of his function in that scheme."[23]

In Plato's view there is inevitable and intolerable conflict when the allegiances of man are plural. Plurality and diversity must therefore have no place in the ideal State. Unity is the condition both of order and genuine freedom. The existence of autonomous economic and social associations can lead only to social disorder, to paralyzing conflict in the consciousness of the individual, and to continuous subversion of the unity of life and society which Plato prized. Plato's hostility is directed, then, not against the individual as such but against the social group. His distrust of the autonomous family is matched by his fear of an independent or private religion, and of an independent art, music, and education. All membership and cultural activity must be related closely and continuously to the monistic political community.

When we pass from the Athens of Plato to the Rome of Cicero and Caesar, we observe similar conflicts of allegiance and association. Especially after the civil wars of the first century B.C. do we see an almost ceaseless conflict between the State and the intermediate unities of family and other forms of association. From its earlier, almost absolute status in Roman society, the authority and functional autonomy of the family, literally the *patria potestas*, declined almost continuously under the increasing centralization of political power.

In this process the demands of war exerted great influence. Whatever the stresses and strains arising from economic dislocation, they were relatively small as compared with those caused by the mounting incidence of war and the readjustments in internal polity which resulted from war. The military reforms of Marius, especially, were of profound consequence to the traditional structure of Roman society. The professionalization of the old militia into a standing army, the increasing autonomy and centralization of military command, the growing allure of military service with its promised rewards—all led to the formation of what was in fact a new association in Roman society, an association based upon the imperatives of battle, upon the eagle of the legion. As freedom from the control of the Senate increased, the whole machinery of the Roman army was at the disposal of the man possessing military command. Out of the civil wars in the first century B.C. Augustus emerged as unchallenged military ruler, and what we observe in the principate that followed, and for that matter for the remainder of Roman history, is a society based upon the army. The emperor, as Rostovtzeff writes, "ruled wholly through the army and for so long as the army was willing to keep him and obey."[24] The most fundamental change that took place in Rome during the century that stretched between Marius and Augustus was the shift of real authority in society from the Senate, and the family system which supported it, to the army. And thereafter in the same proportion that the State became militarized, society became increasingly politicized.

"Relations between the State and the individual became ever more direct. The various situations in which the juridical person found himself affected him alone, and there was no more need to break or form any bond with a jealous and exclusive family group. Being no longer the foundation of the Republic, the *familia* ceased to interpose between the individual and the State."[25] In Rome, during the centuries following the civil wars, we cannot help but see the parallel tendencies of centralization of power in society and the individualization of the traditional social structure. There were, especially during the Augustan age and the later age of the Antonines, periods when the individual seemed the chief beneficiary of institutional change. These were periods of cultural and economic efflorescence. But there were other periods when the central power of the State seemed to crush even the individual. In fact, however, there was always a persistent affinity between centralization and individualism, and during later ages the central power of the State was the most vivid reality in Rome.

As in Attican history it was the intermediate association that became increasingly the object of governmental suspicion. "By the time of the Christian emperors," James Muirhead writes, "the last traces disappeared of the *familia* as a corporate aggregate of persons and estate subject absolutely to the power and dominion of its head. . . . All that remained of the *patria potestas* in Justinian legislation is what is sanctioned in modern systems."[26] What was true of the family was true of other types of association in Roman society. "One of the chief objects of Caesar and Augustus was to prevent the formation of new associations, and to destroy those which had already been formed. . . . The Empire . . . was trying, out of homage to an exaggerated idea of the State, to isolate the individual, to snap every moral tie between man and man. . . ."[27] Although, as modern research has demonstrated, imperial Rome was alive with associations of every sort (and it was within this welter of associations that the Christian Church took form), it remains true, as Gibbon wrote, that Roman policy "viewed with the utmost jealousy and distrust any association among its subjects . . . and the privileges of private corporations, though formed for the most harmless of beneficial purposes, were bestowed with a very sparing hand."[28] The existence of any stable social group had to be regarded as a potential barrier to that consolidation of political power sought from the time of Augustus on, and if such a group could not be obliterated it must be made, as in the case of the gilds, a part of the official machinery of the State.

Five

Here, then, in the conflict between the central political power and the various authorities intermediate to the individual and the State, lies the most fateful of all the conflicts of authority and allegiance which, together, form so large a part of the history of institutions. We do not have to appeal to any immanent spirit or dialectic to appreciate the revolutionary role of the State in history. We see it in such concrete occurrences as the Cleisthenean reforms in ancient Athens, in the founding of Roman law, in the establishment of the King's Peace in the eleventh and twelfth centuries, in the conflict of the political power with the universities, the gilds, the Church, in the enclosure acts, and in the whole development of an administrative bureaucracy that gradually absorbed functions and authorities formerly resident in other associations.

In historical terms the State is the outgrowth of war. In its earliest form, everywhere, it is essentially a military organization. But it does not long remain a purely military association. For the consolidation of authority and the gaining of revenue necessary to military effectiveness inevitably bring political power into conflict with other associations that lay claims to obedience and property. The State may conflict now with clan, now with church, now with class, or village community or gild, or university, depending on necessities inherent in the historical situation.

For long periods of time the conflict may not be obvious. The inroads of political power are restrained by difficulties of communication, by custom, by inertia, and by the frequently formidable nature of ecclesiastical, kinship, or economic institutions. In other periods the conflict flares up and is starkly revealed by decrees and enactments, by constitutional crises, even by civil wars and revolutions. But always in the history of politics, in one degree or another, we see the conflict that is created necessarily by the existence, on the one hand, of associations, local, sectional, or functional, each claiming limited jurisdiction over its members, and, on the other, an association that identifies itself with *all* persons in a given territory and seeks to consolidate all important authorities within that territory.

We see this conflict vividly today in such an area as India. Here the ancient authorities of caste, village, and family are slowly being absorbed by a political administration based upon Western standards. In terms of the functions wielded and allegiances commanded, the State grows stronger, the other associations weaker. In India no more than in the history of modern Europe is this simply a process of crude power expansion. As a process it is bound up with the creation of a system of positive rights of individuals and of important humanitarian gains, with the reduction of inefficiencies and corruptions on the local level, and with the liberation of millions of individuals from caste and religious authorities which have become oppressive.[29] In the new State there are millions of Indians who can look forward to a life politically free, if frequently less secure in a social and psychological sense than any they have known before. But these characteristics of the new order do not hide the often profound conflicts that arise between new agencies of government and traditional social groups. Nor do they obscure the rapidly changing balance of power between central political authority (historically weak in its contact with the individual and in functions performed) and the traditional authorities of caste, village, and joint family.

This, in conclusion, is the revolutionary essence of the State: the combination of social dislocation and political reassimilation; of liberation with power; of loss of old status with the gaining of new. Who can doubt that from this conflict of State with other associations in society have come some of the most important humanitarian gains and personal liberties in Western culture? But who can doubt, either, that from this same conflict, from this same, still ongoing process of revolution, have come problems of balance of authority in society and problems of associative and personal freedom which are very nearly overwhelming at the present time?

What has been described in abstract terms in the preceding chapter can be made more vivid and telling by a brief examination of the theory of sovereignty as it develops from Bodin, through Hobbes, to Rousseau.[1] Each of these influential minds represents a distinct stage in the history of Western political power. Each is a kind of mirror reflecting the massive changes that took place between 1500 and 1800 in the principal spheres of authority and allegiance.

The theory of each man holds, successively, ever greater implications of destruction to the intermediate authorities of society, ever greater implications of centralized political power, and ever greater implications of cultural and social leveling of the population.

In Bodin we observe the emergence of the sovereign from the whole network of restrictions imposed by medieval custom and religious author- ity. But, for all of Bodin's ascribing to the sovereign unconditional and imprescriptible powers, the sovereign remains weak—weak because first the sovereign is made identical with the monarchy alone; and second because Bodin is unwilling to accept the consequences to other associations in society of his own definition of sovereignty.

In the writings of Hobbes, in the seventeenth century, the sovereign becomes much stronger. In formal terms the sovereign has the same attributes ascribed by Bodin, but the locus of sovereignty is shifted from the king to the legal State. Now the sovereign is made into a kind of atmosphere of duties and obligations shared by everyone. Each individual, apart from his natural state, exists only in the contemplation of the sovereign. All customs, traditions, and relationships not founded by the State itself become objects of suspicion. In Bodin's thought society and State were distinct logically and historically. But in Hobbes, State and society are one and the same.

With Rousseau, in the eighteenth century, comes the most formidable and revolutionary of all theories of sovereignty. It is conceived as nothing less than the exalted will of the people, omnipotent and omnipresent. All other forms of relationship are abolished, leaving only the State itself as the community of man's interests and aspirations. Only in the State can the individual find tranquillity and relief from discord and unhappiness. Sovereignty, for Rousseau, is not a mere legal thing; it is the sum total of all virtues and even freedoms.

Two

Of Bodin[2] it has been well said that he had ceased to be medieval without becoming modern. But so had France itself. The age of Bodin was the age of the military triumph of the monarchy over the competing powers of the nobility and the Church. But the triumph was a bare one, and it was set in a scene that was, socially at least, not too different from the France of two centuries earlier. Despite the military might of the monarchy that had grown out of the Hundred Years' War, such associations as the gilds, monasteries, the feudal classes, the communes, and the Church continued to exert vast influence in human lives. Numerous systems of law existed at all levels; traditions and customs hemmed in monarchical power at every turn, and the diversity of culture in France was matched by the diversity of allegiance and authority.

In the middle of the sixteenth century, chiefly in Paris, there arose a group of men who called themselves the Politiques—men who were dedicated to action in behalf of the central power of the monarch at the expense of all other social and moral authorities in France. In their opinion, the disorder of France could be checked only by the clear supremacy of a morally and religiously neutral power, vested in the king himself, extending over every other associative relationship in France. Already there were clear indications that the royal power, through its control of the newer modes of warfare and its growing, if still slight, appeal to the people, was the only power in France capable of checking the divisive tendencies in the population. Among other needs, however, was that of a systematic theory to give it rationality and universal acceptance. This Bodin attempted to supply.

His work is indeed a curious amalgamation of ideas which would have been perfectly suited to the intellectual atmosphere of the thirteenth century and of ideas which logically belong to the century following his own. As a moral philosopher he tended to remain rooted to the soil of medieval pluralism and autonomy of groups. As a practical politician his impulses place him with Hobbes in the next century or with some even more devoted Erastian. The latter impulses dominate his work, but the confusions and contradictions which so many of his commentators have written about make plain the underlying conflict in his own thought. He could not easily relinquish his belief in the ethical priority of all those relationships founded upon kinship and religion and occupation.

Yet as one of the *Politiques* Bodin was deeply aware of problems that could be solved only by a strong political limitation of the rights and powers claimed by the various corporations and groups in France. The conflicting jurisdictions of various spheres of law, the excessive duplication, the divisive influences of customs and allegiances that were either local or stemmed from authorities outside France, the bitter religious conflicts of power, the economic disunities—all of these, he felt, could be checked or terminated by raising the power of the king above all other powers in the realm.

"Majesty or sovereignty," he declares, "is the most high, absolute and perpetual power over the subjects and citizens in a Commonweale." This absolute and perpetual power belongs to the monarch. His power is inalienable and imprescriptible. It cannot be limited by custom within the realm or by edict from without. The king is not below the law, as medieval lawyers like Bracton had declared, but always above the law. The law of the land is simply the command of the sovereign.

Despite some bitter remarks in Bodin concerning the Roman law and the lawyers of his own day who were proclaiming its superiorities, it is plain that behind Bodin's own conception of the sovereign lies the model afforded by the *Corpus Juris*. The Roman emphasis upon legal centralization, upon the superiority of the ruler to all other forms of authority, including custom, and the general political perspective of Roman law could not but have had strong appeal to one of the *Politiques*.

The basic attribute of sovereignty is the power to give laws to citizens collectively and severally without the consent of a superior, an equal, or an inferior. For the France of the sixteenth century this attribute could be translated into reality only by declaring all powers, that of the Church included, all customs, however ancient and sacred, and all persons, however exalted in economic, social, or religious eminence, subject to the will of the king.

More specifically, it meant a challenge to those associations and corporations which lay intermediate to the individual and the king. Here too the influence of Roman law is manifest. "Every corporation or college," Bodin declares, "is a lawful community or consociation *under sovereign power*." That sovereign control of all intermediate associations is to be exacting and detailed is attested by the following injunction: "Where the word lawful importeth the authority of the sovereign, without whose permission there can be no college: and is referred not only unto the power of meeting together: but unto the place also where it ought to meet, unto the time and manner of meeting, and to what things ought to be entreated of, in their assembly."

This is the aspect that is, above all others, the most revealing of Bodin's problems and his perspectives: the sovereign's relation to corporate bodies. The history of the preceding two centuries in France had been characterized by growing assertion of monarchical rights of chartering, approving, and regulating the activities of associations. But even in the late sixteenth century the powers possessed by these bodies were formidable. And it was one of Bodin's prime objectives to limit their collective rights and subordinate them one and all to the power of the king.

It follows that no association within the commonwealth can be allowed to enjoy an independent existence in the sphere of public law. Merchant law, canon law, gild law, all of these reflections of corporate association are subordinate to the law of the king. Whatever compulsion any association can exert over its members has its origin in the authorization of the sovereign. Associations do not even possess the right to own property. Nor can they be said to possess the right of collective legal responsibility. With Innocent IV, Bodin declares these associations *persona ficta*.

What we see, then, in the pages of Bodin's great political treatise, is the unfolding of a view of society that possesses distinctly modern implications. The political, rather than the religious or the economic power, is made foremost. Legal pluralism is replaced by legal monism. Only that authority is legally binding which stems from, or is countenanced by, the king. Gone is the doctrine of the two swords, gone also the conviction that only through religious mediation can the power of the State be made morally right. For Bodin the State has its own justification directly from God. Like the Protestants whom Bodin detested in most respects, he makes the State ethically autonomous. In all these respects Bodin belongs logically with the moderns.

But there is another side to Bodin's theory that places him much more securely among social philosophers of earlier centuries. And this is, first of all, his sharp distinction between State and society, and, second, his devotion to the moral and social qualities of all intermediate associations ranging from family to corporation. Only in the philosophy of Althusius in the century following Bodin do we find an appreciation of intermediate association that matches Bodin's. And Althusius was scarcely recognized. For, as we shall see, the whole tendency of social thought down to the time of Burke in the late eighteenth century was to deprecate, even dissolve, all forms of association that could not be rationalized by natural law or by the will of the State.

But in Bodin's thought there is a keen and frequently brilliant insight into the sociological aspects of human association—status, membership, custom, and moral control. His impatience with legal diversity and his profound devotion to the king did not cause him to lose sight either of the moral or the historical properties of the society in which he lived. We see this in his meticulous distinction between legal and social authority.

The family, the civil associations, the corporations and fraternities are all, in his mind, logically and historically antecedent to the state. It is impossible to read the long discussion which Bodin offers on social groups without realizing the value he ascribes to them as agencies of solidarity and control. The associations, for purposes of trade, religious worship, security and fellowship, were the bonds of human society before any political ties were established, and they have continued to perform functions indispensable to social life. It is this distinction between social and political relationships that marks Bodin as a transitional figure.

Unlike the State which rests upon force the social groups in society rest upon the reciprocal principle of friendship (*amicitia*). The principle of mutual responsibility is the very structure of these associations. Man is a social being by nature and these associations are but manifestations of his instinct for sociability. "Whereby it is plainly to be seen, the societies of men among themselves, to have been at first sought out for the leading of their lives in more safety and quiet: and them first of all to have sprung from the love which was betwixt man and wife: from them to have flowed the mutual love betwixt parents and their children: then the love of brothers and sisters one towards another: and after them the friendship between cousins and other kinsmen: and last of all the love and good will which is betwixt men joined in alliance: which had all at length grown cold, and been utterly extinguished, had it not been nourished, maintained, and kept by societies, communities, corporations and colleges: the union of whom hath for long time in safety maintained many people, without any form of a commonwealth, or sovereign power over them."

It is folly to wonder whether the commonwealth could exist without these groups. "To demand whether communities and colleges be necessary in a commonweale is as much as to demand, whether that a commonweale can be maintained and upholden without love and amity, without which the world itself cannot long stand." He is scornful of those who argue "that all corporations and colleges are out of a commonweale to be excluded and banished; not considering that a family and the very commonweale itself are nothing else but communities."

It is true that some corporations involve a risk of disorder; but to advocate the elimination of all corporations on that account is sophistical in logic and dangerous in practice. The suppression of all corporations would be a distinct act of tyranny, not to be countenanced by wise rulers. "Whereby it appeareth, tyrants always to have hated the corporations and communities of the people, and by all means endeavoured to have them utterly extinguished." The best-constituted, the most prosperous of kingdoms are those in which there is a flourishing diversity of associations and groups. From these the State draws powers of order that give reinforcement to its own legal nature, and from them the citizens derive protection that would be wanting in the absence of the *collegia* and *corpora*. Particularly does Bodin praise the gilds. In their collective operations lie both economic stability and prosperity.

But of all forms of associative life it is the family that Bodin most venerates. It is his devotion to the economic and legal solidarity of this group that forms the high point of the medievalism which persists in his thinking, and, as more than one student has observed, this same devotion destroys the very foundations of the political sovereignty that he has been so careful to build up and make supreme.

Bodin will not tolerate the thought that the political sovereign should be supreme over the individual members of the family and over its customs and property. Sovereignty he has defined as absolute, imprescriptible, and perpetual. But when he comes to deal with the family these qualities of sovereignty become sharply restricted. The public law must not cross the threshold. The children, the wife, the dependents and servants, together with all property, are solely in the custodianship of the father. He grants the law of the commonwealth no rights of pre-emption, eminent domain, or discipline over the possessions and persons of the family. The family, rather than the individual, is the real unit of Bodin's State, as it is the unit from which, historically, all society stems. Even the father's right of life and death over members of the family must be restored or upheld. "It is needful in a well-ordered commonweale to restore unto parents the power of life and death over the children, which by the law of God and Nature is given them." Similarly, in all matters of education, training, religious worship, and political participation, the will of the father shall be supreme, shall not be abridged by even the most absolute of sovereignties.

It is chiefly the family ownership of property that Bodin defends, for, only in its economic solidarity can the social and moral virtues of the family remain intact. If the State were given the power to alienate property, through interference with customs of inheritance, there would then be no limit to the State's capacity for the enslavement of man. The moral structure of the family would dissolve. The State itself would become weak.

Thus despite his clear sense of the need for political unity in the State, despite his insistence upon the legal supremacy of the king over every custom, corporation, and association, the actual conception of society which unfolds before our eyes is not very different from what existed in the minds of medieval philosophers. The society Bodin offers us is not one of abstract, legally discrete, individuals, each individual attached directly to the sovereign. It is a society, instead, composed of families, each of which exists under the imprescriptible authority of the father, each of which is held to be immune to the authority of the sovereign in all matters. It is a society articulated in numerous and varied associations, colleges, and sodalities. It is a society founded, for all of Bodin's leanings to Roman law, upon the primacy of custom and kinship and association.

To observe the logical confusions in Bodin's theory of sovereignty is not, however, the point of the present discussion. What is of greater interest is simply the presence of the two strands of thought, unreconciled, conflicting, but reflecting clearly the issues foremost in the history of modern sovereignty.

Three

In the political writings of Thomas Hobbes[3] most of these conflicts of sentiment and confusions of logic are absent. Few writers have had more influence upon the development of the modern centralized State than Hobbes. The modern State, someone has observed, is an inverted pyramid, its apex resting upon the 1651 folio edition of Hobbes's *Leviathan*. Even those contemporaries and later writers who were most sharply opposed to his conclusions were yet unable to remain aloof from the political principles and perspectives that lay behind the conclusions.

The *Leviathan* made its appearance exactly seventy-five years after the publication of Bodin's great work. It is considerably beyond that span of time in clarity of idea and rigor of logic. Like Bodin, Hobbes takes his theoretical departure from the problem of order and from the assumption that the political State is necessarily the determining environment of human conduct. But beyond this point of departure the two political theorists have little in common. In Hobbes's conception of the State and its law, in his treatment of the foundations of social order, and in his theory of internal associations there are few if any remaining evidences of the medieval image of society that Bodin had been unable to shake free of.

Gone, in Hobbes, is the troubled affection for associations based upon locality, interest, and faith. Gone also is the profound veneration for kinship, for the inviolable household, for the imprescriptible authority of the house-father. Neither the family, the church, nor any other system of authority is allowed by Hobbes to intervene in any significant way between the individual and the absolute power of the State. Where Bodin, like all the medieval lawyers and theorists before him, had rested his political edifice upon the foundations of social custom and historical use and wont, Hobbes relentlessly eradicated every element of social purpose and loyalty that did not proceed directly and logically from the presumed nature of the individual or from the explicit command of the sovereign. For Hobbes there are but two essential elements of civil society: the individual and the sovereign. All else is expunged in the interests of practical order and theoretical simplicity.

Hobbes's philosophy of government has to be seen not merely in terms of the political and constitutional struggles that dominated the England of his time but also in the brilliant light of seventeenth-century doctrines of natural law. No longer were philosophers content to rest their principles of man and society upon either the revealed wisdom of the church or upon historical precedent. Everything had to be derived from the pure resources of reason, from the rigorous development, in theoretical terms, of potentialities that reason taught lay everywhere in the nature of man. No relationship among men, no right, no authority could be admitted into political systems that did not proceed clearly from what was held to be the fundamental law of nature.

In the social thought of the seventeenth century all relationships were suspect. Man was the solid fact; all else was ephemeral. As the physical scientists of the day dealt with physical atoms in space and relegated to secondary or subjective status all of those qualities and essences medieval philosophers had accepted as fundamental, so the social philosophers sought to build theoretical systems upon human atoms alone. Relationships of tradition and inherited morality were either expelled from theory or were rationalized into relationships proceeding ineluctably from man's pre-social nature.

Given originally a prepolitical state of nature, a social vacuum, as it were, in which the individual was isolated and free, the problem chosen by almost every natural-law theorist was: how did man emerge from this socially empty state of nature and by what means? The answer invariably lay in appeal to some form of contract. Contract, conceived as free agreement among self-interested individuals, became the seventeenth-century rationalist's prime response to problems of social cohesion that had commonly been answered in terms of Christian morality or historically derived status by medieval philosophers.

Ernest Barker has perceptively suggested that the seventeenth-century philosophy of natural law was in certain significant respects a kind of subtle rationalization of the principles of Roman law. It adhered to the same conception of the primacy of the individual and individual will in legal matters. It made relationships of contract fundamental in the constitution of society. And, as in the Roman codes, natural-law philosophy in the seventeenth century gave the political State the position of absolute supremacy over all other forms of human association. Roman lawyers ascribed an essentially derivative role to social groups in the State, and natural-law philosophers similarly ascribed a derivative role to all forms of association lying intermediate to the individual and the sovereign. All the symmetry of design and centralization of function and authority to be seen in Roman law are clearly apparent in seventeenth-century natural law.

All of this is fundamental in Hobbes's approach to a scientific explanation of society. The method of geometry never ceased to fascinate his mind, and his conceptual arrangement of individuals, both in the state of nature and in civil society, looks like nothing so much as it does the geometer's arrangement of lines and angles in a geometrical demonstration. For Hobbes, the abstract individual, contract, and the power of the State are fundamental. All else is to be derived rigorously from these assumptions or else discarded.

The intellectual advance of Hobbes beyond Bodin, in the construction of a theory of the absolute State, is apparent in the enormous increase in functional significance that Hobbes gives to the relationship of the State to man. For Bodin, the State did not create order; it merely reinforced the stability that already lay in the nonpolitical associations of men. But Hobbes denies that any form of social order ever existed or can exist apart from the sovereign structure of the State. Before the advent of the State there was only the condition of nature. "In such condition, there is no place for

Industry; because the fruit thereof is uncertain . . . no Navigation, nor use of the commodities that may be imported by Sea; no commodious Building; no Instruments of moving, and removing such things as require much force; no Knowledge of the face of the Earth; no account of Time; no Arts; no Letters; no Society; and which is worst of all, continuall feare, and danger of violent death; And the life of man, solitary, poore, nasty, brutish, and short."

It was the emergence of the political State, through the instrumentality of contract among all of these miserable creatures, that first brought upon the earth any form of society whatsoever. And it is the theoretical reinforcement of this redemptive State that engages all of Hobbes's efforts throughout his *Leviathan*. He does not shrink from making the State's power absolute over man because, first, the contract made it absolute, and, second, apart from its absoluteness, there could be no protective society, and man would sink once again into the dismal condition of fear and brutishness that had characterized his beginnings.

Here, then, in his identification of the State with all association and culture, lies the foundation of the political edifice which Hobbes builds. Unlike Bodin, he does not recognize any pre-political order of society based upon kinship, religion, and other associations within which the sociability of man is nourished. For Hobbes there is no middle ground between man as a helpless, isolated creature of fear and man as the citizen of the absolute State. And, unlike Bodin, Hobbes manifests little sympathy for the customs, traditions, and moralities that exist outside the framework of sovereign law. Law, writes Hobbes, is "to every Subject, those Rules which the Commonwealth hath Commanded him, by Word, Writing, or other sufficient Sign of the Will, to make use of, for the Distinction of Right and Wrong." For the rigorous mind of Hobbes law was not in any way dependent upon the social institutions of a people. Law was the command of the sovereign, nothing else. Among the diseases of the State, he declares, one of the greatest is the belief "that every private man is judge of Good and Evil actions." This was true in the fearful state of nature, "but otherwise it is manifest, that the measure of Good and Evil actions, is the Civill Law."

Nor was there any question in Hobbes's mind about the need to centralize all authority in the State. Division and multiplicity of authority can have no place in a stable order. "For what is it to divide the Power of the Common-wealth, but to Dissolve it; for Powers divided mutually destroy each other." He treats with contempt those writers who hold that since "there be three Soules in man; so there also . . . may be more Soules (that is, more Sovereigns) than one, in a Common-wealth." Authority in a society is unitary and indivisible, or else it is nothing. And, finally, Hobbes gives the death blow to that most cherished of all medieval legal doctrines, the doctrine that the political ruler is below the law. It is, he declares, "repugnant to the nature of the Common-wealth . . . that he that hath the Sovereign Power, is subject to the Civill Lawes." Bodin had stated the same principle, but his own essentially medieval conception of a nonpolitical society had made it impossible for him to develop the principle fully. No such limitations are to be found in the *Leviathan*.

With the monolith of power that Hobbes creates in the State, there is little room left for associations and groups. Hobbes does not see in these the multifold sources of sociability and order that Bodin had found in them. They are breeding areas of dissension, of conflict with the requirements of the unitary State, not reinforcements of order and justice. He compares associations within the State "which are as it were many lesser Common-wealths in the bowels of a greater" to "wormes in the entrayles of a naturall man." Economic monopolies of any kind, he detests. In the body of the commonwealth these associations "breedeth there an Inflammation, accompanied with a Fever, and painfull stitches."

He is suspicious of the universities, for these teaching bodies, he declared, have ever tended toward the support of ideas and actions that are not in the best interests of the State's unity. All teaching establishments should give their first devotion to, and be instruments of, the commonwealth. Large associations founded upon mutual aid and protection, especially those in the upper classes, similarly arouse his distrust. "Leagues of subjects (because Leagues are commonly made for mutual defence), are in a Common-wealth (which is no more than a League of all the Subjects together) for the most part unnecessary, and savour of unlawfull designe." Gilds, even those of beggars, not to mention the more powerful ones, are regarded by Hobbes as potential infringements upon the autonomy of the individual as well as upon the majesty of the sovereign. All such associations seek to represent their members in matters of protection and security. But in the State, correctly formed, the sovereign himself is the absolute and sufficient representative of his subjects. Therefore "no other can be representative of any part of them, but so forth as he shall give leave." And this leave is to be given sparingly, grudgingly.

The meager treatment of the family that Hobbes gives us is in marked contrast to the extensive discussion that Bodin had offered. For Bodin, one of the chief reasons for family solidarity was the protection of the right of property. But Hobbes specifically declares that all property derives in law from the permission of the sovereign. And the kind of parental authority that Bodin had claimed, together with legal inviolability of the household, is, for Hobbes, unthinkable. The parent, Hobbes declares, "obligeth his Children and Servants as farre as the Law permitteth, though not further, because none of them are bound to obedience in those actions, which the Law hath forbidden to be done." But Hobbes is not content to place the family's authority under the strict regulation of the State. He must also do to the family what earlier legal theorists had done to ecclesiastical and economic corporations: that is, individualize them through the fiction of perpetual contract. In discussing the nature of "Dominion Paternall," he insists that it "is not so derived from the Generation, as if therefore the Parent had Dominion over his Child because he begat him; but from the Child's Consent, either expresse, or by other sufficient arguments declared." In short, contract is, in Hobbes's rigorous terms, the cement of even the family itself. Not from custom, or from divine law itself, does the solidarity of the family proceed. It proceeds from, and can be justified by, voluntary agreement, either express or implied.

The conclusion is inescapable that for Hobbes the sole purpose of the family is that of procreation. He does not conceive it, as did Bodin, as the true source of man's moral nature, as the model of all forms of association. In Hobbes's system of thought everything proceeds from atomistic individuals, their instincts and reason, and from contractual agreements among them. There is no place for relationships of ascribed, historically given, status.

But of all associations, it is the Church that Hobbes fears the most. By reason of its tenacious hold upon men's spiritual allegiances, the Church will always be a divisive force within the commonwealth unless it is made strictly subordinate to the political power. It is unthinkable that an autonomous spiritual authority should exist. To grant corporate freedom to the Church would be to set up "Supremacy against the Soveraignty; Canons against Lawes, and a Ghostly Authority against the Civill." An autonomous Church would mean nothing less than a divided sovereignty within the State, and this, as we have seen, is for Hobbes the most deadly of all diseases afflicting the body politic. "For seeing the Ghostly Power challengeth the Right to declare what is Sinne it challengeth by consequence to declare what is Law, (Sinne being nothing but the transgression of the Law)."

How far Hobbes measured himself as a Christian is debatable. Whether he was, as many of his contemporaries bitterly denounced him, an atheist, or whether he was a believer at heart and opposed only to the authoritarian aspects of institutional Christianity is a matter we need not consider here. What alone is of importance in this connection is to mark the heavy blows Hobbes gave to the medieval idea of an autonomous Church. The religious life of the people must always be governed by the head of the State. A Church Hobbes defined as "a company of men professing Christian Religion, united in the person of one Sovereign; at whose command they ought to assemble, and without whose authority they ought not to assemble." From this it follows that any supposition or claim of a universal Church is fallacious and evil. "There is on Earth, no such universall Church, as all Christians are bound to obey; because there is no power on Earth, to which all other Common-wealths are subject. . . . There is therefore no other Government in this life, neither of State, nor Religion, but Temporall; nor teaching of any doctrine, lawfull to any Subject, which the Governour both of the State, and of the Religion, forbiddeth to be taught: And that Governor must be one; or else there must needs follow Faction, and Civil war in the Common-wealth between the Church and State."

Above all other religions it was Roman Catholicism that Hobbes feared and hated the most. For, it was this Church, and most especially its militant Jesuits, that in Hobbes's time provided the strongest challenge to the development of national Christianity. But Hobbes can be severe toward Protestants as well. He denounces "Factions for government of religion, as papists, protestants, etc. . . . as being contrary to the peace and safety of the people, and a taking of the Sword out of the hand of the Sovereign." In truth Hobbes was agreeable to the existence of any religion, irrespective of its dogma, provided it placed itself unquestioningly under the State. And, conversely, he opposed any religion, Catholic or Protestant that did not so place itself.

Despite the severity of Hobbes's attitude toward all associations, despite the centering of all authority in the State, it yet remains true that for him the power of the State was not an end in itself. Too many students of Hobbes have read him through the pages of his enemies, rather than through his own statements. Despite the rigorousness of the theory, when compared with that of Bodin, despite the powerful animus against autonomous associations and the limitations put upon religion and all other autonomous systems of morality, it is the *individual* whom Hobbes has in his mind as the embodiment of virtue. Hobbes did not seek the extermination of individual rights but their fulfillment. This could be accomplished only by removing social barriers to individual autonomy. In his eyes the greatest claim of the absolute State lay in its power to create an environment for the individual's pursuit of his natural ends.

Too often the eighteenth-century emphasis on the natural order and the natural rights of individuals has been described as a reaction to the seventeenth-century political system of Hobbes. Locke is made the philosophical source of this other contemplation of nature. Actually, although Locke, by virtue of his later position with respect to Hobbes, could give more explicit emphasis to individual rights, the fact remains that it was Hobbes's own brilliant sketching of the political environment of individualism that made the later system possible. In many senses Locke is a derivative thinker. Hobbes was his master in all important respects.

However extreme the *Leviathan* may be, however savage its rejection of pluralism, localism, sectionalism, what Hobbes always has in mind is the creation of an impersonal environment of law within which individuals may pursue rationally their proper interests. It is not the totalitarian State that Hobbes gives us but the necessary political environment of the natural system of liberty which was to become identified later with the Enlightenment in France and England. Later theorists such as Locke could give more space to the rights themselves. But Hobbes, with the spectacle of a still potent residue of medievalism before him, had to give the greater part of his attention to the political environment itself.

Nor can Hobbes be described simply as the voice of the "middle class." That his theory of the State was a powerful factor in bringing into existence the new entrepreneur and the new system of economic relationships is a good deal less an indication of his affection for the middle class than it is of his hatred for the economic groups that were hindrances both to the new middle class and to the attainment of a unified and impersonal political order. Hobbes could write bitterly about the representatives of the new economic order and condemn sharply their treatment of the poor. He was no more concerned with deliberately furthering their interests than he was with furthering consciously the interests of the Protestants. What gives continuity to the political theory of Hobbes and both economic rationalism and Protestant individualism is the Hobbesian environment of impersonal law in which both could flourish. We may add also the common dislike of intermediate social and moral associations.

Only the invincible economic determinist would see in the pages of the *Leviathan,* with their brilliant and eloquent portrayal of the impersonal, absolute, and imprescriptible State, a piece of ideology reflecting the alleged interests of the middle class. In light of Hobbes's plain distrust of the market place, and of his preference for the rural countryside, in light of his explicit condemnation of the political practices of the merchants and manufacturers of his day, of his ascribing to them the blame for the civil war, and of his general hatred for their acquisitive and exploitative proclivities, and above all in the light of the relentless political direction of his writings, it is difficult to understand interpretations that relegate his beliefs to the vague categories of economic determinism. If there is any element of reluctant praise in Hobbes for a class of men whose activities he despised, it is because he could see that this class, by reason of the very tenuousness of its internal social relationships and by the absence of any sense of *noblesse oblige,* could never become, as the older aristocracy had been, a threat to the unity of the political State. Hobbes's early affection was for the aristocracy, but through the iron logic of his political thought he cast this affection aside. The landed aristocracy, with its large retinues and its rooted allegiances, must constitute a perennial threat to political unity. Hence the notable shift in his thinking regarding such matters as *honor.* But it is nonsense to suppose that his affection for the landed aristocracy was transferred to a middle class. It went, ruthlessly and rigorously, to the State itself. It would be far more correct to say that Hobbes's appreciation of the middle class—thin and reluctant as it was—came from the logic of his politics rather than to say that his politics came from a middle-class orientation of thinking.

The State that Hobbes gives us is an aggregate of individuals, each free to pursue his proper interests through contract and intellectual agreement, each free from the artificial constraints of class, church, gild, or any other form of intermediate association. And in view of the still ascendant authorities cast over the lives of individuals by such bodies as the legal corporations, the boroughs, the monopolies in trade, not to mention the whole tissue of traditional relationships of church, family, and local community, Hobbes felt, not without some justification, that only with an absolute sovereign could any effective environment of individualism be possible.

Four

By far the most rigorous and revolutionary theory of sovereignty is that of Rousseau.[4] Like Bodin and Hobbes, Rousseau takes his departure from perceptions of social disorder. Where Bodin had defined the role of the State as that of a referee among competing groups and associations, and where Hobbes had described the major purpose of the State as that of providing an impersonal environment for the release of individuals from the confinements of class and religion and for the creation of a morality based upon individual virtue, Rousseau sees the State as the most exalted of all forms of moral community. For Rousseau there is no morality, no freedom, no community outside the structure of the State. Apart from his life in the State, man's actions are wanting in even the minimal conditions of morality and freedom. The State and the people are basically one. Only the State can provide the environment of equality, freedom, and tranquillity for which man's nature calls.

Rousseau is the first of the modern philosophers to see in the State a means of resolving the conflicts, not merely among institutions, but within the individual himself. The State becomes the means of freeing man from the spiritual uncertainties and hypocrisies of traditional society. It is a spiritual refuge even as the Church was a refuge from life's uncertainties in earlier ages of Europe. We cannot understand the structure of Rousseau's ideal State, or the immense appeal his political vision has continued to exert in subsequent decades, except by recognizing the moral and social conditions that Rousseau took for his point of departure. And these he epitomized under the word *uncertainty.*

"What a train of vices must attend this uncertainty!" he wrote in his early *Discourse on the Arts and Sciences.* "Sincere friendship, real esteem, and perfect confidence are banished from among men. Jealousy, suspicion, fear, coldness, reserve, hate and fraud lie constantly concealed under that uniform and deceitful veil of politeness; that boasted candour and urbanity, for which we are indebted to the light and leading of this age." His loathing for the vices of the society around him in Paris, expressed so passionately in the first discourse, was expressed more skillfully and with no diminution of intensity in his second discourse, *The Origin of Inequality.* Here the hatred of cultural stratification, and of all the psychological traits that go with it, matches the earlier expression of hatred for hypocrisy and the fear of uncertainty. The kind of uncertainties that had emerged in intellectual society as the result of modern changes in economy and religion excited his opposition in exactly the same measure that similar changes had excited the opposition of Plato two thousand years earlier in Athens. Like Plato, Rousseau made the *emancipation* of the individual from the tyrannies and uncertainties of ordinary society the major theme of all his endeavors. And like Plato too he found in the structure of the absolute State the perfect conditions for the reconciliation of freedom and order.

Two entities dominate Rousseau's thought: the individual and the State. In his mind they are simultaneously sovereign and, together, the only basis of a just human order. The result is the confluence of a radical individualism on the one hand and an uncompromising authoritarianism on the other. The parallel existence of these strands of thought in Rousseau's works has been the basis of numerous charges of inconsistency, charges which are, however, not true. The ideas of Rousseau, contradictory though they may appear to be at first sight, compose one of the most logically articulate systems of thought in the history of political theory. The authoritarian strain so plain in the *Political Economy* is the perfect complement of the individualism so manifest in his discourse on *The Origin of Inequality.* Both strains come together in the *Social Contract* and make of that work a manifesto which served with equal adequacy the libertarian principles of

'89 and the authoritarian principles of '93. The harmony of the two strains of thought becomes apparent when we realize what each is directed against.

The individualism of Rousseau's thought is not the individualism of a William Godwin; it is not the libertarian assertion of absolute rights against the *State*. Rousseau's passionate defense of the individual arises out of his opposition to the forms and observances of *society*. "What excites Rousseau's hatred," Professor Vaughan has commented, "is not the state, but society of any sort, quite apart from the civic ties by which in fact it is held together. His ideal alike in the discourses and in *Émile*, is no doubt individual freedom: freedom, however, not in sense of immunity from control of the state but in that of withdrawal from the oppressions and corruptions of society." It is this ideal which animates the educational philosophy of *Émile*—the belief in the goodness and perfectibility of the individual when he is protected from the corruption of society. It is, perhaps above all others, the basic theme of the *Confessions*. The splendidness of isolation from society is a leitmotif which recurs again and again in the passages of that work. The ideal lies implicit in *The Origin of Inequality* where each stage of advancement that removes the individual from the isolation which was his existence in the condition of nature is marked as a point on the way to degeneration. It is not the political state which inspires Rousseau's hostility but the harshness, inequalities, and dissensions of civil society. In a letter to Mirabeau, he writes: "It is of the essence of society to breed a ceaseless war among its members; and the only way to combat this is to find a form of government which shall set the law above them all."

The traditional bonds of society, the relationships we generally speak of as social, are the ties that to Rousseau symbolize the chains of existence. It is from these he desires to emancipate the individual; their gross inequalities he desires to replace with a condition of equality approximating as nearly as possible the state of nature. "Each citizen would then be completely independent of all his fellow men, and absolutely dependent upon the state: which operation is always brought by the same means; for it is only by the force of the state that the liberty of its members can be secured." There is no other single statement in all Rousseau's writings that better serves as the theme of his political philosophy than this. In it is incorporated the essential argument of the discourses and the *Social Contract*. His ideal is independence for the individual, but independence, it will be observed, not from the State but from fellow members of society.

The function of the State is made apparent by the same statement. Its mission is to effectuate the independence of the individual from society by securing the individual's dependence upon itself. The State is the means by which the individual can be freed of the restrictive tyrannies that compose society. It is the agency of emancipation that permits the individual to develop the latent germs of goodness heretofore frustrated by a hostile society. By entering into the pure state, Rousseau declares, "Man's actions receive a moral character which was wanting to them before," and "from a stupid and limited animal he now for the first time becomes a reasoning being and a man." The State is thus of the essence of man's potential being, and far from being a check upon his development, it is the sole means of that development. Through the power of the State, man is spared the strife and tyranny that arise out of his selfish and destructive passions. But in order to emerge from the dissensions of society, and to abide in the spiritual peace of the state, there must be "an absolute surrender of the individual, with all of his rights and all of his powers, to the community as a whole."

Rousseau's emphasis upon the community has been too often interpreted in a sense foreign to his own aim. Commentators have occasionally written of his "community" as the revival of a concept that had disappeared with the Middle Ages. The mystic solidarity that Rousseau preaches is not, however, the solidarity of the community existing by custom and unwritten law. The social community, as it existed in the thought of Thomas Aquinas or, later, in the theory of Althusius, is a community of communities, an assemblage of morally integrated minor groups. The solidarity of this community arises out of the moral and social observances of the minor groups. Its unity does not result from being permeated with sovereign law, extending from the top through all individual components of the structure. Rousseau's community however is a *political* community, one indistinguishable from the State and sharing all the uniformitarian qualities of the State. It is, in his mind, a moral unity, but it is a unity conferred by the sovereign will of the State and directed by the political government. Thus the familiar organic analogy is used to indicate the unitary structure of his political community. The same centralization of control existing in the human body must dominate the structure of the community; unity is conferred by the brain, which in Rousseau's analogy represents the sovereign power. The General Will is the analogue of the human mind, and as such must remain as unified and undiversified as the mind itself. The *volunté générakz*, as he is careful to indicate, is not synonymous with the *volunté de tous*, the will of all. It is the will of the political organism, an entity with a life of its own quite apart from that of the individual members of which it is built.

In its suprahuman reality it is always right, and while the *volunté de tous* may be often misled, the General Will never deviates from the strictest rectitude. The General Will is indivisible, inalienable, and illimitable. It demands the unqualified obedience of every individual in the community and implies the obligation of each citizen to render to the State all that the State sees fit to demand. This preeminence of the State in the life of the individual is not, however, despotism; it is the necessary basis of true individual freedom. "In order that the social contract shall be no empty formula it tacitly implies that obligation which alone can give force to all the others: namely that anyone who refuses obedience to the General Will is forced to it by the whole body. This merely means that he is being compelled to be free." In this last phrase is revealed, clearly, the relation between individualism and authoritarianism in the thought of Rousseau. The same rationale of values that leads him to restrict morality to life within the State compels him similarly to regard the State as the sphere of freedom. The individual lives a free life only within his complete surrender to the omnipotent State. The State is the liberator of the individual from the toils of society.

The totalitarian implications of Rousseau's thought do not arise merely out of the severity of his theory of sovereignty. The most common form of criticism—that the theory sets up an illimitable power—is applicable to all monistic theories of sovereignty. In any social theory where the sovereign State exists as a concept there is implicit at least the idea of potentially unrestricted power. What gives uniqueness to Rousseau's doctrine is not so much its severity as its subtle but explicit identification with freedom. What has connoted bondage to the minds of most men is exalted as freedom by Rousseau. To regard the power structure of the State as a device by which the individual is only being compelled to be free is a process of reasoning that sets Rousseau apart from the tradition of liberalism. The phraseology of liberalism in this case merely intensifies the authoritarianism which underlies it. What Rousseau calls freedom is at bottom no more than the freedom to do what the State in its omniscience determines. Freedom for Rousseau is the synchronization of all social existence to the will of the State, the replacement of cultural diversity by a mechanical equalitarianism. Other writers have idealized such an order in the interests perhaps of justice or of stability, but Rousseau is the first to invest it with the value of freedom. Therein lies the real distinctiveness of his theory of sovereignty.

It is in the bearing of Rousseau's General Will upon traditional society, however, that the full sweep of its totalitarian significance becomes manifest. It has been made clear that the object of Rousseau's dislike is society, and the special merit of the State lies in its power to emancipate the individual from traditional society. The relationship among individuals that forms the General Will and is the true State is obviously an exceedingly delicate one. It must be unitary and indivisible for its nature fully to unfold. In short, it must be protected from the operations of extraneous channels of constraint. "For the same reasons that sovereignty is inalienable, it is indivisible," he writes; "the Will is general or else it is nothing." To achieve a pure sovereignty, one which will be untrammeled by social influences, one which will encompass the whole of man's personality, it is necessary that the traditional social loyalties be abrogated. A unified, General Will is incompatible with the existence of minor associations; hence they must be banished. "When the people, having been adequately informed, hold its deliberation, and the citizens have had no communication among themselves, the whole number of individual opinions will always result in the General Will, and the decision will always be just. But when factions arise, and partial associations are created at the expense of the great association, the will of each of these associations becomes general so far as its members are concerned, and particular in its relation to the state: it may then be said that it is no longer a number of votes equal to the number of men, but equal only to the number of associations. . . . It is therefore essential, if the General Will is to be able to express itself, that there should be no partial society within the state, and that each citizen should think only his own thoughts."

The proscription of all forms of association except what is identical with the whole being of the State—this is Rousseau's drastic proposal. It is not to be regarded as one of these hasty, ill-considered remarks for which

Rousseau is famous. Nor is it true that his banishment of associations is out of harmony with the rest of his thought. We have seen that Rousseau's animus is against society, against the ties that make individuals dependent on one another. We have seen, further, that his conception of sovereignty demands the attributes of unity and indivisibility; the General Will is *general* or else it is nothing. Is it not then logical that the right of nonpolitical association should be sharply restricted? In his earlier *Political Economy,* Rousseau, in almost the same words, had presented this analysis of the effect of associations on the State. There is to be no bond of loyalty, no social affiliation, no interdependence save what is symbolized by the General Will. Society is to be an aggregate of atoms held rigidly together by the sovereign will of the State alone.

The practical implication of this doctrine is made strikingly evident by Rousseau's consideration of religion. A socially independent Church, like any form of nonpolitical loyalty, would constitute an interference with the functioning of the General Will. It would represent a flaw in the spiritual unity Rousseau prized so highly in his political order. Yet it would not do to repress the religious propensities of man, for "as soon as men come to live in civil society they must have a religion to keep them there. No nation has ever endured or ever will endure without religion." But, argues Rousseau, it is not enough that a nation should have a religion. The religion must be identified, in the minds of the people, with the values of national life, else it will create disunity and violate the General Will. It is not enough that a religion should make good men; it must make good citizens. Religion has a responsibility toward civic or political ends before any others. It must reflect, above all, the essential unity of the State and find its justification in the measures it takes to promote that unity.

In light of these criteria, the possibility of Christianity's being the religion of the true State must be rejected. "For Christianity, as a religion, is entirely spiritual, occupied solely with heavenly things; the country of the Christians is not of this world." There are even greater objections to Christianity. "Christian charity does not readily allow a man to think hardly of his neighbors. . . . Christianity preaches only servitude and dependence. Its spirit is so favourable to tyranny that it always profits by such a regime. True Christians are made to be slaves, and they know this and do not much mind: this short life counts for too little in their eyes." It cannot be overlooked that it is the essential humanity in the Christian faith that Rousseau despises. Its very virtues, he tells us, are its vices, for a society of Christians with all its perfections would be neither the strongest nor the most lasting. The very fact that it was perfect would rob it of its bond of union. The disregard of the Christian mind for secular law, for the values of the nation, would be the undoing of that unity indispensable to the true State. The spirit of subserviency which Christianity embodies would prevent any real flowering of the martial spirit. "Set over against Christians those generous peoples who were devoured by ardent love of glory and of their country; imagine your Christian republic face to face with Sparta or Rome; the pious Christians will be beaten, crushed, and destroyed before they know where they are." The ancient Romans were possessed of military valor until Christianity was accepted, "but when the Cross had driven out the eagle, Roman valour wholly disappeared." Christianity, then, because of its pacifism, its depreciation of the State, and because of its concentration upon men rather than citizens, must be replaced by another religion, one which will perfectly embody the measure of nationalist ardor necessary to the State.

There must be instituted a purely civil religion, for which the sovereign should fix the articles of faith. "While it can compel no one to believe them, it can banish from the state whoever does not believe them. . . . [I]f anyone after publicly recognizing these dogmas behaves as if he does not believe them, let him be punished by death: he has committed the worst of all crimes, that of lying before the law." Other faiths will be permitted to exist alongside of the civil religion providing there is nothing in their articles deemed by the sovereign to be inimical to the development of citizenship. "Tolerance should be given to all religions that tolerate others, so long as their dogmas contain nothing contrary to the duties of citizenship." It will be remembered, however, that the criteria of good citizenship are far reaching. Rousseau's prior criticism of Christianity on the ground of its intrinsic irreconcilability with good citizenship should serve as the grain of salt with which to take the protestations of tolerance. The articles of faith of the civil religion as fixed by the sovereign have as their fundamental objective the cementing of the social contract. We have already seen that the most basic values of Christianity at least are not regarded as compatible with the State. We may therefore perhaps speculate on the extent to which tolerance as a practical policy would be deemed commensurate with civil religion.

It is political religion Rousseau extols, one which in essence is indistinguishable from the law of the land. Like his forerunner Hobbes, Rousseau holds sin to be no more than a transgression of civil law, and in that fact lies the inspiriting aim of *la religion civile*. Respect for the sovereign, allegiance to the State alone, and subordination of all interests to the law of the realm—these are the primary attributes of the civil religion proposed by Rousseau. The symbol of *patrie* is uppermost; religion and patriotism will be but two aspects of the same thing.

Hardly less than religion the family itself, as a corporate entity, must be radically adjusted to meet the demands of the General Will. Morality is essentially a civic condition, and without citizens there can be no virtue. "Create citizens, and you have everything you need." To form these citizens is not the work of a day, nor is it a responsibility that can be left idly to the influences of traditional society. The unitary state calls for a remodeling of human nature so that there shall be no irritants to the body politic. "He who possesses the courage to give a people institutions, must be ready to change human nature, to transform every individual, who by himself is a complete and separate whole, into a part of a greater whole from which this individual in a certain sense receives his life and character; to change the constitution of man in order to strengthen it, and to substitute for the corporeal and independent existence which we all have received from nature a merely partial and moral existence. In short, he must take from man his native individual powers and equip him with others foreign to his nature, which he cannot understand or use without the assistance of others. The more completely these natural powers are annihilated and destroyed and the greater and more enduring are the ones acquired, the more secure and the more perfect is also the constitution."

It is necessary to inculcate in the minds of the people from infancy the surpassing claim of the State to their loyalty. "If, for example," Rousseau writes, "the people were early accustomed to conceive their individuality only in its connection with the body of the state, and to be aware of their own existence merely as parts of that of the state, they might in time come to identify themselves in some degree with the greater whole. . . ." The family should not be granted the all-important duty of education, for too great a responsibility hangs in the balance. The traditional educative function should be transferred from the family to the State, so that, as

Rousseau states it, the "prejudices" of the father may not interfere with the development of citizens. However, the disintegration of this age-old basis of the family should in no wise create alarm. "Should the public authority, in assuming the place of father and charging itself with this important function, acquire his rights in the discharge of his duties, he should have little cause to protest; for he would only be altering his title, and would have in common, under the name *citizen,* the same authority over his children, that he was exercising separately under the name of *father,* and would be no less obeyed when speaking in the name of the law than when he spoke in that nature." In this almost incredible statement is to be observed what is surely the ultimate in the totalitarian absorption of society. Family relationship is transmuted subtly into political relationship; the molecule of the family is broken into the atoms of its individuals, who are coalesced afresh into the single unity of the state. "If the children are reared in common in the bosom of equality, if they are imbued with the laws of the state and the precepts of the General Will, if they are taught to respect these above all other things, if they are surrounded by examples and objects which perpetually remind them of the tender mother who nourishes them, of the love she bears them, of the inestimable benefits they receive from her, and of the return they owe her, we cannot doubt that they will learn to cherish one another mutually as brothers. . . ."

It would be difficult to find anywhere in the history of politics a more powerful and potentially revolutionary doctrine than Rousseau's theory of the General Will. Power is freedom and freedom is power. True freedom consists in the willing subordination of the individual to the whole of the State. If this is not forthcoming, compulsion is necessary; but this merely means that the individual "will be forced to be free." There is no necessity, once the right State is created, for carving out autonomous spheres of right and liberty for individuals and associations. Because the individual is himself a member of the larger association, despotism is impossible. By accepting the power of the State one is but participating in the General Will.

Not without reason has the theory of the General Will been called a theory of permanent revolution. It was Rousseau's subtle achievement to clothe the being of the absolute State in the garments of the terminology of freedom. By his paeans to the individual he has been known as the apostle of liberty. By his insistence upon popular sovereignty he has become classified as one of the minds who have helped free the civilized world from despotism. The state is, in Rousseau's mind, the only sphere of liberation from the tyrannies of society. Here the individual may achieve a higher morality and freedom. The individual renounces the social loyalties of traditional society, surrenders to the state the rights of association which are the fundament of religion, family, and community, and by so doing becomes free for the first time. Herein lies the lure of Rousseau's philosophy for absolutists and here too is the essence of the confusion of freedom and authority that underlies contemporary totalitarian philosophies.

From Rousseau comes most of the intellectual devotion to the State that has made the political mentality so influential in social and moral thought during the past century and a half. "I had come to see," he wrote in his *Confessions,* "that everything was radically connected with politics, and that however one proceeded, no people would be other than the nature of its government made it." And in his discourse on *Political Economy,* he declared: "If it is good to know how to deal with men as they are, it is much better to make them what there is need that they should be. The most absolute authority is that which penetrates into a man's inmost being, and concerns itself no less with his will than with his actions. . . . Make men, therefore, if you would command men: if you would have them obedient to the laws, make them love the laws, and then they will need only to know what is their duty to do it. . . . If you would have the General Will accomplished, bring all the particular wills into conformity with it; in other words, as virtue is nothing more than this conformity of the particular wills with the General Will, establish the reign of virtue."

Establish the reign of virtue! This was the moral imperative that was to capture the visions of men of good will everywhere in nineteenth-century Western Europe. But establish it how? Establish it through the sovereign power of the State! Man is born free and good, yet everywhere he lies fettered and corrupt, the product of repressive institutions. Not through kinship, class, church, or association can man be freed, for these are the very chains upon his existence. Only by entering into the perfect *State* and subordinating himself completely to its collective will will it be possible for man to escape the torments and insecurities and dissensions of ordinary society. The redemptive power of the sovereign State—this was Rousseau's burning slogan for the modern world.

In ancient Athens the State had come to take on this guise of community during the period following the disastrous wars with Sparta. Many a reflective mind in that dark period could see in the intensification of the political bond among individuals the sole hope for the recovery of order in the *polis,* for the establishment of a new stability that would forever dispense with the old, but now distracting, ties of family, class, and association. Plato was but one of the more enlightened of those who saw in the power of the State not repressive force but the very basis of moral life, the prime source of true individuality and virtue. In Plato's view, the State, properly conceived, was the most holy of sanctuaries, a refuge from the torments, frustrations, and iniquities that had come to plague Athens as the consequence of spiritual factionalism. "Let this then be the law," declared Plato in *The Laws:* "no one shall possess shrines of the gods in private houses, and he who performs any sacred rites not publicly authorized, shall be informed against to the guardians of the law." Spiritual faith and the State must be as one, else there will be incessant conflict between the two, and man will be, even as he now is, torn by uncertainty and doubt.

It is not surprising to learn from Rousseau that, of all influences upon his mind, Plato's was greatest. In the visions of both philosophers we are given a political structure that is nothing less than community itself, with all its social and spiritual anodynes. In the warming atmosphere of the benign, omnicompetent State man will be able to discard his distractive, conflict-engendering social allegiances. Then, freed of old burdens, will he find surcease from uncertainty and disquiet. He will know at last the meaning of secure status, clear function, and ineffable spiritual release. He will know these in the pure State.

After Rousseau, the State would be regarded by many men as the most implicative of all forms of association. Inevitably the charms of kinship, religion, and cultural association would pale before the brilliance of the new State. No longer would the political relationship be regarded as but *one* of society's bonds. It would be seen as synonymous with society, as the culmination of man's long struggle for a just social order. The new State would be more than an abstract legal framework of rights and duties. It would be community itself, the Political Community.

What is the political community? It is an idea system, and, I believe, the most potent of all idea systems in the complex nineteenth century. We shall not often find it in its fullness in the writings of any single person or in any single pattern of events in the nineteenth century. We must await the twentieth-century totalitarian State for the full realization of the idea of the political community. But we are nevertheless able to descry this system of ideas running throughout the nineteenth century in one or another form, in one or another degree of intensity. It is a kind of brooding omnipresence, giving force and direction to a variety of visions of social redemption. It touches the foundations of modern popular democracy, especially on the Continent; it gives substance and appeal to cultural nationalism; it becomes the context of the socialist movement before the century is ended; it becomes the matrix of the most successful schemes of humanitarianism; it becomes, at times, the context of Christianity itself. In a diversity of ways we see the idea of the political community making its inroads into the minds and acts of the new men of power in the nineteenth century, the men for whom power was but the other face of humanitarian redemption.

Fundamental to the political community is the belief that the normal plurality of authorities and functions in society must be supplanted by a unity of authority and function arising from the monistic State. The power of the State must become the context of the realization of all man's aspirations, even as the Church formed this context in the Middle Ages. There is, second, the view of the people, not as diversified members of social groups and cultural associations, but as an aggregate of atomized particles needing the absolute State for protection and security. Man, in this view, is a timid, insecure, and lonely being apart from his membership in the omnipotent, all-benign State. The power of the State must not be regarded as repressive force. What separates the political community from earlier forms and visions of the State is its insistence that only through absolute, unitary power can man find freedom, equality, fraternity, and virtue. Freedom becomes freedom *from* other institutions, freedom *to* participate in Leviathan. Equality is the mechanical equivalence of talents, functions, and ideas engendered by the State's leveling influence upon all other associations and statuses, and enforced by the iron mold of law. Fraternity is the bond of political brotherhood that must rule out, as its very condition, all other brotherhoods based upon interest, place, or belief. And virtue, what is it? Virtue is, in Rousseau's words, "nothing more than the conformity of the particular wills with the General Will." Power is not power if but formed in the alembic of political imagination; it is freedom, equality, brotherhood, virtue. It is community.

Two

In practical terms, what Rousseau's ideas pointed toward was a two-fold emancipation: first, of the individual from his traditional associative chains; and, second, of the State itself from the mass of feudal customs which, everywhere, limited its real efficacy. For only by extricating the State, the *ideal* State, from the mass of intrusive localisms and partial allegiances descended from the past would it be possible to use its power to emancipate man from these same prejudices and entanglements. What was demanded was a revolutionary liaison between the individual and the omnipotent State. Between the challenge of atomistic individualism and the militant power of the central State, dedicated to human welfare, it would be possible to grind into dust all intermediate associations, reminders and nourishers of the despised past.

It was in a real sense a necessary affinity, for all major social movements are a combination of radical individualism and authoritarian affirmation. New structures of belief and authority cannot be introduced until human beings have been alienated, in one way or another, from the old. Hence the insistence upon individual release from old institutions and social groups, and upon man as the natural embodiment of all virtues. Hence also the emphasis upon the State as the area of reassimilation and upon political power as the instrument.

This affinity between social individualism and political power is, I believe, the most fateful fact of the eighteenth and nineteenth centuries. It forms the very substance of the ideology of the political community; it comprehends the majority of ideas of political humanitarianism. It is impossible to understand the massive concentrations of political power in the twentieth century, appearing so paradoxically, as it has seemed, right after a century and a half of individualism in economics and morals, unless we see clearly the close relationship that prevailed all through the nineteenth century between individualism and State power and between both of these together and the general weakening of the area of association that lies intermediate to man and the State.

Three

It was the French Revolution, following hard upon Rousseau's clamant prophecy, that served to translate so many of the adjurations of the *Social Contract* into hard administrative reality and to bring forcibly to the attention of intellectuals throughout Europe the new perspective of re-demption through political power. However minor Rousseau's influence may have been upon the *causes* of the Revolution, his influence upon the *course* of the Revolution became great. "Hitherto," wrote Sébastien Mercier in 1791, "the *Social Contract* was the least read of all Rousseau's works. Now, every citizen broods over it and learns it by heart."[1]

The tremendous value of the *Social Contract* to the men of the Revolution lay, first, in its extraordinary flexibility. It could serve the authoritarian demands of the Revolution as easily as it could provide an apologetics for the corrosive individualism of the early phases. But its greatest value lay in its ingenious camouflaging of power with the rhetoric of freedom, and in its investment of political power with the essence of religious community. Rousseau had succeeded in *spiritualizing* the political relationship and, in so doing, had removed the State conceptually from the ordinary realm of political intrigue and force. "How are you to know a Republican?" asked Barère late in the Revolution. His answer to his own question might have been taken from the chapter on the Civil Religion. You will know him when he speaks of his country with "religious senti-ment" and of the sovereign people with "religious devotion."[2]

Treatments of the French Revolution fall, generally, into one of two major categories. The Revolution is regarded as the work primarily of individual freedom, or it is regarded as the work of collective power. But the Revolution was both, and each of these aspects must be seen as contributing profoundly to the other. Apart from the emancipation of masses of human beings from the social structures of the old regime, the extraordinary increases of political power that become so noticeable in the final phases of the Revolution are scarcely intelligible. And, similarly, it is only in the context of the Revolutionary government's early impact upon such structures as church, gild, class, and family that we may see the effective conditions of the new individualism in France. Both elements of the Revolution, the socially free individual and the omnipotent nation, are vividly apparent from the very start. The stress upon individual rights that is to be found in the first two articles of the Declaration of the Rights of Man is succeeded, in the third and sixth articles, by a clear insistence that the nation is the source of all sovereignty and that law is the expression of the General Will. But whether from the point of view of the natural rights of the individual or of the celebration of the collective nation, the position of all loyalties and values intermediate to individual and State is made precarious from the outset.[3]

Rousseau had written that it is the force of the State that alone achieves the liberty of its members. Revolutionary legislators took this literally, and the liberty of the individual became the prime justification for the powerful legislative attacks upon old values, old idea systems, and old associations. The same temper of mind that led them to the release of Jews from the ancient ghetto led them also to seek the release of millions of others from the gilds, the Church, the patriarchal family, class, and the local community.

To this militant libertarianism was added an equally militant rationalism. The passion for geometrical symmetry, inherited from Cartesian philosophy, drove them beyond a reform of the currency system, beyond a standardization of weights and measures, to a rational standardization of the very units of men's social and political life. If men were to be made free and wise, there had to be an enforced obliteration of old memories and prejudices embedded in traditional associations and institutions. The calendar had to be reformed, with new names for days and months, in order to remind the people of their emancipation from the old. It was necessary to establish a new educational system and office of propaganda that people might be emancipated, in Rousseau's words, from the prejudices of their fathers. Above all, new unities of law and social function were needed to replace those inherited from the hated Middle Ages. If man was to be put in full possession of natural faculties, he had to be made free of the associations that fettered him and, equally important, placed in new associations that would nurture his emerging rationality and goodness. The rational State, with its own new subdivisions, had to become man's chief area of membership.

Hence the early destruction of the gilds. Hence the prohibition of all new forms of economic association. "Citizens . . . must not be permitted to assemble for their pretended common interests. There is no longer any *corporation* within the State; there is but the particular interest of each individual and the general interest. . . ."

Charitable societies were declared illegal. "It is the business of the nation," declared Le Chapelier, "it is the business of the public officers in the name of the nation, to furnish employment to those who need it and assistance to the infirm." Literary, cultural, and educational societies were also banned for, declared one of the legislators, "A State that is truly free ought not to suffer within its bosom any association, not even such as, being dedicated to public improvement, has merited well of the country."[4]

We observe also the profound changes made in the structure and functions of the family. The legitimate family was conceived, like the State itself, as a small republic, not as a monarchy. Ideals of equality and liberty must prevail there as in the larger society. The oft-written protests of the *philosophes* against paternal authority, as one of the chief barriers to intellectual progress, had their effects on legislators of the Revolution. Paternal authority and the indissolubility of marriage were both declared "against nature and contrary to reason." Marriage was designated a civil contract and numerous grounds of divorce were made available. Strict limitations were placed upon the authority of the father, and, in all cases, the authority of the father was declared terminated when the children reached the age of twenty-one. New property laws were directed against the corporate character of the family, and the *partage forcé* was enjoined, thus preventing the perpetuation of family property in aggregate and insuring the equal division of property among all the children.

In this way, too, was the Church dealt with, for of all structures of traditional society it was the Church that was most feared and hated by rationalists and *politiques*. In the name of *liberté* the Revolution suppressed all perpetual monastic vows and abolished all independent religious orders.

Charitable and educational functions of the Church were discontinued, and property was confiscated. Relationships of status and bond, of whatever type, were terminated by political decree, in order that individuals might be released from priestly tyranny. Bishops and priests were compelled to give up all rights and privileges, and even distinction of dress, and at one point it was decided that such functionaries must be elected to office like regular governmental officials.

Profession, class, the historic commune, the universities, and provinces, all alike came under the atomizing consideration of the legislators of the Revolution. The sovereign aim was the conversion of all collectivities into the individuals who composed them, all social statuses into the natural rights and abilities presumed to underlie them. "France," proclaimed Sieyés, "must not be an assemblage of small nations each with its own democratic government; she is not a collection of states; she is a single whole, made up of integral parts; these parts must not have each a complete existence of its own, for they are . . . but parts forming a single whole."[5]

"The transition of an oppressed nation to democracy," declared the Committee of Public Safety, "is like the effort by which nature arose from nothingness to existence. You must entirely refashion a people whom you wish to make free, destroy its prejudices, alter its habits, limit its necessities, root up its vices, purify its desires."[6] There are few examples in history that match the Revolution in its individualization of ranks and associations, in its forced liberation of masses of human beings. It is one of the most explosive outbursts of individualism in the whole history of the world.

But we must not lose sight of the context of this individualism. The rise of masses of legally autonomous individuals, free to devote their talents to whatever they chose, is but one aspect of a picture which includes also the development of the collective power of the State in France. The individualist aspects of the Revolution are inseparable from the augmentation of State power, which was largely the result of the reduction of other social bodies. The decree of the Committee of Public Safety given above was concluded by the statement: "The State must therefore lay hold on every human being at his birth and direct his education with powerful hand." Only through force could freedom be born.

The real power of political government increased during the Revolution to a point scarcely dreamed of by earlier kings. There is nothing strange in this. It is obvious that any assemblage of people will more willingly suffer the passage of authority from their private associations into the hands of the central government when a pervasive ideology supports the view that such a government is but administering powers always, in theory, revocable by the people. As Ostrogorski has written, such a regime "has on its side the maximum of brute force and moral force. Every law is supposed to be made with the assent of the humblest of citizens, and the citizen who obeys the laws and the custodians of them appears to obey only himself. . . . The fiction of spontaneous assent is thus added to the reality of the most formidable external constraint which can be exerted, constituting in society a power of intimidation from which no one escapes, and to which everyone can fly for refuge."[7]

Four

There is, moreover, the mounting attraction of political power when all other forms of association have been destroyed or weakened. If the individual is prevented, by law or public opinion, from participating in ordinary associations, and if he feels, as men commonly do, the need to belong to something larger than himself, he will seek close membership in the one association that is open to him. In France, before the eighteenth century had ended, this association was the State, and the government overlooked no means by which to bind the people ever more closely to itself. "The Republic," declared a revolutionist in 1794, "must penetrate the souls of its citizens through all the senses." Hence the declaration by such men as Le Pelletier and Robespierre that the State must have primacy of claim upon the young. Hence the meticulous care in designing an educational system that would be financed and directed by the government and made compulsory for all children in France. Hence the incessant emphasis upon the singleness and unity of French culture.

What the spectacle of the Revolution emphasized to many minds in the decades following it was a truth known to every great political leader from Cleisthenes to Napoleon. The State that would become powerful must become identified with the people; it must become *absolutely* identified. The State becomes powerful not by virtue of what it takes from the individual but by virtue of what it takes from the spiritual and social associations which compete with it for men's devotions.

It is in these terms, indeed, that the phenomenon of nineteenth-century nationalism becomes intelligible. All serious students of nationalism are agreed that, in its contemporary form, nationalism is the child of the French Revolution. There is nothing strange in this fact. During the Revolution, as we have seen, there occurred a general sterilization of associative allegiances that were not of the State, a subtle transmutation of social statuses into political status, and a general assimilation of human purposes and devotions into the single structure of the people's State. The loss of older statuses could not help but turn men's eyes to the status of *citizen*. The loss of older memberships could not help but be followed by a growing willingness to make the State itself the primary area of association. "A State becomes a nation," A. D. Lindsay has correctly written, "when instead of its members being primarily divided between sovereign and subjects, government and citizenship become a common task, demanding not passive citizenship but active cooperation from all."[8]

The modern State is not the offspring of the nation. It is far more correct and relevant to say that the nation is the offspring of the State. Nationalism, in the form that has become triumphant in the last century and a half, is no mere development, as is so often argued, of folk ties of tribe, locality, or region. Doubtless the emotional elements which earlier populations found in kinship and region, in local community and church, have been transferred, so to speak, to the nation. But the logical continuity of symbolic transference should not be made the basis of assuming any continuity of social development in this instance. Modern nationalism, as a state of mind and cultural reality, cannot be understood except in terms of the weakening and destruction of earlier bonds, and of the attachment to the political State of new emotional loyalties and identifications.[9] It cannot be understood, that is, apart from those rents and clefts in the traditional structure of human loyalties, caused by economic and social dislocation, which left widening masses of human beings in a kind of psychological vacuum. And it cannot be understood except in terms of the ever more hypnotic appeal exercised by the political association in the hands of men who saw the State as the new and final enclosure of human life and purpose.

In many governments of nineteenth-century Europe there were politicians and philosophers who, in their desire for military and national unity, were willing to pay at least a considerable part of the equalitarian and humanitarian price that was involved. It was thus not always easy to tell from the appearance of a specific social reform whether it had been motivated by basically humanitarian or military-nationalist motives. The abolition of the servile status of the peasant, the limitation of economic powers of the Church, the reduction of traditional class differences, the widening of the electorate, and the amelioration of the economic plight of the people—these were measures that served not merely the purposes of the equalitarian and the humanitarian but the purposes also of the nationalist.

How could the kind of military power be achieved that had made the Revolutionary armies the scourge of Europe as long as the government was remote and indifferent to popular aspirations? The medieval Church had been strong because of what it did for its members. The State must do no less. The medieval Church had sought to bind man spiritually as well as economically, culturally as well as politically, into an undiversified unity of membership that would leave nothing outside it. The State must similarly seek to make itself the harmonious coordinator of all human interests, being no less sensitive to the economic, the charitable, the communal, and the symbolic needs of the people.

Thus Fichte, in the addresses he gave at Berlin after Napoleon had humbled the Prussian people, made unquestionably clear the relation that must prevail between a government and its people if the government would be powerful. The State must assume humanitarian and educative functions; it must create a meaningful ethical bond between itself and the people. In every previous system of government, Fichte declared, "the interest of the individual in the community was linked to his interest in himself by ties, which at some point were so completely severed that his interest in the community absolutely ceased." What is now necessary is "to find an entirely different and new binding tie that is superior to fear and hope, in order to link up the welfare of her whole being with the self-interest of each of her members." This new tie would be the State based upon the people, the political community, successor to the Church in its inclusion of all human needs, desires, and hopes. If only we have the will to create such an order,

Fichte concluded, we shall be able to produce "an army such as no age has yet seen."[10]

The motives behind the vision of the nation-community could vary from militarism to humanitarianism to those of what Matthew Arnold in England called sweetness and light. For in the structure of the political State, properly conceived, Arnold could see the only real hope for the cultural redemption of Western society. For a long time the "strong feudal habits of subordination and deference continued to tell," but now "the modern spirit has almost entirely dissolved these habits, and the anarchical tendency of our worship of freedom in and for itself . . . is becoming very manifest." What, then, "if we tried to rise above the idea of class to the idea of the whole community, *the State,* and to find our centre of light and authority there? We want an authority, and we find nothing but jealous classes, checks, and deadlock; culture suggests the idea of *the State.*"[11]

In France it had been demonstrated that the State can become powerful by its emancipation of human beings from competing allegiances and by its absorption of functions formerly resident in other associations. It had been demonstrated that equalitarian legislation could have as its signal consequence the leveling of all authorities which interposed themselves between a people and government and which, by their existence, perpetually challenged the influence of government.

Between the partisan of social justice and the exponent of national collective power there thus arose a genuine, if mutually repugnant, affinity. The aims of humanitarianism required the obliteration of institutional authorities descended from the past within which men were manifestly unequal and unfree. But the aims of the nationalist required exactly the same obliteration. Whether in the equalitarian interest of the General Will or in the authoritarian interest of the General Will, what was demanded was the removal of the intermediate associations which acted as barriers to national equality and national authority alike. Only thus could there be created a new culture to replace present anarchy, a new order to replace growing lawlessness, and a new community to fill the rapidly forming spiritual vacuum.

Five

The Revolution was distinguished by the triumph of the political relationship and of man's political status over all other relationships and statuses in society. Thus the term "citizen" reached a degree of prestige that threatened all older titles of status in society, and political functionaries enjoyed a new merit. There were many conflicts and resistances, of course. The edicts and enthusiasms of Paris were not easily communicated to other parts of France. But we may say, nevertheless, that the most momentous aspect of the Revolution, in psychological terms, was its systematic depreciation of all the statuses that had characterized traditional French society, and its calculated celebration of the personal qualities and statuses that arose from man's membership in the political order. Not economic man, nor religious man, but *political* man was, in a very important sense, the key figure of the Revolution.

It was the political habit of mind that became compelling in the nineteenth century. One of the most curious conceptions of the nineteenth century in modern writing is that it was the century of the natural economic order, *laissez faire,* and the weak State. In actual fact the State achieved a position of power and direction in human affairs that was unprecedented in European history. Even in England the full advent of industrialism was accompanied by an increase in political law and administration greater, during the decades of the thirties and forties alone, than anything known earlier.[12] Industrially, morally, educationally, and philanthropically, the State became the indispensable context of men's thinking and planning.

Especially was this true on the Continent. There, in the minds of a constantly growing number of reformers, socialists, unitary democrats, and other tacticians of humanitarianism, the liberative power of the State, revealed so dramatically by the Revolution in France, assumed many guises.

In power lay popular unity. But this was an old reflection. What was now so exhilarating was the realization that in political power lay, also, *equality, virtue, justice,* and *freedom itself.* To use the absolute, centralized power of the State against religious and economic tyrannies—was this not a transcendent way of making men good and free? All of this Rousseau had argued brilliantly. All of this had been demonstrated to the admiring gaze of the nationalist, the democrat, and the humanitarian alike, by the incomparable Revolution. Whatever else the Revolution may be, in the various perspectives of historical interpretation, it would be folly to over-look the fact that it was *power*—power in a form hardly known since the days of Caesar and his admiring multitudes.

"After the Revolution," Lord Acton has written, "the purpose of the continental governments formed on that pattern is not that the people should obtain security for freedom, but participation in power." The characterization is apt, but it is highly important to see that, for a growing number of intellectuals and politicians, and even for the masses themselves, such participation in power, with its attendant properties of centralized administration, carried with it implications of joyous release. Of all the subtle alchemies of thought performed by Rousseau and by the guiding spirits of the Revolution, the subtlest and the most potent was the conver-sion of absolute power into the illusion of mass freedom.

What was new, and profoundly exciting, was the sense of achieving freedom through absolute identification with the will of the majority, a will expressed relentlessly and single-mindedly by the government. During the Revolution freedom had come to mean, increasingly, the freedom not so much of individuals taken singly or in small groups but of the *whole* people. The emancipation of the entire people from the tyrannies exercised by church, class, family, and local custom—this was the most potent and revolutionary conception of freedom. And the key to the reality of this conception of freedom lay in the centralizing, absorptive work of govern-ments. When Robespierre announced to the National Convention that the will of the Jacobins was the General Will, he could have cited Rousseau in support of his position. After all, were not the Jacobins motivated by justice? Were they not dedicated to the common weal, to virtue. Were they not, in Rousseau's words, "well-intentioned"? And who else but Rousseau could have prepared the minds of the Convention to accept credulously Robespierre's ringing declaration that the "government of the Revolution is but the despotism of freedom against tyranny"?

This conception of mass participation in power, with its corollary of mass power as mass freedom, has proved to be the most revolutionary of all political doctrines in the modern world. If the power of government is but the reflection of the will of the masses, or, rather, of the interests of the masses, and if the General Will is merely a means of forcing individuals to be free, then does it not follow, as the Jacobins held, that every increase in governmental authority, every increase of *political*—at the expense of religious, economic, and kinship—authority is, *ex hypothesi,* an increase in real freedom for the people?

Hardly less significant was the conception, born also of Rousseau and the Revolution, of the equalitarian properties of power. In the nineteenth and early twentieth centuries this conception was to become a redemptive vision of escape from all the social and cultural inequalities inherited from the past. The belief in the natural equality of human beings was an old one. What Rousseau and the legislators of the Revolution added to it was the view of the State as the indispensable means for the recovery of equality that had been lost in the dark ages of the past.

By its inroads upon the authorities of church, class, and local community the popular State would liberate men—liberate them not only from the oppressions of traditional society but from its intolerable hierarchy. Much of that imagined natural equality which had been lost through the rise of property, the patriarchal family, and ecclesiastical institutions would be restored to man merely through the power of the State used to emancipate men from their historically given statuses.

But even more fascinating than the vision of equality through release from old authorities was the vision of equality *through participation in power*—the same participation that would also confer freedom. If all power in society were transferred from the plurality of traditional institutions, institutions in which individuals had grossly unequal degrees of participation, to the single structure of the State, and if the State were conceived as identical with the people, then it followed that in terms of the exercise of power in society each individual would be equal to every other individual. Rousseau had described this process in his *Social Contract.* In a State of ten thousand people each person would be a subject, but he would also be one ten-thousandth of the sovereign, fully equal to all other men in his possession of authority. And if, in the transfer of functions and authorities from family or gild to the State a man lost his own traditional authority over children or employees, he would not mind since he would be but transferring the rights and duties from an older status to his new status of citizen.

It is this envisagement of power as equality that goes far to explain the appeal the growing tendency toward administrative uniformity and standardization had in many parts of nineteenth-century Europe. The European State had always been, as we have seen, a potentially revolutionary force in this direction. The struggles between king and the feudal authorities arrayed against him had been won, and the victories consolidated, through legal and administrative standardization. But everything that had taken place along this line in earlier centuries was as nothing compared to the spread of administrative uniformity in the nineteenth century. And much of the explanation for this lies in the impetus given by the revolutionary conception of State power as the work of freedom and equality.

Six

Unquestionably, the most dramatic and far-reaching event of the Revolution was the *coup d'état* of the 18th *Brumaire*.[13] For it was this seizure of power and the justification following it that laid the basis for the modern rise of the belief that in *one man*, rather than in any representative body, the real interests and desires of a people are best given expression. Here, too, we are dealing with an idea which, in its essentials, is an old one. The fateful Napoleonic Idea of the nineteenth century is closely related to the ancient Athenian conception of the tyrant and has an even closer connection with the role of Caesar before the masses in the Rome of the first century B.C.

But it is important to see the close relation between the Napoleonic Idea of the nineteenth century and the whole developing conception of the political community with its emphasis upon the political masses, collectivization of power, and centralization of administration. Far from there being any conflict between the idea of one man as the supreme ruler and the idea of the political community, based upon the whole people, there was, in truth, an almost inevitable affinity of interest.

Once the political community was accepted as the highest of all forms of existence, once political virtue was regarded as the most exalted of all forms of virtue, the next problem was that of discovering the technical means of achieving and securing the political community from its enemies. We have already seen the appeal which lay in administrative uniformity and centralization. To Revolutionary legislators and to all their disciples in the following century the forces of evil were represented by the plurality of authorities and memberships which lay outside the realm of the rational State. Reform could proceed only as reason does itself, through a rigorous exclusion of all elements not pertinent to the central objective.

Inevitably the idea of the One acquired fresh appeal for all political rationalists. "To be as One" has echoed down through the centuries from Plato's time. That which promotes unity, system, and simplicity has ever had its transcendent appeal to the rationalist as well as to the mystic. Centralizing, unitary systems of classification have been as deeply involved in Western systems of political action as they have in systems of metaphysics. Despite the manifest pluralism of the universe and the diversity of society, only rarely have philosophers and statesmen made this pluralism and diversity the perspectives of their thought and policy. Much oftener have philosophers sought some one substance or factor from which all else could be deduced and to which it could be related for meaning.

In nineteenth-century political thought one of the most important developments is the conversion of the ideal of oneness into new techniques of centralization. If the interests of a political population could safely be entrusted to five hundred men, why not to one hundred, to fifty, to ten men? Why not, indeed, to *one* man who, by his virtue and devotion to the whole of the people, could be depended on to interpret and give actuality to the will of the people in a way that no cumbersome parliamentary system could? Political government and its bureaucracy were already accepted by the majority of political rationalists as the indispensable means of liberating vast populations from the dead hand of the past. All that was necessary was that such governments remain constantly in touch with the real will of the people.

But here was the stumbling block. For the real will of the people was, as Rousseau had warned, frequently difficult to ascertain. It was not equivalent to the mere "will of all." The real will, the General Will, was more elusive and fundamental. Frequently the General Will of a people was not apparent even to the people themselves.[14] It could only be inferred by a government devoted to the welfare of the people and concerned with the people in their *collective* reality and their political oneness.

But how could a government be in touch with the collective reality of the whole people when it was itself composed of representatives of mere *sections* of the whole? There was also the inevitable obstruction provided by the existence of paid, permanent political functionaries, men who must necessarily come to lose respect for, and even knowledge of, the will of the people. It was thus argued by more than a few politicians and ideologists that popular welfare is more often hindered than helped by ordinary parliamentary processes. Parliamentary government too often becomes government of special and local interests. It is asking too much to suppose that the man who represents only a few hundred square miles, or the bureaucrat who acts as a trained expert in some specialized capacity, can be depended on to represent the real interest of the whole of the people. Moreover, representative government was, as Rousseau himself characterized it, *feudal,* and hence to be distrusted. Genuine sovereignty cannot be represented; it can only be *expressed.*

Here was where the dramatic accession to power of the first Napoleon provided a tantalizing example. Napoleon had come to power, in his own words and in the recognition of large numbers of the people, not to destroy but to fulfill the Revolution. Through his own acumen, through his willingness to act quickly and decisively, and through the subtle interplay of interest that he created between himself and the people, he had come to appear as the very embodiment of the real will of the French masses. And his roots in popular allegiance were deep. Between him and the people, as between Caesar and the Roman masses, there had developed a bond and a mutual understanding that could never have been matched by the cumbersome processes of parliamentary representation. Because of this bond the work of governmental reorganization, the rationalization of law, and the achievement of humanitarian gains for the masses had been made relatively easy. Granted that Napoleon had frequently been ruthless in his extermination of dissent, that he had sought upon occasion to make the writing of history and literature serve the ends of his rule. But what was this against the fact that he had represented faithfully the General Will?

Robert Michels has ably described this whole point of view under what he calls "Bonapartist ideology." "Once elected, the chosen of the people can no longer be opposed in any way. He personifies the majority, and all resistance to his will is antidemocratic. The leader of such a democracy is irremovable, for the nation, having once spoken, cannot contradict itself. He is, moreover, infallible, for *l'Elu de six millions de suffrages exécute les voluntés du peuple, il ne les trahi pas.'* It is reasonable and necessary that the adversaries of the government should be exterminated in the name of popular sovereignty, for the chosen of the people acts within his rights as representative of the collective will, established in his position by a spontaneous decision. It is the electors themselves, we are assured, who demand from the chosen of the people that he should use severe repressive measures, should employ force, should concentrate all authority in his own hands. One of the consequences of the theory of the popular will being subsumed in the supreme executive is that the elements which intervene between the latter and the former, the public officials, that is to say, must be kept in a state of the strictest possible dependence upon the central authority, which, in its turn, depends upon the people. The least manifestation of liberty on the part of the bureaucracy would be tantamount to a rebellion against the sovereignty of the citizens. . . . Bonapartism does not recognize any intermediate links."[15]

Thus the same affinity that had developed between the political processes of power and the goals of humanitarianism developed with greater intensity between the latter and the fascinating vision of one man, equipped, like Rousseau's Legislator, with courage and insight and virtue. "The great soul of the legislator," Rousseau had written, "is the only miracle that can prove his mission." Some may doubt and scoff, but "the true political theorist admires . . . the great and powerful genius which presides over things made to endure."

Only in the serene and unprejudiced regard of one man could the real will of a people be made manifest. Only to such a man could the real interests and aspirations of a people be entrusted. Only the man who represented not sections, not localities, not partial interests, but the *whole* of the people, the people in their mystic political oneness, would be able to save the people from the corruptions and oppressions always threatening to spring up, like noxious weeds, in the crevices of the new State. In his person, if he could but be found, lay the ultimate realization of that redemption promised by the political community.

Seven

We are familiar enough with the idea of the political community, with its elements of redemptive power, in the writings of the nineteenth-century zealots of nationalism. The names of such men as Jahn, Wagner, Mazzini, Maurras, and Treitschke come readily to mind. But the major channels of the idea of the political community are to be found in writings and movements which were not, in intent at least, nationalist at all. The idea of political power was most successfully disseminated, not by the writers who saw national power itself as the primary goal, but by those who saw in political power the sole means of realizing cherished social and moral objectives connected with popular welfare.

This is the point that is crucial. The modern State and the whole ideology of the political community have become significant, influential, not through worship of naked power but because of the promise which seemed to lie in political power for the salvation of man—for the attainment of moral goals that had eluded mankind for thousands of years. Not to the writings of power worshipers or reactionaries must we look for the source and diffusion of the ideology of the political community in the nineteenth century, but to those men who, like Bentham and Marx, were eminently rational and whose goals were the release of mankind from its long bondage to oppression, misery, and ignorance.

Thus in Bentham, despite an early repudiation of Rousseau and the Revolution on the grounds that both had elevated imaginary natural rights of individuals instead of the real *interests* of men, we cannot miss (at least with the guidance of Halevy's great study[16]) the very real influence exerted upon his thought and upon the ideas of his followers by the idea of the centralized, rational, political community. We may be inclined, on first consideration, to regard as somewhat comical and unrepresentative his expressed desires to legislate (from the recesses of his study) for all India, to be the ruler of Mexico, or to become the benevolent intellectual power behind a Continental despot. Yet the relation of these aspirations to similar aspirations on the Continent, and what is more important, their relation to the central elements of his own ethical system, makes them less comical and more representative than might at first be thought.

The State as conceived by Bentham, Halévy has written, "is a machine so well constructed that every individual, taken individually, cannot for one instant escape from the control of all the individuals taken collectively." Here, indeed, is the essence of the General Will. But, as in the writings of Rousseau and in the speeches of the Jacobins, what is central and directive is not the primary worship of power. Rather, it is the principle, so fundamental in Bentham's political theory, that only *because* of the control exerted collectively is it possible for each individual to be taken individually. Only through the elevation of political power to the point where it supersedes all other powers and constraints, to the point where it becomes the sole power in men's lives, is it possible to create that scene of rational impersonality demanded by the needs of individual liberation. It is no contradiction to be reminded of Bentham's hostility to many of the existent political and administrative structures of his time, of his incessant zeal for the liberation of individual reason. Granted the supremacy of the individual in Bentham's ethics and granted also his relentless opposition to many aspects of the English State, his larger system of thought nevertheless seems unified only when we see that the prime object of his endeavors is the discovery of that political system in which such irrationalities as the common law and the rotten boroughs can be eliminated, and in which the indvidual, emancipated from all his institutional fetters, can achieve the life of perfect reason.

Quite apart from his early reflections on the possible moral achievements of political legislation, the idea of the centralized administrative State logically becomes central in Bentham's thought when he finds it necessary to supplement "natural" and "sympathetic" identifications of interest by recourse to what he calls "artificial" identification. The first two are based upon the principles of hedonistic psychology. But the third is the direct reflection of the vision of the political community, the community rationally and impersonally organized, omnipotent and monolithic. It may be true, as some unkind critic has suggested, that whereas Bentham began with self-evident natural interest he was forced to conclude with the policeman and the penitentiary. But the fact remains that for Bentham, as for Rousseau, the policeman and penitentiary were but means of "forcing individuals to be free."

Behind Bentham's constantly developing reliance upon the omnipotent, benevolent political community lay always the vision of a society in which men would be freed from the tyrannous and stultifying traditions that had come down from the Middle Ages. Hence his almost fanatical desire to see exterminated not only the rotten borough and the functionless aristocracy but also the Inns of Court, the Church, the common law, the semi-public corporations, such universities as Oxford and Cambridge, the jury system, the parish, and even the traditional family.

The logic of his political rationalism became relentless. It even demanded that the testimony of husband against wife, of wife against husband, be admitted in legal cases. For what is the value of an immunity that is based upon mere sentiment and, more often than not, impedes the function of clear reason. His logic demanded the abolition of the jury system. How preposterous to suppose that right will ever be determined by the mere counting of votes among twelve people. Right must be determined, in legal matters as it is in mathematical problems, by the sovereignty of reason, not by custom and headcounting. And this sovereignty of reason must be made manifest by the sovereignty of the single judge, alone omnipotent, subject only to the limitations provided by his perception of the will of the whole people. Similarly, for the immunities of lawyer-client relationship, doctor-patient, and priest-communicant relationship, Bentham had nothing but contempt. Such immunities were of a piece with the whole fabric of customary observances handed down from the Middle Ages and, by their existence, constituted a barrier both to the emancipation of the individual and to the will of the people. "Every man his own lawyer," as Halévy has pointed out, has in Bentham's theory a significance remarkably like Luther's insistence upon "every man his own priest." The implied individualism is a reflection of the hatred for all intermediate relationships.

Centralization of administration became almost an obsession with Bentham. In his later years he saw nothing good in government that did not become focused in the mind of one man. He extended advocacy of his celebrated panopticon principle from the context of prison administration, in which it first took form, to the supervision of factories, schools, and hospitals. He compares the position of the central inspector to "divine omnipotence" and stoutly defends the garrison-like discipline as an indispensable means of liberation as well as efficiency.

With this advocacy of centralization in the light of reason went not merely a radical individualism that insisted on the release of human beings from all connecting relationships founded upon tradition, but also an emphasis upon the collective nature of legitimate power. The only recognized authority in society must be that which springs clearly from the will of the whole people, taken in their political unity. Bentham's conception of the State is as relentless in its demand as his conception of the individual. The State and its power must extend to all areas of society now covered by the network of custom and tradition. Bentham had as little use as Rousseau for the principle of division of powers and separation of function. The people must be represented by a single body, a unified legislature, which will be omnicompetent. Such a body will work tirelessly toward the extermination of all relationships and beliefs that now separate individuals from their sense of membership in the rational political order.

The passionate spirit of Bentham's logic died early, but the political habit of mind among English intellectuals and reformers was nevertheless given a profound stimulus by his doctrines as they were passed down through such men as Grote and Chadwick. Not a little of the actual course of administrative reform during the nineteenth century in England must be seen in terms of Bentham's stress upon political centralization and standardization, and upon the removal of social functions and authorities not proceeding clearly from the State itself. More than most countries England remained, as a whole, aloof to the charms of rational centralization in the nineteenth century, but, despite this, we can see the consequences of the ideology of the political community. We see them in the gradual reduction of the influence of the parish, of the role of the "great unpaid" in the administration of justice and charity, and of the whole of that body of custom which, by its subtle permeation of formal processes of government, had for so long made English polity the despair of Continental jurists nurtured by doctrines descended from Roman law. We see them in the creation of new administrative districts challenging for the first time in centuries the autonomy and functional importance of the older unities of class and local community. We see them concretely and symbolically in the conversion of registration of births and deaths from ecclesiastical to political responsibility. We see the consequences, finally, in the steady expansion of the English electorate during the nineteenth century, through the removal of age-old restrictions against political participation.[17]

Such changes were clearly in the direction of increased efficiency of governmental operation and in the humanitarian interests of the people. Most of them were of a piece with such changes as those involved in the reforms in the Poor Law and the abolition of the rotten boroughs and were manifestly on the side of welfare and justice. No one familiar with the heavy toll exacted upon family, village, and personal security by emerging English industrialism in the nineteenth century, or with the painful details of ecclesiastical and upper-class indifference to the plight of the masses, can doubt that in such changes lay a promise of future political relief which not even the trade union or the cooperative could match. All of this is clear and undeniable. But equally undeniable is the fact that even in England where the conservative forces were strongest, where the "smaller patriotisms" of village and class remained more alive than in France or Prussia, the ideology of the political community became steadily more appealing. As in France, the power of the State over its people rose in direct proportion to its services to them.

Eight

Similarly, in the writings of Karl Marx the vision of omnicompetent power in the service of human welfare becomes almost blinding. Despite the predominantly economic cast of Marx's analysis of society and his philosophy of history, there is much reason for insisting that Marx's greatest importance lies in his willingness to translate the moral values of socialism into the structure of the centralized, political power. Whatever else Marxian socialism may be in ethical and historical terms, it is plainly a significant chapter in the history of political collectivism.[18]

The extreme collectivism and centralization of contemporary Soviet Russia are by no means distortions and corruptions of the Marxian philosophy of power. They are clearly rooted in the ideas of strategy and tactics that Marx and Engels were led to formulate in anticipation of revolutionary demands. The anarchists and French socialists against whom Marx and his followers fought so savagely were well aware of this aspect of Marx, and the words Bakunin first applied to Rousseau—"the true founder of modern reaction"—were as often applied to Marx himself by later anarchists.

Much has been made of the asserted Marxian disavowal of the State. It has been widely supposed that Marx held the State in disdain, that he regarded it and its power as a purely transitory phenomenon, dependent wholly upon the economics of exploitation. With the disappearance of capitalist classes, there would then be no need for the anachronism of the State and its machinery. Engels declared that "the authority of the government over persons will be replaced by the administration of things and the direction of the processes of production. The state will not be 'abolished,' it will wither away." But Engels prefaces these words with the statement: "The first act of a State in which it really acts as the representative of the whole of society, namely the assumption of control over the means of production on behalf of society, is also its last official act as a State." From this curious piece of reasoning it would appear that what disappears is not the State, in any sense that has had significance since the eighteenth century, but a special form of government. What Marx and Engels chose to label the "state" was actually a form of *government* that the French Revolution and subsequent nationalism had made largely obsolete—the simple vertical relation between an institutionally remote government and the people.

The unpopularity of the idea of the State, especially among the anarchists and the followers of Proudhon, led Marx and Engels, as a means of broadening their own popular following, to borrow some of the terminology of the anarchists, all the while combating vigorously both the anarchist and syndicalist movements. The "withering away of the State" was in part a terminological trick by which to steal some of the anarchist thunder and, in part, a piece of self-deception which resulted from confusion between the legal state as a centralized structure of power, and a particular form of state regarded for tactical and definitional purposes as part of the exploitative apparatus of the capitalists. As more than one student of Marx has been forced to conclude, Marx was never above letting tactical necessities influence his description of the universe itself.

Marx's own summary toward the end of the *Manifesto* of action to be taken and of the political significance of that action is instructive in this connection. "The proletariat will use its political supremacy to wrest by degrees all capital from the bourgeois, to centralize all instruments of production in the hands of the State, i.e., of the proletariat organized as the ruling class; and to increase the total of productive forces as rapidly as possible." In his list of the steps that will be a necessary part of the Revolution in "the most advanced" countries, the following are included: "Centralization of credit in the hands of the State, by means of a national bank with State capital and an exclusive monopoly. Centralization of the means of communication and transport in the hands of the State. Extension of factories and instruments of production owned by the State; the bringing into cultivation of waste lands, and their improvement. . . . Establishment of industrial armies, especially for agriculture. Combination of agriculture with manufacturing industries; gradual abolition of the distinction between town and country, by a more equal distribution of population over the country. . . . When in the course of development, class distinctions have disappeared, and all production has been concentrated in the hands of a vast association of the whole nation, the public power will lose its political character. Political power, properly so called, is merely the organized power of one class for oppressing another. . . ."

If we consider the State in terms which were made perfectly familiar by Hobbes and Rousseau and in light of the institutional realities of organized political government in the nineteenth century the final words have an almost naive ring. It would appear in fact that what is terminated is not the State but merely "the organized power of one class for oppressing another"— a quite different thing. To suppose that the public power would lose its political character when all production had been "concentrated in the hands of a vast association of the whole nation" was to miss entirely the nature of the political State that was developing in Marx's own time. Subsequent socialists have been all too willing to follow the reasoning by which a powerful, centralized, "vast association of the whole nation" could be declared bereft of political character simply because, like Rousseau's General Will, it reflected in theory no domination by a privileged social class minority. Marx's goal is the political community, centralized and absolute.

The Jacobin roots of Marxian socialism are clearly observable, although for obvious reasons Marx and his followers treated the French Revolution as a climax of the bourgeois rise to power. The Jacobins may not have been socialists, but there is little to separate their more radical views of property and wealth from the views of the later Marxians. Many of the recorded Jacobin speeches express ideas that are closer to those of the Communists of 1917 than to any set of "bourgeois" aspirations. The highly centralized conception of democracy held by the Jacobins, which could justify the most ruthless governmental actions by a few individuals on the ground that they spoke for the mass, was appropriated by the Marxian socialists in their theory of the relation of the party to the masses. Democratic centralism of present-day Communism owes much to the Jacobins. All of this Lenin had in mind when he declared in his *State and Revolution* that communism is the more perfect development of democracy.

Marx had as little use as Rousseau or Robespierre for the natural pluralism of society, for the difference between town and country, for localism, for autonomous association—whether religious or economic—and for the family. For Marx, as for the Revolutionary democrats and the Philosophical Radicals, differences of locality, religion, and grouping must be abandoned in favor of a rational, centralized society. The practical result, as A. D. Lindsay has written, is that society is treated by Marx as though it had but a single center. "The smaller associations within the State are treated not as subordinate forms in which the general will finds expression but as rivals to it."

Unlike most of the classical economists, Marx was sufficiently the historian to be aware at least of the existence of the institutions of traditional society. From Hegel he derived his interest in the impact of the historical process upon social classes, communities, gilds, families, and throughout the *Manifesto* and in many parts of *Capital* there are unsurpassable descriptions of the devastating social effects the rise of capitalism had on them.

But from Marx's point of view these associative aspects of human life were in large part mere expressions of a defunct social order—feudalism. In *Civil War in France* he wrote approvingly of the "gigantic broom of the French Revolution at the end of the eighteenth century, which swept away all these relics of medievalism." He was keenly aware of the influence of the traditionalists upon the social thought of his own time and wrote bitterly of the medievalism which "even donned proletarian apparel and learned the language of socialism." Marx and Engels despised pluralism as being ineffectual and archaic. It was this feeling that led Marx, in a letter to Engels, to hope fervently for the Prussian victory over France in 1870, on the ground that by the defeat of France, the new national predominance would shift the center of gravity of socialism from France to Germany, where the theory of centralization was much stronger.

Marx's view of the socially forward nature of history led him, as the determinist, to regard with hostility the traditional affiliations of family, community, association, and religion. The historical process, for Marx, was inevitable and could only take human relationships on to newer forms. He could write with all the bitter fervor of the prophet in his descriptions of the misery of the people and the consequences of industrialism, but in the glimpses we have been given of the future order imagined by Marx, there is little room either for cultural plurality or for decentralization of authority. In terms of his philosophy of history Marx could be brilliantly aware of the pluralism of history and of the facts of social allegiances and the clash of opposed classes. He could also write some devastating descriptions of contemporary bureaucracies. But when it came to setting down even in meager form his conception of the beginnings of socialist society, he could see the future only in Rousseauian terms of "a vast association of the whole nation" and in terms of techniques of extreme politicization and centralization. With Marx the socialist movement became clearly and almost irrevocably political or national socialism.

A generation of Marxists sought ingeniously to remove from this vision of the future the grounds for the anarchists' charges of political despotism in a new form. Thus Lenin persuasively put the initial process of socialist reconstruction in the beguiling language of natural administration. "The bookkeeping and control necessary for this have been simplified by capitalism to the utmost, till they have become the extraordinarily simple operations of watching, recording and issuing receipts, within the reach of anybody who can read and write and knows the first four arithmetical rules. . . . When most of the functions of the State are reduced to this bookkeeping and control by the workers themselves, it ceases to be a 'political' state. The public functions are converted from political into simple administrative functions. . . . The whole of society will have become one office and one factory with equal work and pay."

How far such a statement reflected Lenin's real views of the administrative problems of socialism, and how far it is to be regarded as camouflage for purposes of disarming pluralist and anarchist objections to Marxian socialism, is not easily determinable. Lenin's attitude toward the local and functional associations among the Russian peasants and workers—the villages, the cooperatives, and certain forms of the trade unions movement—was far from cordial. Unlike some of the Russian socialists who sought to preserve the communalism of the village and the already established cooperative and to make the achievement of universal socialism an outgrowth of these, Lenin, like most of the Bolsheviks, took the attitude that they were legacies of medievalism and hence to be destroyed.

Whether Lenin's contempt for what he called the flabbiness of the village and for the inherent particularizing and conservative influences of such functional associations as cooperative and trade union was based upon a rationalist faith, akin to Bentham's, in the universal potentialities of administration in each individual, or whether it was based upon themes of revolutionary, despotic centralization which earlier pre-Marxian Russian Nihilists had sounded, is of no great moment here. What is important is the fact that, given Marx's conception of the practical sphere in which socialism was to be realized—the vast association of the whole nation—it was inevitable that the political complexion of Marxism, its dependence upon the techniques of centralized power based upon a presumed will of the people, would become ever more pronounced. And given also a philosophy of history that saw the future emerging as inexorably out of the present as the present had out of the past, a philosophy of history that ridiculed the possibility of altering, through morality and knowledge, the design of history, it was equally inevitable that ensuing generations of Marxists would accept the major realities of the present as, in one degree or another, the major realities of the future. Heavy concentrations of industry, mass electorates, administrative centralization, the sterilization of cultural diversities, the eradication of social autonomies, and the conversion of social authority into administrative power—all this seemed a part of historic design and as relevant to the socialist future as to the capitalist present. All that was necessary was a revolutionary *coup de grâce* administered to a dying class in whose hands now lay, temporarily, the control of these progressive realities.

Nine

The nineteenth century has been called the Century of Great Hope. Innumerable historians have characterized its dominant qualities in the words of progress, democracy, freedom, and the liberation of reason from the shackles of superstition and ignorance. There is no need to quarrel with any of these characterizations. The nineteenth century was each and all of them. But it was something else, too, something that touched upon and, in one way or another, involved all of these moral values, something that we are only now beginning to understand clearly.

It was the century of the emergence of the political masses: masses created in widening areas by the processes of social destruction bound up with the increasing penetration of political power into all areas of society; masses created by the impact of a factory system that, in the essentials of its discipline, frequently resembled the military State itself; masses devoid, increasingly, of any hope for relief from the established, traditional institutions of society—family, church, and class.

Between the State and the masses there developed a bond, an affinity, which however expressed—in nationalism, unitary democracy, or in Marxian socialism—made the political community the most luminous of all visions. In it lay salvation from economic misery and oppression. In it lay a new kind of liberty, equality, and fraternity. In it lay right and justice. And in it, above all else, lay community.

What gave the vision of the political community added brilliance was the fact that so many of its elements—rational centralization of authority, the mass electorate, equality, political participation, unity, and so forth—could seem to be the elements of inexorable progress. Diversity, localism, regionalism, administrative decentralization—were not these the central elements of the despised Middle Ages, elements that were, as Michelet once insisted, being expunged remorselessly and eternally by the beneficent hand of Progress? All that did not serve the interests of the emerging new State, its unity and centralization, could be treated scornfully as unrealistic, as unprogressive, as an outcropping of the past. "Reactionary" and "Utopian" became, in equal degree, the appropriate epithets for all the ideas that did not begin with recognition of the historic inevitability of the political community and its dominant values.

"I think," wrote the brilliant Tocqueville in 1840, "that the species of oppression by which democratic nations are menaced is unlike anything that ever before existed in the world; our contemporaries will find no prototype of it in their memories. I seek in vain for an expression that will accurately convey the whole of the idea I have formed of it; the old words *despotism* and *tyranny* are inappropriate: the thing itself is new, and, since I cannot name it, I must attempt to define it.

"I seek to trace the novel features under which despotism may appear in the world. The first thing that strikes the observation is an innumerable multitude of men, all equal and alike, incessantly endeavouring to procure the petty and paltry pleasures with which they glut their lives. Each of them, living apart, is as a stranger to the fate of all the rest; his children and his private friends constitute to him the whole of mankind. As for the rest of his fellow citizens, he is close to them, but he does not see them; he touches them, but he does not feel them; he exists only in himself and for himself alone; and if his kindred still remain to him, he may be said at any rate to have lost his country.

"Above this race of men stands an immense and tutelary power, which takes upon itself alone to secure their gratifications and to watch over their fate. That power is absolute, minute, regular, provident and mild. It would be like the authority of a parent if, like that authority, its object was to prepare men for manhood; but it seeks, on the contrary, to keep them in a perpetual state of childhood: it is well content that people should rejoice, provided they think of nothing but rejoicing. For their happiness such a government willingly labors, but it chooses to be the sole agent and the only arbiter of that happiness; it provides for their security, foresees and supplies their necessities, facilitates their pleasures, manages their principal concerns, directs their industry, regulates the descent of property, and subdivides their inheritances: what remains, but to spare them all the care of thinking and all the trouble of living?

"Thus it every day renders the exercise of the free agency of man less useful and less frequent; it circumscribes the will within a narrower range and gradually robs a man of all the uses of himself. The principle of equality has prepared men for these things; it has predisposed men to endure them as benefits.

"After having thus successively taken each member of the community in its powerful grasp and fashioned him at will, the supreme power then extends its arm over the whole community. It covers the surface of society with a network of small, complicated rules, minute and uniform, through which the most original minds and the most energetic characters cannot penetrate, to rise above the crowd. The will of man is not shattered, but softened, bent, and guided; men are seldom forced by it to act, but they are constantly restrained from acting. Such a power does not destroy, but it prevents existence; it does not tyrannize, but it compresses, enervates, extinguishes, and stupefies a people, till each nation is reduced to nothing better than a flock of timid and industrious animals of which the government is the shepherd.

"I have always thought that servitude of the regular, quiet, and gentle kind which I have just described might be combined more easily than is commonly believed with some of the outward forms of freedom, and that it might even establish itself under the wing of the sovereignty of the people."[1]

Here, in these paragraphs, lies one of the most astonishing prophecies to be found anywhere in political literature. It is nothing less than a picture, nearly a century in advance of the reality, of the totalitarian community. But it is more than a mere prophecy. It is an analysis of the nature of totalitarianism that has not been improved upon by even the most brilliant of contemporary students of the subject.

What makes Tocqueville's analysis immeasurably superior to all but a few others is that it does not seize upon the transparently horrible, the grotesque, the obviously irrational, as the essence of totalitarianism. It does not limit itself to brutalities which, however abhorrent and real in totalitarian society, are nevertheless practiced by totalitarian rulers only against minorities already disliked and discriminated against by majorities. It does not fix upon aspects that are but incidental or variable in the structure of totalitarianism.

The merit of Tocqueville's analysis is that it points directly to the heart of totalitarianism—the masses; the vast aggregates who are never tortured, flogged, or imprisoned, or humiliated; who instead are cajoled, flattered, stimulated by the rulers; but who are nonetheless relentlessly destroyed as human beings, ground down into mere shells of humanity. And the genius of his analysis lies in the view of totalitarianism as something not historically "abnormal" but as closely related to the very trends hailed as progressive in the nineteenth century.

Two

Nothing can come from analyses of totalitarianism based upon elements that are incidental, or that vary from one country to another. Totalitarianism has unfortunately become one of those omnibus words used to absorb, indiscriminately, every element of past and present that we regard as detestable. Because totalitarianism is the major evil of our century, there is a strong tendency to make it the summation of all manifestly evil aspects of the past and the embodiment of all lesser evils of the present. But, however gratifying to our moral sensibilities, this is a dangerous mode of analysis. We had better direct our attention to qualities that might be supposed to have deep and wide appeal to large aggregates of human beings, qualities that, however corrupt, have meaning and relevance and can come to be regarded by masses of people as a part of the very design of history. Totalitarianism is an affair of mass attitudes. Its success depends on incorporating into new structures of power those values with the widest appeal to a population. It cannot be reduced, in its fundamentals, to such manifestly abhorrent facts as racial extermination, capitalist enslavement, or military dominance.

Hideous as were the systematic killings and torturings of millions of Jews by the Nazis, there is still no justification for making anti-Semitism the essence of totalitarianism. The reality of Soviet Russia, more ruthless and more efficiently totalitarian in many ways than even Hitler's Germany, should make this fact evident. Racialism is not the essence. That racialism, as a doctrine, was closely associated with Nazism has nothing to do with the structural foundations of totalitarianism and everything to do with the fact that race happened to be an evocative piece of imagery in Germany. Race may be the central image held up before the masses in a totalitarian country, but the image might as well be the proletariat, the fatherland, or suffering humanity.

We must recognize that there is no single intellectual image intrinsic to the totalitarian design. There is no single spiritual or cultural value inherently incapable of being made into the central image of a totalitarian society. It can as well be racial equality as inequality, godly piety as atheism, labor as capital, Christian brotherhood as the toiling masses. What is central is not the specific image held up to the masses but, rather, the sterilization and destruction of all other images and the subordination of all human relationships to the central power that contains this image.

Nor are poverty and economic distress, as such, the crucial factors leading to the rise of totalitarianism. Such analyses too are undiscriminating efforts to make the larger evil simply the sum of lesser evils. Poverty may, in certain circumstances, be a powerful basis of appeal for the totalitarian leader. It may be used as a piece of concrete symbolism for all the real and imaginary deprivations and frustrations of a population. But mere poverty itself does not automatically impell men to the acceptance of totalitarian power. What is decisive is the social context, the sensations of disinheritance and exclusion from rightful membership in a social and moral order. These may or may not accompany poverty.

Nor can the effective source of totalitarianism be confined to any one class or section of the population. For a long time, Marxism had the regrettable effect of convincing even well-informed observers that all the massive changes which took place in Germany after 1933 were simply "reactionary" efforts of a group of men known as capitalists to maintain an existing economy. Because in its early phases some highly placed industrialists contributed financially to the Nazi Party, and learned too late that rootless men always betray, the legend arose that totalitarianism is indistinguishable from predatory efforts of capitalists.

But we must recognize that totalitarianism can as easily be the work of industrial managers, who are themselves revolting against the capitalists, or of labor leaders, scientists, church leaders, or any group of intellectuals who may find themselves strategically placed to accomplish through revolution or bureaucracy the transition from free society to totalitarianism.

Least of all can totalitarianism—in whatever form it has taken, Nazi or Fascist included—be regarded seriously as a "reactionary" movement. Totalitarianism may not be revolutionary in the sense the word possessed in the nineteenth century, but in none of its forms can it be placed in the conservative category of reaction. To describe totalitarianism as simply the effort of a minority to maintain, through force, existing institutions of society misses grotesquely the sweeping dislocations and atomizations actually involved in such a movement as Nazism. Far from being, as it is sometimes absurdly argued, a lineal product of nineteenth-century Conservatism, totalitarianism is, in fact, the very opposite of it.

Nor can totalitarianism be reduced to the operation of force and terror. That these exist, and horribly, in every totalitarian country is beside the point. The essence of totalitarianism lies in its relation to the masses, and to the masses the leaders never bring the satanic arts of the torture chamber and the exterminations of the concentration camp. The totalitarian order will use force and terror, where necessary, to destroy organized *minorities*— refractory labor unions, churches, ethnic groups—but to the masses of individuals who are left when these social relationships are destroyed, a totally different approach is employed. It is an approach based upon the arts of psychological manipulation—cajolery, flattery, bribery, mass identification with new images, and all the modern techniques of indoctrination.

We merely delude ourselves if we suppose that there is always necessary conflict between totalitarian governments and the desires and aspirations of the masses. Here the recent words of Hannah Arendt are illuminating. "In view of the unparalleled misery which totalitarian regimes have meant to their people—horror to many and unhappiness to all—it is painful to realize that they are always preceded by mass movements and that they 'command and rest upon mass support' up to the end. Hitler's rise to power was legal in terms of majority rule and neither he nor Stalin could have maintained the leadership of large populations, survived so many interior and exterior crises, and braved the numerous dangers of the relentless intra-party struggles, if they had not had the confidence of the masses."[2]

The totalitarian leader is never loath to identify himself with the "will and wisdom" of the masses. No intellectual defense against totalitarianism could be more futile than that which sees the States of Hitler and Stalin as operating in open contempt and hatred of the people. Such States may plead with, flatter, and persuade, but they never openly insult the people. It was this dependence upon popular support that permitted Mussolini to call his Fascism "an organized, centralized, authoritarian democracy," and Hitler to refer to the Third Reich as "Teutonic democracy based upon the free choice of the leader." We do not have to be reminded of the ceaseless efforts of the Soviet leaders to identify their policies and actions with the tradition of democracy in the West and of their incessant attempts to maintain popular support of these policies.

There are two other misconceptions, greater than any of the foregoing, each of which precludes an understanding of totalitarianism. The first consists of the view of totalitarianism as some sort of vast irrationality, a kind of collective derangement. Here we are victims of the supine optimism that has characterized so much of Western thought during the past two centuries. We insist upon making the irrational and the evil interpenetrating essences of one another. Because totalitarianism is manifestly evil we suppose that it is also fundamentally irrational. And because we have thus proved it to be irrational we comfort ourselves with the belief that it must be destroyed by its own departure from reason.

The total State is evil, but we merely delude ourselves if we do not recognize in it elements of almost overpowering rationality. In terms of basic organization it is at least as rational as the huge industrial corporation, the mass political party, or the mammoth bureaucracies of all modern governments. Indeed the total State would be inconceivable without a background, in some degree, composed of these and related elements. We might as well conceive of selling the Rotary Creed to savages on the banks of the Amazon as disseminating Nazi or Communist creeds to populations unfamiliar with the basic and overt manifestations of economic and political rationalism.

The total State is rational in that it recognizes in human personality certain basic needs for security and recognition and strives through every art and technique to satisfy those needs in calculated political terms. It is rational in that it seeks to eliminate from culture all of those ceremonial, ritualistic, or symbolic features inherited from the past that constitute by their existence obstructions to the achievement of a perfect mobilization of popular will. New ceremonies and symbols will be created by totalitarian rulers, but these will be made to fit as closely into the total design of political power as manipulative intelligence can contrive. Old complexities of language and syntax will be removed, where necessary, in the interests of a more rational structure of communication readily assimilable by all members of the population; ancient legal procedures will be abolished or streamlined in the interests of a more rational and remorseless legal code; superfluous or irrelevant forms of recreation will be outlawed, subtly or forcibly as circumstances may require, and replaced by new forms harmonious with the purposes of the State. Horrible as were the Nazi concentration and extermination camps, in moral terms, we cannot miss the essential rationality of their operation. They were rational not merely in the ruthless efficiency of their techniques but in their calculated separation of victim and overseer alike from all the emotional and spiritual aspects of personality.

To start out with the assumption that totalitarianism is irrational, and hence doomed to self-destruction, is to start out with an extremely unintelligent view of a form of society that has used all the rational arts of modern public administration, economic management, and social psychology to maintain itself and to make its identity ever more emphatic in the minds of its people.

Equally fatal to our understanding of totalitarianism is the assumption, drawn from the philosophy of Progress, that this form of society represents some kind of historical abnormality or deflection from the appointed course of history. Here also we are in the presence of the typical confusion between the morally good and the historically inevitable. Because we, for so long, saw in political freedom, rights, and justice the basic elements not merely of moral goodness but also of historical necessity, there are many who persist in regarding such movements as Nazism and Soviet Communism as deviations from the normal development of civilization.

Related to this view are the efforts to place totalitarianism in the category of primitivism, of antique tribalism. Such efforts are a part of the larger perspective of moral philosophy that makes all evil a mere reversion to the past, as though there were some inevitable link between time and moral states. The total State, it is said, is nothing more than a reversion to the infancy of civilization. It is the product of certain dark forces, buried beneath the superego man has acquired through centuries of moral progress, now manifesting themselves in Nazism and Communism. This view may be gratifying to sensibilities nourished by the idea of Progress, but it is as delusive as the idea that totalitarianism is a vast collective irrationality. To explain all evil as simply a reversion to the past is, as Reinhold Niebuhr once observed, like describing individual insanity as simply a reversion to childhood.

What is most dangerous in this whole view is the supposition that totalitarianism is a kind of monstrous accident, an interruption of the normal, a deflection that must be set right by the operation of the so-called laws of historical progress. But if there are any laws of unilinear progress, we have not discovered them, and there is no more justification in purely historical terms for regarding totalitarianism as an abnormal development than there is for so regarding democracy, or liberalism.

Three

There are two central elements of totalitarianism: the first is the existence of the masses; the second is the ideology, in its most extreme form, of the political community. Neither can be fully described apart from its relation to the other, for the two exist always, in modern society, in sensitive interaction with each other. What works toward the creation of the masses works also toward the establishment of the omnicompetent, absolute State. And everything that augments the power and influence of the State in its relation to the individual serves also to increase the scope of the masses.

The masses are fundamental to the establishment of totalitarian society. On this point all serious students of the subject, from Peter Drucker to Hannah Arendt are agreed.

"Masses," writes Dr. Arendt, "are not held together by consciousness of common interest, and they lack that specific class articulateness which is expressed in determined, limited, obtainable goals. The term masses applies only where we deal with people who either because of sheer numbers, or indifference, or a combination of both, cannot be integrated into any organization based on common interest, into political parties, or municipal governments, or professional organizations, or trade unions."[3]

The essence of the masses, however, does not lie in the mere fact of numbers. It is not the quantitative but the qualitative aspect that is essential. A population may be vast, as is that of India, and yet, by reason of the stability of its social organization, be far removed from the condition of massdom. What is crucial in the formation of the masses is the atomization of all social and cultural relationships within which human beings gain their normal sense of membership in society. The mass is an aggregate of individuals who are insecure, basically lonely, and ground down, either through decree or historical circumstance, into mere particles of social dust. Within the mass all ordinary relationships and authorities seem devoid of institutional function and psychological meaning. Worse, such relationships and authorities come to seem positively hostile; in them the individual can find not security but despair. "The despair of the masses," concludes Peter Drucker, "is the key to the understanding of fascism. No 'revolt of the mob,' no 'triumphs of unscrupulous propaganda,' but stark despair caused by the breakdown of the old order and the absence of a new one."[4]

When the masses, in considerable number, already exist, as the consequence of historical forces, half the work of the totalitarian leader has been done for him. What remains but to complete, where necessary, the work of history, and to grind down into atomic particles all remaining evidences of association and social authority? What remains, then, but to rescue the masses from their loneliness, their hopelessness and despair, by leading them into the Promised Land of the absolute, redemptive State? The process is not too difficult, or even too violent, providing the masses have already been created in significant size by processes that have destroyed or diminished the social relationships and cultural values by which human beings normally live and in which they gain not merely their sense of order but their desire for freedom.

But where the masses do not already exist in great numbers, and where, through the accident of quick seizure of power, the totalitarian mentality comes into ascendancy, then it becomes necessary to *create* the masses: to do through the most ruthless force and in the shortest possible time the work that has been done in other areas by the operation of past processes.

Here is where the most shocking acts of totalitarianism become manifest—not in its attitude toward the already existing masses, but toward those human beings, still closely related by village, church, or family, or labor union, and whose very relationships separate them from the indispensable condition of massdom. Such relationships must be ruthlessly destroyed. If they cannot be destroyed easily and inexpensively by propaganda and intimidation, they must be destroyed by all the techniques of the torture chamber, by enforced separation of loved ones, by the systematic obliteration of legal identities, by killing, and by the removal of large segments of a population to labor camps.

The violence and the horrors of Soviet Russia, in many ways greater perhaps even than those of Nazi Germany, have arisen from the fact that in Russia, down to the beginnings of the First World War, the masses scarcely existed. The ancient relationships of class, family, village, and association were nearly as strong as they had been in medieval times. Only in small areas of Russia were these relationships dissolving and the masses beginning to emerge.

The political inertia of the large majority of the Russian people under the Czars, the relative impotence of postwar government, and the general state of disorganization in the cities made it not too difficult for the disciplined Communists to capture power in 1917. But the consolidation of that power was quite a different problem. The realization of what Marx had called "the vast association of the whole nation" called for drastic steps— for the rapid industrialization of rural areas, for eradication of political opposition, and for the extreme centralization of power which alone could make these and other steps possible.

But, of far greater import, this realization also called for a change in the very structure of the people, its values, incentives, motivations, and allegiances. The new Communism could not thrive on popular values and relationships inherited through the ages. If the classless society was to be created, it was necessary to destroy not only old classes but old associations of any type. It was necessary, as Stalin saw the problem, to accomplish in a short time the atomization and dislocation that had been proceeding in Western countries for generations.[5]

Hence, beginning in the nineteen-twenties, the destruction of all traditional associations, the liquidation of old statuses. Hence also the conversion of professional and occupational associations into administrative arms of the government. The hopes of older Russian intellectuals, who had supposed that socialism in Russia might be founded upon the communal institutions of the peasantry, supplemented by the emerging workers' organizations in the cities, were proved fatuous. For the new rulers of Russia realized that the kind of power requisite to the establishment of the Marxian order could not long exist if any competing associations and authorities were allowed to remain. The vast association of the nation, which Marx had prophesied, could come into being only through the most absolute and extensive central political power. And, for the establishment and maintenance of this power, the creation of the undifferentiated, unattached, atomized mass was indispensable.

Four

We may regard totalitarianism as a process of the annihilation of individuality, but, in more fundamental terms, it is the annihilation, first, of those social relationships within which individuality develops. It is not the extermination of individuals that is ultimately desired by totalitarian rulers, for individuals in the largest number are needed by the new order. What is desired is the extermination of those social relationships which, by their autonomous existence, must always constitute a barrier to the achievement of the absolute political community.

The individual alone is powerless. Individual will and memory, apart from the reinforcement of associative tradition, are weak and ephemeral. How well the totalitarian rulers know this. Even constitutional guarantees and organic laws dim to popular vision when the social and cultural identities of persons become atomized, when the reality of freedom and order in the *small areas* of society becomes obscure.

The prime object of totalitarian government thus becomes the incessant destruction of all evidences of spontaneous, autonomous association. For, with this social atomization, must go also a diminution of intensity and a final flickering out of political values that interpose themselves between freedom and despotism.

To destroy or diminish the reality of the smaller areas of society, to abolish or restrict the range of cultural alternatives offered individuals by economic endeavor, religion, and kinship, is to destroy in time the roots of the will to resist despotism in its large forms. In its negative aspects totalitarianism is thus a ceaseless process of cultural nihilism. How else can the individual be separated from the traditions and values which, if allowed to remain intact, would remind him constantly of his cultural past? A sense of the past is far more basic to the maintenance of freedom than hope for the future. The former is concrete and real; the latter is necessarily amorphous and more easily guided by those who can manipulate human actions and beliefs. Hence the relentless effort by totalitarian governments to destroy memory. And hence the ingenious techniques for abolishing the social allegiances within which individual memory is given strength and power of resistance.

Totalitarianism is thus made possible only through the obliteration of all the intermediate layers of value and association that commonly nourish personality and serve to protect it from external power and caprice. Totalitarianism has been well described as the ultimate invasion of human privacy. But this invasion of privacy is possible only after the social contexts of privacy—family, church, association—have been atomized. The political *enslavement* of man requires the *emancipation* of man from all the authorities and memberships (obstructions to popular will, as the Nazis and Communists describe them) that serve, in one degree or another, to insulate the individual from external political power.

The destruction of the independent labor unions in Nazi Germany was followed by the prohibition of independent economic organizations of every kind. It was not the fact of labor that was central; it was the social fact of *union*. All autonomous organizations were destroyed and made illegal:

professions, service clubs, voluntary mutual aid groups, fraternal associations, even philatelist and musical societies. Such organizations were regarded, and correctly, by the totalitarian government as potential sources of future resistance, if only because in them people were brought together for purposes, however innocent, that did not reflect those of the central government. As organizations they interposed themselves between the people as a society and the people as the masses.

Despite the fact that the early Nazis used the symbolism of family and religion for its possible sentimental appeal, the actual realities of family and religion were as remorselessly attacked by the government and Party as were the labor unions.[6] The shrewd totalitarian mentality knows well the powers of intimate kinship and religious devotion for keeping alive in a population values and incentives which might well, in the future, serve as the basis of resistance. Thus to emancipate each member, and especially the younger members, from the family was an absolute necessity. And this planned spiritual alienation from kinship was accomplished, not only through the negative processes of spying and informing but through the sapping of the functional foundations of family membership and through the substitution of new and attractive political roles for each of the social roles embodied in the family structure. The techniques varied. But what was essential was the atomization of the family and of every other type of grouping that intervened between the people as society and the people as a mindless, soulless, traditionless mass. What the totalitarian must have for the realization of his design is a spiritual and cultural vacuum.

Five

Totalitarianism is an ideology of nihilism. But nihilism is not enough. No powerful social movement can be explained in negative terms alone. There is always the positive goal and absorptive association for which all the destructive and desolative actions are but a preparation, a clearing of the way. We should miss the essence of the total State if we did not see in it elements that are profoundly affirmative. The extraordinary accomplishments of totalitarianism in the twentieth century would be inexplicable were it not for the immense, burning appeal it exerts upon masses of individuals who have lost, or had taken away, their accustomed roots of membership and belief.

The atomization of old values and associations does not leave for long an associational vacuum. The genius of totalitarian leadership lies in its profound awareness that human personality cannot tolerate moral isolation. It lies, further, in its knowledge that absolute and relentless power will be acceptable only when it comes to seem the only available form of community and membership.

Here we have the clue to that fatal affinity of power and individual loneliness. Early in his career Hitler sensed this affinity and wrote in his *Mein Kampf:* "The mass meeting is necessary if only for the reason that in it the individual who in becoming an adherent of a new movement feels lonely and is easily seized with the fear of being alone, receives for the first time the picture of a greater community, something that has a strengthening effect upon most people." Knowing the basic psychological truth that life apart from some sense of membership in a larger order is intolerable for most people, the leaders of the total State thus direct their energies not just to the destruction of the old order but to the manufacture of the new.

This new order is the absolute, the total, political community. As a community it is made absolute by the removal of all forms of membership and identification which might, by their existence, compete with the new order. It is, further, made absolute by the insistence that all thought, belief, worship, and membership be within the structure of the State. What gives historical identity to the totalitarian State is not the absolutism of one man or of a clique or a class; rather, it is the absolute extension of the structure of the administrative State into the social and psychological realm previously occupied by a plurality of associations. Totalitarianism involves the demolishment of autonomous social ties in a population, but it involves, no less, their replacement by new ones, each deriving its meaning and sanction from the central structure of the State.

The total State is monolithic. It is not convincing to argue, as have some of even the best students, that the power of the Party in the total State, paralleling at every point the powers of the formal bureaucracy, is proof of the contrary. In the first place, the totalitarian Party is regarded as but a necessary transitional step in the attainment of a formal governmental structure that will be, ultimately, free of any distractive allegiance, Party included. The Party may hold heavy powers over the actual bureaucracy, but its essential function is catalytic. It is designed to bring not only the people as a whole but the bureaucracy itself into line with the basic purposes of totalitarian society. In the second place, with all allowance for the so-called "dual state" created by the powers of the Party, what is crucial is the fact that the Party is dedicated to the same ends which are sovereign over the whole population and the official bureaucracy. The Party may be outside the formal sphere of governmental administration, but it is never outside the range of ends that are absolute and exclusive in the whole society.

Nor is any other form of association. The monolithic cast of the totalitarian State arises from the sterilization or destruction of all groups and statuses that, in any way, rival or detract from the allegiance of the masses to State.

It is characteristic of the total State, as Peter Drucker has pointed out, that the distinction between ordinary civil society and the army is obliterated. The natural diversity of society is swept away, and the centralization and omnicompetence native to the war band become the organizing principles of human life. We have already noted the power of war, in the twentieth century, to inspire a sense of moral community. This power is exploited to the full in totalitarian society. Every decision is converted into a military decision, dependent for its meaning upon the strategies and tactics of war. Every difficulty, every obstacle, is translated by totalitarian leadership into the imagery of war against evil, of defense against aggression. Every significant deviation from official policy—in art and in politics, in science and economy—is ruthlessly exterminated in the name of unity and preparedness. All relationships are conceived eventually in the likeness of those of the garrison.

To convert the whole of society into the ordered regularity of the army may seem a fair estimate of the objectives of Communist and Nazi totalitarianism. But, basically, there is little choice between these objectives and those that seek to convert society into the ordered regularity of the factory, the bureau, or the asylum. We must not be led astray by the analogy of the army. It is not war, anymore than it is race or economic class, that is central. What is central is simply the absolute substitution of the State for all the diversified associations of which society is normally composed.

In the totalitarian order the political tie becomes the all-in-all. It needs the masses as the masses need it. It integrates even where it dissolves, unifies where it separates, inspires where it suffocates. The rulers of the total community devise their own symbolism to replace the symbolism that has been destroyed in the creation of the masses.

The communal likeness of power is indispensable, for power that seems remote and inaccessible will be, no matter how ruthlessly it is imposed, unavailing and ineffectual. At every stage the power of the government must seem to proceed from the basic will of the people. The government thus chooses to bend, soften, and corrode the will to resistance in preference to forcible and brutal breaking of the will. For in the latter lie dread possibilities of overt resistance which might serve to dramatize opposition and create the potent symbolism of martyrdom.

New meanings must therefore be created for popular assimilation. Even new "memories" must be fabricated to replace the memories which, by their continual reminder of a past form of society, would ceaselessly militate against the new form. New conceptions of good and evil, of truth and falsehood, of freedom and tyranny, of the sacred and the secular, must be established in the popular mind to replace those lost or destroyed. History, art, science, and morality, all of these must be redesigned, placed in a new context, in order to make of a power a seamless web of certainty and conformity. Totalitarian power is insupportable unless it is clothed in the garments of deep spiritual belief.

But the spiritual transformation of a people, the creation of new meanings and symbols, cannot proceed apart from the creation of new social contexts of belief and meaning. Here is where the real genius of the totalitarian order becomes manifest.

The atomization of old groups and associations is accompanied by the establishment of new forms of association, each designed to meet the needs and to carry on the functions that were embedded in the old forms of social grouping. To these new associations, each based upon some clear and positive function, inevitably go the allegiances of the masses. In these groups, reaching down to the most primary levels of relationship, lies escape from the intolerable emptiness and demonic nature of mass society. Such groups, in time, come to seem the very difference between membership and isolation, between hope and despair, between existence and non-existence.

From them come, for constantly widening aggregates, the anesthetic release from sensations of alienation, hostility, and irrationality. These associations are not only the context of personal identification and belonging; they are also the indispensable contexts of totalitarian indoctrination.

As old cultural values and spiritual meanings become dim and unremembered through the destruction or erosion of social relationships that once made them vivid, so, in the totalitarian order which replaces the old, new meanings and values are given root and solidity in new associations and memberships. With new social status comes in time a new set of allegiances, new values, even new perceptions.

Powerful and unprecedented as it is, totalitarian domination of the individual will is not a mysterious process, not a form of sorcery based upon some vast and unknowable irrationalism. It arises and proceeds rationally and relentlessly through the creation of new functions, statuses, and allegiances, which by conferring community, makes the manipulation of the human will scarcely more than an exercise in scientific social psychology.

The superficial evidences of the old political structure may be left intact. There may well be a parliament or legislature. Old civil service positions, old titles of office may be left undisturbed. There may be periodic elections or plebiscites, and the terminology of freedom may be broadcast unabatedly. There may be left even the appearance of individual freedom, provided it is *only* individual freedom. All of this is unimportant, always subject to guidance and control, if the primary social contexts of belief and opinion are properly organized and managed. What is central is the creation of a network of functions and loyalties reaching down into the most intimate recesses of human life where ideas and beliefs will germinate and develop.

All the rational skills of modern social manipulation, borrowed from every quarter of modern, large-scale economic and political society, go into the process of reassimilation. New organizations based upon place, work, and interest are created. The same force that seeks constantly to destroy the social substance of the old family is concerned with the establishment of new organizations designed to assimilate each sex and each age group of the family. Labor unions are either remade into agencies of the State, or new labor organizations are created to replace the old. New professional, scientific, and artistic groups are created—even new associations for the varied hobbies of a people.

As the totalitarian psychologist well knows, within these new formal associations based upon clear function and meaning, there will inevitably arise over a period of time the vastly more important network of new *informal* relationships, new interpersonal allegiances and affections, and with them a new sense of personal status, which will reach like a chain from the lowliest individual to the highest center of government.

But the new groups, associations, and formal statuses are without exception agencies of the State itself. They are plural only in number, not in ultimate allegiance or purpose. What we must recognize is that each association is but a social and psychological extension of the central administration of the State. Each exists as a primary context of the political repersonalization of man that follows the nihilistic process of social depersonalization. Each is the instrument, ultimately, of the central government, the psychological setting that alone makes possible the massive remaking of the human consciousness. All such groups, with their profound properties of status, are the means of implementing whatever image—race, proletariat, or mankind—surmounts the structure of the absolute, monolithic, political community.

Nothing could be more delusive than the supposition that the totalitarian political order is without roots in the allegiances of vast numbers of human beings, that it is a flimsy structure at best. The amazing evidences of militant, collective power and of fanatical will to resist revealed by the Germans during the Second World War should demonstrate irrefutably that, even within the mere six years which intervened between the Nazi rise to power and the outbreak of the war, the successes of mass manipulation had been considerable. From these we might well ponder the undoubtedly greater successes of the Russian rulers in their three decades of almost uninterrupted creation of the will-less, cultureless masses and the assimilation of these masses into cohesive primary groups, each an agency of central governmental policy, each the seed-bed of popular allegiance.

The monolithic reality of totalitarianism is revealed when, through military defeat, there is complete disorganization of the central government. For, from this central disorganization proceeds the inevitable collapse of all those forms of intermediate society which were dependent on central power and which were the contexts of human life. Then the masses are left nakedly revealed, stripped of the memberships, statuses, and associations created for them by the totalitarian rulers.

Twice in the twentieth century Germany has been defeated by enemy powers, but the consequences of the second defeat have been vastly different from the consequences of the first. The collapse of the central government in 1918 was scarcely more than just that. The internal *private* governments of Germany—business associations, labor unions, churches, municipal administrations, and the like—even though some of their effectiveness had been damaged by the war effort, were still capable of exercising independently a measurable stabilizing influence upon the German people. But at the end of the Second World War Germany was, in huge areas, a social as well as a physical rubble. Twelve years of Nazism, the extermination of autonomous social functions and memberships, the incorporation of the masses into organizations each of which was a division of the central government—all of this left, when military defeat had destroyed that central government, scarcely more than an aggregate of atomic human particles, hopeless, will-less, and ground down into chronic despair.

This is the true horror of totalitarianism. The absolute political community, centralized and omnicompetent, founded upon the atomized masses, must ceaselessly destroy all those autonomies and immunities that are in normal society the indispensable sources of the capacity for freedom and organization. Total political centralization can lead only to social and cultural death.

PART THREE

COMMUNITY AND THE
PROBLEM OF FREEDOM

"The real tragedy of existence," Hegel once wrote, "is not the conflict between right and wrong but between right and right." The present crisis of freedom and organization in Western society would be easier to resolve if it were plainly the outcome of opposed forces of manifest good and manifest evil. But who can doubt that the mounting anxiety and the widespread sense of moral conflict in contemporary liberal thought are the consequence of a state of mind which sees the things we value opposed by other things we value as well as by what we hate.

On the one hand we prize equalitarian democracy, moral neutrality, intellectual liberation, secular progress, rationalism, and all the liberating impersonalities of modern industrial and political society. On the other we continue to venerate tradition, secure social status, the corporate hierarchies of kinship, religion, and community, and close involvement in clear moral contexts. Conflicts between these sets of values seem to become ever more pressing. We esteem rationalism but we shrink from disenchantment.

The result of intellectual and moral conflict is written large in the thought of the contemporary liberal. The last two decades have undoubtedly produced a greater effusion of disillusionment and doctrinal abdication than any similar period in modern history. Never have past, present, and future seemed more discontinuous in terms of ideals and hopes. Whatever the basic intellectual significance of existentialism, its present popularity, especially in Western Europe, is one more example of the flamelike attraction that moral atomism and solipsism have for the disinherited and the alienated. When even the ideas of humanitarian liberalism are consigned by the intellectual to the same charnel house that holds the bones of capitalism and nationalism, his emancipation is complete. He is now free—in all his solitary misery.

To observe this is not to write in complacent irony. More and more it appears that only the stupid and the blind can hold fast to social and moral creeds with the same degree of assuredness that marked the intellectual's faith of even a decade ago. In few ages have ideals changed so suddenly and drastically from vital symbols of faith and action to mere museum pieces. The convinced socialist, like the convinced atheist, has ceased to be the recognized standard-bearer of radicalism. He has become simply irrelevant. His position, among intellectuals, is no longer given even the dignity of attack.

As one secular hope after another has failed, the liberal finds himself in the position described by Matthew Arnold. The sea of faith is once more

> *Retreating, to the breath*
> *Of the night-wind, down the vast edges drear*
> *And naked shingles of the world.*

But now it is the long, withdrawing roar of liberalism and secularism that is heard, not Christian orthodoxy.

To regard all evil as a persistence or revival of the past has been a favorite conceit of liberals nourished by the idea of Progress. For several centuries Western liberal thought has been buoyed up by the assumption that history is a more or less continuous emancipation of men from despotism and evil. Past, present, and future have been convenient categories into which to fit precisely the moral qualities of bad, good, and best. Present evils could be safely regarded as regrettable evidences of incomplete emancipation from the past—from tribalism, from agrarianism, religion, localism, and the like. In one form or another the theory of cultural lag has been the secular approach to the problem of evil.

This chronological categorization of morality has not, to be sure, disappeared even in the present time of troubles. But more and more people of a reflective disposition, without losing entirely their distrust of the past and their faith in the future, are coming to see a large element of uncertainty, of Devil's brew, in the aspects of society that are most plainly "modern" and that point most directly to the future. To look into the future as far as one can see is now more likely to produce the black pessimism of an Orwell or Koestler than the enthusiasm of a John Reed.

One of the most dismaying features of the present intellectual scene is the reluctant abdication of some of the values and faiths that have been among the highest glories of Western civilization: the dignity of the human being, the faith in the people, and the possibilities of reason based upon human experience. The reasons for this abdication are not far to see. As values these seem to possess less and less relation to the area of actual choices and realities that lies before us. But the consequences of the abdication are nonetheless tragic.

We cannot overlook the crisis of belief regarding the nature of man himself. At the beginning of the present century the great economist, Alfred Marshall, declared that "the average level of human nature has risen fast in the last fifty years." How many could now be found who, far from agreeing with this judgment, would not instead wonder whether the level of human nature has not sunk abysmally? Two world wars within a quarter of a century together with revelations of the extermination and torture of untold numbers of people in some of the most civilized of modern areas have done much to reawaken in the modern intellectual a respect for the ancient dogma of original sin. More and more of us have come to feel, with Melville, Hawthorne, and Dostoevsky, that in men's souls lie deep and unpredictable potentialities for evil that no human institutions can control.

There is a perceptible weakening of faith in the power of man to set the conditions of the good life. "We are faced," a recent Gifford lecturer has declared, "with a spiritual conflict of the most acute kind, a sort of social schizophrenia which divides the soul of society between a non-moral will to power served by inhuman techniques and a religious and moral idealism which have no power to influence human life."[1] If there is any inference to be drawn from the recent secular literature of disillusion it is the inference that supports and reinforces this judgment. In many minds there is a growing conviction that between our moral ideals and our available techniques for achieving them there is a constantly widening gulf.

It is hard to overlook, too, the mounting distrust of organized action in behalf of even our most cherished ideals. For, in the twentieth century, there have arisen, under the guise of humanitarian purposes, intensities of tyranny and stultifications of human personality that are unprecedented in

Western history. Even if we do not agree wholly with Acton's celebrated maxim that all power corrupts, we have been made unavoidably aware of the fact that the striving for power, however benign in intent, often creates corruptions of the ideals behind the striving.[2] The growing distrust of the authority that must lie within any organized action produces a state of mind which affirms with Shelley that

> *The man*
> *Of virtuous soul commands not, nor obeys;*
> *Power, like a desolating pestilence,*
> *Pollutes whate'er it touches; and obedience,*
> *Bane of all genius, virtue, freedom, truth,*
> *Makes slaves of men and of the human frame,*
> *A mechanized automaton.*

In many minds lies the paralyzing belief that we have reached a point in the struggle for human justice where some kind of demonic compulsion leads to the supremacy of techniques and instruments of power over even the most exalted of ideals.

So too has the age-old problem of evil reappeared and become once more disturbing to rationalist complacency. The events and transformations of the present century, especially in Communist dominated Europe, have given rise to the suspicion that some of the worst evils of the age arise out of ideas and elements we have long hailed as good. And no odor, Thoreau once wrote, is so bad as that arising from goodness tainted.

What is so disturbing is the suspicion that the abhorrent nature of certain forces in our society arises from the very tradition of secular humanitarianism itself. It was this suspicion that gave George Orwell's *Nineteen Eighty-four* its peculiar flavor of horror. For, as amorphous suspicion in a group can lead to distrust of even the most trusted of men, so can suspicion of certain values lead to a wholesale dissolution of moral trust.

Two

More than anything else it is the massive spectacle of totalitarianism, especially in its Communist form, that has brought dismay to the minds of those men who were prepared to find in the mid-twentieth century a realization of earlier visions of emancipation and freedom. Few Western liberals now doubt the evil in Soviet Russia and the world Communist movement. Both represent the most efficiently ruthless concentration of power and subversion of human personality that the Western world has yet seen. Yet, who can doubt that Communism has its appeal, everywhere, to men of the utmost good will? Who can doubt that its success depends in large degree upon its capacity for offering refuge to the hungry sheep, hope to the hopeless, and faith to the disillusioned? And who can doubt, finally, that, making all allowance for the awful gulf between practice and preachment, twentieth-century Communism does have a demonstrable historical connection with social movements and ideals which we in the West continue to prize?

If Communist despotism were unadorned, if it did not have, in the memory of living man, roots in the humanitarian tradition, if it did not depend on the historic slogans of secular humanitarianism for so much of its appeal, the present sense of crisis would be, perhaps, less acute.

Is it democracy that we would point to as the crucial difference between the cultures of the West and the Communist tyranny of the East? Totalitarian Russia stridently reiterates its popular foundations, and appeals, not without success, to the political tradition of Rousseau and Robespierre. Is it freedom? There is, we are told by Communist apologists, almost in the words of Rousseau and of the Jacobins, a "higher freedom" than that of the bourgeois West, a freedom of the people as a whole from the tyrannies of minority elements within it. Is it liberation? What is Communism—in Czechoslovakia, Eastern Germany, and China—but a process of forcible liberation of human beings from the shackles set upon them by landlords, trade union leaders, capitalists, and educational systems? Is it not, again to use the words of Rousseau, a process of "forcing men to be free"?

Is it the common man? There is scarcely any tyranny in the contemporary world, Fascist or Communist, that does not defend its most wanton invasions of personal or associative liberty by an appeal to the common man. Is it equality? The leveling of populations, the radical atomization of every kind of religious, economic, academic, and cultural association within the State, is justified in the name of equality; and if new forms of political hierarchy arise, these, it is said, in the word if not the spirit of Bentham, are but temporary artificial barriers to the redevelopment of exploitation and superstition.

Is it reason? Only the naive persist in treating the Communist and Fascist States, with their technically advanced schemes of scientific management and bureaucratic custodianship of cultural life, as irruptions of the irrational. Immoral and degenerative, we may say, but not irrational! Nor would we dare claim, with painful memory of the assurance and tenacity with which the Russians and the Germans fought in the recent war, that intensity of faith alone is the clue to the kind of cultural salvation which most of us continue to believe in.

It is no wonder that the spectacle of totalitarianism, especially in its Communist form, has done so much to create doubt in many minds of the value of the symbols on which Western liberal humanitarianism has so long depended. For we cannot overlook the triumph of a despotism behind the iron curtain that is carried to ever greater successes by the very slogans we have cherished in the West for generations. Despite the manifest corruptness of the process, despite the blatant hypocrisy of the New Barbarism, there is nevertheless forced upon us at times the nerveless disillusionment that can come only from the experience of seeming to be betrayed by all we have trusted most.

But despite the traumatic effect of contemporary Communism upon the liberal mind, I do not think the spectacle of Communist corruption of liberal values is primary in the process of creeping disillusionment which now seems to threaten paralysis of liberal will and action. The major elements of this disillusionment, unhappily, come from within and are merely quickened in their action by the external shocks that Communism has provided. In large part, the present crisis of liberal thought in the West comes, I believe, from the increasing loss of correspondence between the basic liberal values and the prejudgments and social contexts upon which the historic success of liberalism has been predicated.

It is a commonplace in the study of language that the meanings of words and sentences depend on understandings which exist prior to the utterance of the words themselves. It is equally true that all explicit, formal judgments of value contain, and indeed depend on, certain prejudgments which give the formal judgments their roots of meaning and their possibility of communication. Without some kind of agreement upon the unspoken but efficacious prejudgments, all efforts to derive meaning from and to reach agreement about the explicit, exposed judgments are fruitless. Most of the world's conflicts of faith and action take their departure from lack of agreement about prejudgments rather than from dissension about formal judgments; and these are never within reach of the semanticist.

Finally, it is but an extension of the foregoing to suggest that the communities of assent on which the spoken word depends, and the silent prejudgments which give meaning and efficacy to formal judgments of value, are themselves reinforced and contained by the more tangible communities of interest and behavior that compose a social organization. No one of these three sets of elements is causative or even crucial. They exist as inseparable aspects of the one unified phenomenon. What the philosopher Whitehead has written on the problem of symbolism is pertinent here.

"There is an intricate expressed symbolism of language and act which is spread throughout the community, and which evokes fluctuating apprehension of the basis of common purpose. The particular direction of individual action is directly correlated to the particular sharply defined symbols presented to him at the moment. The response of action to the symbol may be so direct as to cut out any effective reference to the ultimate thing symbolized In fact, the symbol evokes loyalties to vaguely conceived notions, fundamental for our spiritual natures. The result is that our natures are stirred to suspend all antagonistic impulses, so that the symbol procures its required response in action. Thus the social symbolism has a double meaning. It means pragmatically the direction of individuals to specific actions; and it also means theoretically the vague ultimate reasons with their emotional accompaniments, whereby the symbols acquire their power to organize the miscellaneous crowd into a smoothly running community."[3]

But do not some of the profoundest problems of liberal democracy arise at the present time from the weakening of both of these aspects of the symbolism that has been embodied in the Western liberal tradition? On all sides it is apparent that the direction of individuals' "specific actions" has become confused and chartless. Increasingly, the way is left open for cynical manipulation of the words and phrases that have been, historically, inseparable from the liberal heritage. For fewer and fewer people is it possible to "suspend all antagonistic impulses, so that the symbol procures its required response in action." And it is the very decline of "vague ultimate reasons with their emotional attachments" that has become the major difficulty in our perspectives of freedom.

"A mind that is oriented," writes Susanne Langer, "no matter by what conscious or unconscious symbols, in material and social realities, can function freely and confidently even under great pressure of circumstance and in the face of hard problems. Its life is a smooth and skillful shuttling to and fro between sign-functions and symbolic functions, a steady interweaving of sensory interpretations, linguistic responses, inferences, memories, imaginative prevision, factual knowledge and tacit appreciations. . . . In such a mind, doubts of the 'meaning of life' are not apt to arise, for reality itself is intrinsically 'meaningful': it incorporates the symbols of Life and Death, Sin and Salvation. For a balanced active intelligence, reality is historical fact and significant form, the all-inclusive realm of science, myth, art, and comfortable common sense. . . .

"The mind, like all other organs, can draw its sustenance only from the surrounding world; our metaphysical symbols must spring from reality. Such adaptation always requires time, habit, tradition, and intimate knowledge of a way of life. If, now, the field of our unconscious symbolic orientation is suddenly plowed up by tremendous changes in the external world and in the social order, we lose our hold, our convictions, and therewith our effectual purposes. . . . All old symbols are gone, and thousands of average lives offer no new materials to a creative imagination. This, rather than physical want, is the starvation that threatens the modern worker, the tyranny of the machine. The withdrawal of all natural means for expressing the unity of personal life is a major cause of the distraction, irreligion, and unrest that mark the proletariat of all countries."[4]

Now, I cannot help thinking that the symbolic nightmare into which contemporary liberalism has been plunged, a nightmare that the brilliant writings of such men as de Jouvenel, Orwell, Koestler, and Mumford have made so vivid, is not the result, as Miss Langer suggests, of the nature of technological development or of alienation from old nature-symbols, though these may well be deeply involved; rather, it is the consequence of that centralization of social function and authority with which we have been concerned throughout this book. I do not deny that symbolic disruptions and dislocations of prejudgments may and do come from many types of intrusion into personal value systems. But the disruptions and dislocations we are most closely concerned with here, those which have made the quest for community and certainty so ominous an aspect of our age, come from the kinds of social disruption that have been the consequence of a system of power which has converted the historic plurality of allegiances and meaningful memberships into, increasingly, a kind of social monolith. In the process of conversion, old values and old symbols have had their social roots made desiccate.

The basic values of modern liberalism have been two—the individual and the moral sovereignty of the people. As values they are as noble today as they were when they were first brought into existence as the elements of modern liberal democracy. But they have become, manifestly, loose and wavering in their appeal. Worse, as we have seen, they have become the potent elements of modern Communist and Nazi despotism. We find ourselves baffled by the problem of not merely making them remain vivid values in our own society but of combating the uses which Communists today make of them throughout the world.

In the remaining two chapters of this book I shall consider in more detail the contexts of historic individualism and democracy and some of the problems created by disruptions in these contexts. Here, however, it is important to stress the close dependence of the whole conscious liberal heritage, with all its basic propositions, upon the subtle, infinitely complex lines of habit, tradition, and social relationship that have made this conscious heritage more than a mere set of formal propositions, that have made it instead a potent body of evocative symbols, striking deep chords in human appreciation and remembrance. The formal, overt judgments of liberalism have rested, historically, not merely upon processes of conscious reason and verification, but upon certain prejudgments that have seldom been drawn up for critical analysis until the most recent times. And these prejudgments have, in turn, been closely linked with a set of social relationships within which their symbolic fires have been constantly kept lighted through all the normal processes of work, function, and belief. It is the disruption of the relationship among judgment, prejudgment, and social context that confronts us at the present time—a disruption caused in very large part, as I believe, by the cultural mechanization and sterilization that have accompanied modern centralization of power.

When we consider either the "individual" or the "people," we are dealing, plainly, with ideal types. They are moral abstractions. This in no way lessens their potential efficacy, but it does call attention to the fact that their actual efficacy as symbols depends on the means by which they are translated concretely into the goals and actions of day to day living. Today, the formal values of individual and people remain as clamant as they ever were in the days of Montesquieu or Jefferson. But what have drastically changed are the contexts both of the *assimilation* of these values into everyday life and of their *realization* in any effective way in the nation at large.

Whereas modern liberalism began in the eighteenth century with an image of man as inherently self-sufficing and secure beyond the effects of all social change, the contemporary image of man is, as we have seen, almost the very opposite of this. And whereas in the eighteenth century the image of the people that glowed in the minds of such men as Jefferson was composed of elements supplied, actually, by a surrounding society strong in its social institutions and memberships, the image of society that now haunts man is one composed of the disunited, despairing masses.

We continue to ring changes on themes handed down from the eighteenth century without realizing that the power of the bells to stir consciousness is always limited by what already lies *within* consciousness. When this has become altered, no amount of frenzied change-ringing will suffice. For the symbols of liberalism, like the bells of the church, depend on prejudgments and social tradition.

Of all the philosophies of freedom in modern Western society, the most generally accepted and the most influential has been individualism. Whether with respect to economic, religious, or intellectual autonomies, the dominant assumption has been that the roots of these freedoms lie in the individual himself. The philosophy of individualism is based on a belief, Ramsay Muir has written, "in the value of the human personality and a conviction that the source of all progress lies in the free exercise of individual energy."

No fault is to be found with the declared purposes of individualism. As a philosophy it has correctly emphasized the fact that the ultimate criteria of freedom lie in the greater or lesser degrees of autonomy possessed by *persons.* A conception of freedom that does not center upon the ethical primacy of the person is either naive or malevolent. We have seen how another conception of freedom, the one that finds freedom in conformity to the General Will, in participation in collective identity, is the root of the totalitarian view of freedom and order. Any freedom worthy of the name is indubitably freedom of persons.

But from the unquestioned ethical centrality of the person it does not follow that the philosophy of individualism, as we have inherited it from the eighteenth and nineteenth centuries, is equally valid. For individualism is more than an ethic, historically; it is also a psychology and an implied theory of the relation between man and his institutions. And most of our difficulties with the philosophy of individualism at the present time come from our unconscious efforts to make the ethical aspect of individualism remain evocative when we have ceased to hold to the psychological and sociological premises of this philosophy.

Secular individualism of the eighteenth century arose on the basis of an image of man very different from the image prevalent in contemporary thought and action. And, as a philosophy, it existed in and was given unrecognized reinforcement by a social organization, the fundamentals of which no longer exist.

When the basic principles of modern liberalism were being formulated by such men as Locke, Montesquieu, Adam Smith, and Jefferson, the image of man luminous in the philosophical mind was an image constructed out of such traits as sovereign reason, stability, security, and indestructible motivations toward freedom and order. Man, abstract man, was deemed to be inherently self-sufficing, equipped by nature with both the instincts and the reason that could make him autonomous.

What we can now see with the advantage of hindsight is that, unconsciously, the founders of liberalism abstracted certain moral and psychological attributes from a *social organization* and considered these the timeless, natural, qualities of the *individual,* who was regarded as independent of the influences of any historically developed social organization. Those qualities that, in their entirety, composed the eighteenth-century liberal image of man were qualities actually inhering to a large extent in a set of institutions and groups, all of which were aspects of historical tradition. But, with the model of Newtonian mechanics before them, the moral philosophers insisted on reducing everything to human atoms in motion, to natural individuals driven by impulses and reason deemed to be innate in man.

Given this image of man as inherently self-sufficing, given the view of institutions and groups as but secondary, as shadows, so to speak, of the solid reality of man, it was inevitable that the strategy of freedom should have been based upon objectives of release and the emancipation of man from his fettering institutions. The philosophy of individualism, in short, began with the Christian-Judaic stress upon the ethical primacy of the person; but from that point it became a rationalist psychology devoted to the ends of the release of man from the old and a sociology based upon the view that groups and institutions are at best mere reflections of the solid and ineffaceable fact of the individual.

What was born in the eighteenth century and confirmed, as it seemed, by the French Revolution, was carried full-blown into the nineteenth century. Whole systems of economic, religious, and intellectual freedom were founded on the assumption that the essence of human behavior lies in what is *within* man, not in what exists between man and his institutions. All the basic manifestations of society—altruism, sympathy, economic gain, and the like—were held to be mere unfoldings of certain deeply rooted drives born in man and presided over by his sovereign reason.

The rationalist dichotomy of man and society was crucial to the ends of the liberal reformers of the eighteenth and nineteenth centuries. How else could the moral imperatives of emancipation be fulfilled except by the premise of man's fundamental separateness and his self-sufficiency? The demands of freedom appeared to be in the direction of the release of large numbers of individuals from the statuses and identities that had been forged in them by the dead hand of the past. A free society would be one in which individuals were morally and socially as well as politically free, free from groups and classes. It would be composed, in short, of socially and morally *separated* individuals. Order in society would be the product of a natural equilibrium of economic and political forces. Freedom would arise from the individual's release from all the inherited personal interdependences of traditional community, and from his existence in an impersonal, natural, economic order.

Thus, in Bentham's terms, the fundamental cement of society would be provided not through institutions but through certain "natural" and "sympathetic" identifications of interest arising in almost equal part from man's instinctual nature and from his sovereign reason. What Bentham was later to invoke as an "artificial" identification was, to be sure, the strong, sovereign State. But, for Bentham as for all the Utilitarians who followed him, the role of the State was conceived essentially as a kind of impersonal setting for the free play of personal interest. It might be a strong State. Indeed, as we have seen, the power of the State becomes very great in Bentham's philosophy. But whatever its omnipotence, the major function of the State consists, for Bentham, in the eradication of all the interdependences of society inherited from the past that act to repress the atomic, presocial instincts *and reason* of the individual. Between Bentham's political theory and his psychology of the individual there was the closest affinity. They are two sides of the same coin.

"It is not strange," George P. Adams trenchantly observes, "that this self-discovery and self-consciousness of the individual should have steadily mounted higher as the environment of individuals more and more takes on the form of an impersonal, causal, and mechanical structure. For the mobility and freedom of the individual can be won only as he becomes detached from his world; his world becomes separated from him only when organized and defined in objective and impersonal terms."[1]

Here, of course, the role of the new State was influential in men's conception of the individual units of society. If all authority becomes objectified, externalized, that is *centralized,* in the increasingly remote and impersonal State, the consequences to the primary forms of authority with which man has traditionally and subjectively identified himself are profound. They cease to be important. Their moral *virtues* are transferred, as it were, to him, even as their historic *authorities* have been transferred to the State.

The conception of society as an aggregate of morally autonomous, psychologically free, individuals, rather than as a collection of groups, is, in sum, closely related to a conception of society in which all legitimate authority has been abstracted from the primary communities and vested in the single sphere of the State. What is significant here is that when the philosophical individualists were dealing with the assumed nature of man, they were dealing in large part with a hypothetical being created by their political imaginations.

By almost all of the English liberals of the nineteenth century freedom was conceived not merely in terms of immunities from the powers of political government but, more significantly, in terms of the necessity of man's release from custom, tradition, and from local groups of every kind. Freedom was held to lie in emancipation from association, not within association.

Thus in what is perhaps the noblest of individualistic testaments of freedom in the nineteenth century, John Stuart Mill's essay *On Liberty,* there is the clear implication that membership in any kind of association or community represents an unfortunate limitation upon the creative powers of the individual. It is not Mill's *definition* of individuality that is at fault.

This is matchless. The fault lies rather in his psychological and sociological conception of the *conditions* necessary to the development of individuality.

Mill is generous in his praise of localism, association, and the "smaller patriotisms" when he is discussing administrative problems of centralization. But in matters pertaining to the nature of man and motivations he is too much the child of his father. For him as for the elder Mill, individuality is something derived from innate qualities alone and nourished solely by processes of separation and release.

Two

What we have learned under the guidance of studies in modern social psychology, with the dismaying spectacle before us of enlarging masses of insecure individuals seeking communal refuge of one sort or another, is that the rationalist image of man is theoretically inadequate and practically intolerable. We have learned that man is not self-sufficing in social isolation, that his nature cannot be deduced simply from elements innate in the germ plasm, and that between man and such social groups as the family, local group, and interest association there is an indispensable connection. We know no conception of individuality is adequate that does not take into consideration the myriad ties which normally bind the individual to others from birth to death.

As an abstract philosophy, individualism was tolerable in an age when the basic elements of social organization were still strong and psychologically meaningful. In fact, whatever its theoretical inadequacy, the philosophy of individualism may be said to have had a kind of pragmatic value in an age when the traditional primary relationships were, if anything, too strong, too confining. Today, however, the philosophy of individualism lacks even pragmatic justification. For the prime psychological problems of our age, the practical problems that is, are those not of release but of reintegration.

All the testimony of contemporary sociology and psychology joins in the conclusion that individuality cannot be understood save as the product of normatively oriented interaction with other persons. Whatever may lie neurologically embedded in the human being, the product of physical history, we know that a knowledge of man's actual behavior in society must from the outset take into consideration the whole stock of norms and cultural incentives which are the product of *social* history. The normative order in society is fundamental to all understanding of human nature. "The normative order," writes Kingsley Davis, "makes the factual order of human society possible."[2] We do not see, think, react, or become stimulated except in terms of the socially inherited norms of human culture.

But the normative order of values and incentives is itself inseparable from the associative order. Culture does not exist autonomously; it is set always in the context of social relationships. Only thus do the ends and patterns of culture make themselves vivid and evocative to human beings. And we have learned that with the dislocation of the social relationships which immediately surround the human being there occurs also a disruption of his cultural or moral order. Hence, as we have seen, the calculated destruction, in totalitarian countries, of the tangible social structures of human life. For, with the obliteration of these, the task of normative nihilism is made easy.

The greatest single lesson to be drawn from the social transformations of the twentieth century, from the phenomena of individual insecurity and the mass quest for community, is that the intensity of men's motivations toward freedom and culture is unalterably connected with the relationships of a social organization that has structural coherence and functional significance. From innumerable observations and controlled studies we have learned that the discipline of values *within* a person has a close and continuing relationship with the discipline of values supported by human inter-relationships. "Only by anchoring his own conduct . . . in something as large, substantial, and super-individual as the culture of a group," wrote the late Kurt Lewin, "can the individual stabilize his new beliefs sufficiently to keep them immune from the day to day fluctuations of moods and influences of which he, as an individual, is subject."[3]

The intensity of personal incentive, whether in the context of psychiatric therapy or in the day to day life of the normal human being, tends to fluctuate with the intensity of meaningful social relationships. This is what we have learned from studies of motivation in learning, from studies of character formation, and from observation of personal morale in all kinds of stress situations. This is what we have learned, through the researches of such men as Elton Mayo and F. J. Roethlisberger, about the performance of individual workers in industry. Between the vitality of incentives to production and the vitality of the worker's informal social relationships in the work room of the factory there is a crucial relationship.[4]

So too, in the recent war, it was made clear that the combat effectiveness of military units and, conversely, the incidence of combat fatigue and neurosis, had much less to do with the calculated indoctrination of "why we fight" values than with the solidarity and sense of relatedness to others in the military unit itself. Whatever the individual soldier's greater or less comprehension of, and devotion to, the purposes of the war, whatever the degree of hatred of the enemy in the breast of the individual soldier, what he actually fought on and was spiritually supported by was his sense of relatedness to others in his platoon or company. It was this concrete association, nourished by innumerable stimuli, that made combat and privation tolerable when belief was weak and understanding unclear.[5]

The philosophy of individualism, John Dewey wrote a generation ago, "ignores the fact that the mental and moral structure of individuals, the pattern of their desires and purposes, change with every great change in social constitution. Individuals who are not bound together in associations, whether domestic, economic, religious, political, artistic, or educational, are monstrosities. It is absurd to suppose that the ties which hold them together are merely external and do not react into mentality and character, producing the framework of personal disposition."[6]

As we have learned from the recent literature of the concentration camp and from studies of uprooted and displaced persons, moral conscience, the sense of civilized decency, will not long survive separation from the associative ties that normally reinforce and give means of expression to the imperatives of conscience. Separate man from the primary contexts of normative association, as the nineteenth-century individualist enjoined in effect, and you separate him not only from the basic values of a culture but from the sources of individuality itself.

All of this, I repeat, is well enough known at the present time in the literature of sociology and social psychology. Yet there remains a curious inability to recognize the implications of what is known when we come to deal with such matters as cultural, economic, and religious freedom. We continue, too many of us, to deal with practical problems in these areas and to interpret in terms of perspectives created originally on the basis of certain premises regarding the nature of man which have by now been largely repudiated. It is as though we continued to hold tenaciously to a derived proposition in geometry long after we had discarded the axioms upon which it could alone rest.

Three

Much of the argument of the individualist with respect to the nature of freedom derives from the apparent fact that the most intellectually creative ages in history have been ages of the widespread release of individuals from ties of traditional values and relationships. Ages of cultural achievement, great periods of economic prosperity, and epochs of religious awakening have been interpreted as periods of extreme individualism.

The birth of new ideas, of art forms, of technologies, the discovery of new sources of wealth, all of this has behind it—so the argument runs—the individual escaping his social group, his class, family, and community. Such relationships may give security but do not excite the imagination. Great ages of intellectual achievement are always ages of disorder, for the displacement of moral and social cohesion is but the reverse side of the release of the creative individual. To read the funeral oration of Pericles, the speeches in the plays of the Elizabethan dramatists, or the essays of Francis Bacon, is to be put in touch with a vision of the illimitable vistas that lie before men who have emancipated themselves from tradition, and who have struck off the restrictive ties of binding social relationships. In the fact of a *separation* between the individual and authority has commonly been found the secret of the cultural freedom and prosperity of the world's great ages.

In his interesting book, *The Open Society and Its Enemies,* K. R. Popper has recently held up to us once again the rationalist's view of the problem of freedom as it manifests itself in cultural achievement. Like many before him, Popper sees the great age of Athens in the fifth century B.C. and the modern Renaissance in Western Europe as ages of "individualism." What is central to Popper is the vision of a society in intellectual ferment, in persistent critical self-analysis, and in a perpetual outburst of individual expression. These are ages, he argues, recently released from the dead hand of tradition, membership, and tribalism. For Popper the greatness of Athens was at its very apogee when the Sophists and Socrates, among others, were declaring their relentless hostility toward all forms of moral or social interdependence. Such nihilistic declarations were of a piece, Popper seems to believe, with the effective psychological conditions that underlay the whole efflorescence of genius in the drama, in art, philosophy, sculpture, and architecture in Athens of the fifth century B.C. In all of these spheres the cake of custom, the net of the past, was being broken, and man, absolute man, emerged to make his contributions.

The rationalist argument is a plausible one and inevitably attractive to all who find the greatest repressions of society to lie in the smallest and most personal of interdependences. But it raises certain difficulties.

We readily grant that it is the freedom of *persons* which is crucial in any period of intellectual achievement. Great works of art or literature are not created by anonymous organizations. They are the concrete results of personal performance. But from the obvious centrality of the *person* in intellectual or cultural achievement it follows neither that such achievement is the sole consequence of innate *individual* forces, nor that it is the result merely of processes of *separation.* We may grant that there is, in the achievement of any great work, whether it be a painting or a treatise in metaphysics, a relatively high degree of detachment in the mind of the artist or philosopher. But this does not justify our emphasizing only the psychological and social facts of individuation which the rationalist has made central in his interpretation.

We are not justified in disregarding the profoundly important interdependences between the artist and his city, his locality, his religion, or the various other communal influences that give his work its inspiration and direction. The greatness of Athenian tragedy may have been the consequence, in considerable degree, of an increasing detachment which made it possible for an Aeschylus, a Sophocles, or Euripides to dramatize the great moral problems of their time. But these tragedies were also the consequence of profound and deeply evocative relationships with the communal contexts of Greek religion, kinship, and the community. To emphasize one set of psychological facts at the expense of the other is small contribution to that total picture of the conditions of cultural achievement which we seek.

The case of rationalist individualism would be stronger as an explanation of cultural achievement in the world's great ages if there were not every reason for applying the term "individualistic" even more surely to those ages which, by universal assent, must be regarded as ages of cultural decadence and morbidity. If individual detachment and release are the crucial elements of cultural achievement, we should expect to find a constant increase in the quality of the Athenian culture that extended beyond the age of Pericles into the age following the Peloponnesian Wars. In any tangible sense of the word, *this* was the age of moral and social "individualism." This age, which Sir Gilbert Murray, Rostovtzeff, and Glotz have described for us in such melancholy fashion, was assuredly an age of individualism, measured in terms of the individual's release from the constraints and symbolism of the past. But it was increasingly an age of cultural sterility, of "failure of nerve," of philosophical morbidity. It is also pertinent to observe that this was an age of mounting political despotism.

Neither personal freedom nor personal achievement can ever be separated from the contexts of community. These are the contexts not of mechanical restraint but of the incentives and values that men wish to express in enduring works and to defend against wanton external aggression. This is not to deny the role of the individual, nor the reality of personal differences. It is assuredly not to accept the argument of crude social determinism—which asserts that creative works of individuals are but the reflection of group interests and group demands. It is merely to insist on the fundamental fact that the perspectives and incentives of the free creative mind arise out of communities of purpose. The artist may alter these, reshape them, give them an intensity and design that no one else has ever given them or ever will give them, but he is not thereby removed from the sources of his inspiration.

What Livingston Lowes has written on the creative process in his *Road to Xanadu* is relevant here. "'Creation,' like 'creative,' is one of those hypnotic words which are prone to cast a spell upon the understanding and dissolve our thinking into haze. And out of this nebulous state of the intellect springs a strange but widely prevalent idea. The shaping spirit of Imagination sits aloof, like God, as he is commonly conceived, creating in some thaumaturgic fashion out of nothing its visionary world. . . . [But] we live, every one of us—the mutest and most inglorious with the rest—at the center of a world of images. . . . Intensified and sublimated and controlled though they be, the ways of the creative faculty are the universal ways of that streaming yet consciously directed something which we know (or think we know) as life. Creative genius, in plainer terms, works through processes which are common to our kind, but these processes are superlatively enhanced."[7]

Only in the modern European world, and largely under the influence of romantic intensifications of the individualist hypothesis, has there arisen in popular form the myth of the artist as solitary, lonely, and dependent for his genius only upon what he spins from his inner consciousness. The notion that artistic achievement is always connected in some degree with rootlessness and alienation, that art itself is asocial, has been singularly effective in disguising the actual contexts of creative imagination.[8]

Not by setting up an imaginary release from communities of belief and purpose do we look into the springs of intellectual creativeness and freedom. The free artist, scientist, or teacher is always, in some degree, involved in the contexts of communication and association. His may be a detached position; he may be the recipient of impulses sent out from a variety of fields; he may live, more than do most of us, toward the periphery of his community and thus be in more sensitive nearness to other communities. But what is crucial to the creator is not release or separation, not inward withdrawal, but imagination feeding upon diverse social and cultural participation. For the artist as for all of us the sense of creative freedom demands an environment that is concrete and plural in its cultural manifestations.[9]

Four

Nor does economic freedom rest upon the lone individual. It never has. But because some of the principal problems of early nineteenth-century economic development were provoked by the persistence of certain rigid social structures, a whole ideology of economic freedom arose on the basis of the eighteenth-century atomistic view of man. Society was envisaged by the classical economist as being, naturally, an aggregate of socially and culturally emancipated individuals, each free to respond to the drives that lay buried within his nature. Economic freedom would be the result, it was declared, of the same conditions that produced economic equilibrium: masses of autonomous, separated individuals, a minimum of social constraint of any kind, and a reliance upon the automatic workings of the free market.

But here too we are in the presence of the typical failure of the rationalist to recognize the social memberships of men in society and the dependence of human motivations upon these memberships. What we observed in an earlier chapter regarding the social contexts of economic motivations has as much pertinence to the problem of freedom as it does to the problem of order.

There is indeed a sense in which the so-called free market never existed at all save in the imaginations of the rationalists. What has so often been called the natural economic order of the nineteenth century turns out to be, when carefully examined, a special set of political controls and immunities existing on the foundations of institutions, most notably the family and local community, which had nothing whatsoever to do with the essence of capitalism. Freedom of contract, the fluidity of capital, the mobility of labor, and the whole factory system were able to thrive and to give the appearance of internal stability only because of the continued existence of institutional and cultural allegiances which were, in every sense, precapitalist. Despite the rationalist faith in natural economic harmonies, the real roots of economic stability lay in groups and associations that were not essentially economic at all.[10]

Most of the relative stability of nineteenth-century capitalism arose from the fact of the very *incompleteness* of the capitalist revolution. Because large areas of Europe and the United States remained predominantly rural and strongly suffused by precapitalist relationships and desires, a large measure of national stability coexisted with the rise of the new industrial cities and the new practices of manufacture and commerce. Through ingenious processes of rationalization this institutional stability was converted by the economic rationalist into an imaginary equilibrium of the market place. The struggle of man against man, the individual striving for gain and success, the conversion of real property into shares of industrial wealth, unrestrained competition, and complete freedom of contract—all of this, it was imagined, had in it the materials of stability as well as freedom.

But there has never been a time when a successful economic system has rested upon purely individualistic drives or upon the impersonal relationships so prized by the rationalists. There are always, in fact, associations and incentives nourished by the non-economic processes of kinship, religion, and various other forms of social relationships.

Unfortunately, it has been the fate of these external institutions and relationships to suffer almost continuous attrition during the capitalist age. First the gild, the nucleated village, and the landed estate underwent destruction. For a long time, however, the family, local community, tangible property, and class remained as powerful, though external, supports of the economic system which the rationalists saw merely as the outcome of man's fixed instincts and reason. But, in more recent decades, as we have already seen, even these associations have become steadily weaker as centers of security and allegiance. Modern rationalization and impersonalization of the economic world are but the other side of that process which the Hammonds called the "decline of custom" and which we may see as the dislocation of certain types of social membership. The result, as Joseph Schumpeter wrote a decade ago, "shows so well that the capitalist order not only rests on props made of extra-capitalist material but also derives its energy from extra-capitalist patterns of behavior which at the same time it is bound to destroy."[11] And in this whole process the directive role of the political State becomes ever greater.

Now, one may write persuasively about creeping totalitarianism and, conversely, about the felicities of the free market, as Hayek and others have recently done. No one can seriously question the abstract superiority of a society in which freedom of economic choice exists compared to a society in which it does not. Moreover, only the willfully blind will fail to mark the danger to economic freedom created by increasing political controls at the present time.

But, ultimately, human institutions depend for their preservation on the strength of the allegiances which such institutions create in human beings. To divorce economic ends from the contexts of social association within which allegiance to these ends can be nourished is fatal. Not all the asserted advantages of mass production and corporate bigness will save capitalism if its purposes become impersonal and remote, separated from the symbols and relationships that have meaning in human lives.

As the vividness and meaning of the symbolism of capitalism wane, so do the human desires to maintain it. This symbolism has always been closely embodied in the social structures within which human beings have lived, structures which have had a close and determining relation to the economic ends of capitalism. Incentives to economic freedom, like those of economic production, are the product not of instincts but of social relationships and of tangible norms and institutions.

But the recent history of capitalism, especially in its vast corporate forms, has tended to weaken steadily the symbolic and the normative aspect of economic life. Schumpeter has described it well: "The capitalist process, by substituting a mere parcel of shares for the walls of and the machines in a factory, takes the life out of the idea of property. . . . Dematerialized, defunctionalized and absentee ownership does not impress and call forth moral allegiance as the vital form of property did. Eventually there will be *nobody* left who really cares to stand for it—nobody within and without the precincts of the big concerns."[12]

Economic freedom cannot rest upon moral atomism or upon large-scale impersonalities. It never has. Economic freedom has prospered, and continues to prosper, only in areas and spheres where it has been joined to a flourishing associational life. Economic freedom cannot be separated from the non-individualistic contexts of association and community of moral purpose. Capitalism has become weakest, as a system of allegiances and incentives, where these social resources have become weak and where no new forms of association and symbolism have arisen to replace the old.

Put in this light is it not obvious that the rise of the modern labor union and the cooperative have been powerful forces *in support* of capitalism and economic freedom? Despite many businessmen's opposition to these associations, they, as Lenin and his fellow Marxists realized with dismay, actually *reinforce* capitalism. The labor union and the cooperative are foremost among new forms of association that have served to keep alive the symbols of economic freedom. As such, it should be remarked, they have been the first objects of economic destruction in totalitarian countries. In such associations the goals of production, distribution, and consumption can be joined to the personal sense of belonging to a social order. The individual entrepreneur, it may be observed, is less dangerous to the totalitarian than the labor union or cooperative. For in such an association the individual can find a sense of relatedness to the entire culture and thus become its eager partisan.

These and related associations are the true supports of economic freedom at the present time. Not to the imaginary motives of the individualist but to the associational realities of the labor union, the cooperative, and the enlightened industrial community must we look for the real defenses against political invasions of economic freedom. But unfortunately there are still large areas of the economy and large segments of public opinion that are inclined to treat such associations as these as manifestations of collectivism, all of a piece with the authoritarian State. The mythology of individualism continues to reign in discussions of economic freedom. By too many partisans of management the labor union is regarded as a major obstacle to economic autonomy and as partial paralysis of capitalism.

But to weaken, whether from political or individualistic motives, the social structures of family, local community, labor union, cooperative, or industrial community, is to convert a culture into an atomized mass. Such a mass will have neither the will, nor the incentive, nor the ability to combat tendencies toward political collectivism. The transition from free capitalism to forced collectivism is easy and will hardly be noticed when a population has lost the sense of social and moral participation in the former. Everything that separates the individual from this sense of participation pushes him inevitably in the direction of an iron collectivism, which will make a new kind of participation both possible and mandatory.

Capitalism is either a system of social and moral allegiances, resting securely in institutions and voluntary associations, or it is a sand heap of disconnected particles of humanity. If it is, or is allowed to become, the latter, there is nothing that can prevent the rise of centralized, omnicompetent political power. Lacking a sense of participation in economic society, men will seek it, as Hilaire Belloc told us, in the Servile State.

Five

In religion, no less than in other areas of faith and action, the desire for freedom is inseparable from the ties of close association. I do not deny that the meaning and values of religion exist ultimately in the consciousness of the individual human being alone. And it is plain in the historical record that religions die when they are allowed to become divorced from individual purposes, when the letter and the ritual become ends in themselves. So much is true, but there is nevertheless a profound relevance in those contemporary efforts, as we have seen in an earlier chapter of this book, to strengthen the associative, the symbolic, and the hierarchical aspects of modern, especially Protestant, religion.

The experience of the present century, especially in Europe, has taught us that the religions most likely to survive the manipulations of hostile governments are those that are most strongly supported by the foundations of community and clear social status. In Nazi Germany, as we have learned, the religions most deeply rooted in hierarchy and ritual proved to be the most successful in holding the faiths of their individual members and in insulating these members from the spiritual appeals of totalitarian leaders. Where visible religious ties were weak, where faith was unsupported by the sense of communal membership, where the individual alone was conceived to be the sole vessel of grace, defenses against the powerful organizational ethos of totalitarianism were too often lacking.

In the non-totalitarian West, during the past few decades, it has become apparent, I believe, that the uncertainties and tensions of our urban-industrial society are met more successfully by religions strong in the values of community and tradition than by those that seek to rest upon individual faith alone. The perennial quest for meaning, never so urgent as in our own day, cannot help but be eased by the presence of landmarks formed of clear symbols and ritual that arise out of communal tradition.

The desire for religious freedom can be no greater than the desire for religious *order*. Lacking a clear sense of religion as a way of life, as an area of articulate membership, of status and collective meaning, man is not likely to care for long whether he is free or not free in religious pursuits. In any event, despots have never worried about religion that is confined mutely to individual minds. It is religion as community, or rather as a plurality of communities, that has always bestirred the reprisals of rulers engaged in the work of political tyranny.

Historians who have stressed the profound *social* appeal of early Christianity have not erred.[13] Great as was the early Church's spiritual message of hope, evocative as were its doctrines of salvation in the City of God, the remarkable successes of Christianity among the atomized masses of the Roman Empire cannot be separated from the earthly security which the tightly organized, communally oriented, Christian groups offered. The new religion of Christianity gave to its members a profound sense of social status and collective involvement as well as a burning message of deferred salvation.

During the Protestant Reformation, as we have seen, much of the emphasis upon the church visible was transferred to the church invisible, and the individual man of faith replaced the corporate Church as the repository of divine guidance. Much of the theology of Protestantism, like the theory of economic rationalism, was founded upon an assumption of the individual's inherent, indestructible stability of purpose. Because for the religious, as well as the economic, reformer the corruptions of society seemed to flow from an excess of associative membership and works, the individual alone became the *summum bonum* of religious life. Faith in God and incentives toward religious piety were held by the early Protestants to lie in the self-sufficing individual, even as incentives toward work were declared by the economic rationalist to be similarly embedded in the very nature of the individual. Hence, the Protestant leaders gave little direct attention to the social reinforcements of conscience and faith.

But in the contemporary world we have learned that individual faith unsupported is likely to dissolve altogether under the acids of materialism and the invasions of political power. We have learned that large numbers of nominal Christians are prone, when conditions become desperate, to forsake mere creed for mass movements that make central the values of organization and status. Even when the lure of totalitarianism is not strong, when there is no alternative collective escape, individual faith that is unsupported communally often tends to collapse into self-doubt and frustration.

"We have reached the point," observes Reinhold Niebuhr, "where the more traditional and historic churches, with their theological discipline, are more successful in evoking a genuinely Christian faith than the churches which dispensed with these disciplines. American Protestantism cannot regain its spiritual vitality without seeking a better synthesis between religious spontaneity and religious tradition and discipline."[14]

Equally important is the relation between religion and other forms of community. Early Protestant leaders were dealing with individuals whose basic motivations and prejudgments had been well formed by the traditional family and local community, as well as by the historic medieval Church.[15] In the present world we cannot do this so easily, for, as we have seen, these unities have become weakened under the impacts of modern political and industrial history. The union of family, local community, and religion is strong wherever religion has flourished, for motivations toward religious zeal cannot be nourished by the structure of the church alone. In the contemporary world the continuing reality of religion as an integrating force will depend on the successful fusion of religious impulse and religious organization with all forms of social life that implicate the lives of human beings. However fundamental and ultimately justifying are the private devotions within religion, the success of religion among large numbers of people, like the success of any structure of human faith, depends on the degree to which spiritual creed and values are integrated with *associative* purposes.

Six

Despotism never takes root in barren soil. When, in the first century, the Emperor Augustus decreed that an image of himself should be placed upon the hearth, along with the images of the sacred Lares and Penates, thus extending the symbolism of the State to the very roots of domestic society, he was taking a step that would never have been feasible a century or two earlier when Roman society was organized in terms of the solidarity of the family. Only because, during the century preceding the triumph of Augustus, the basic social unities of the Roman community had become weakened under the harsh impact of war and economic distress was it possible for this political invasion of the household to take place. The entrenchment of *Imperator Caesar divi filius Augustan,* in the privacy of individual consciousness is a fact understandable only in light of the creation of masses of socially "free" individuals. Despite our admiration for the cultural effects of the emergence of the individual during the Augustan age of letters, we cannot help but see the relation between this growing intellectual and moral individualism and the incessant centralization of political power.

Nor can we help but see the same fatal combination of individualism and political power in the modern era. The inadequacy of individualism as a theory of freedom lies plainly written in the conditions we see spreading in the Western world today: on the one hand, enlarging masses of socially "free," insecure, individuals; on the other, the constant increase in the custodial powers of a State that looms ever larger as the only significant refuge for individuals who insist upon escaping from the moral consequences of individualism. The value of the dignity of man is perhaps more vocal today than it has ever been, but the plain fact is that the means of reinforcing this value seem ever more remote. As a philosophy of means, individualism is now not merely theoretically inadequate; it has become tragically irrelevant, even intolerable.

It is absurd to suppose that the rhetoric of nineteenth-century individualism will offset present tendencies in the direction of the absolute political community. Alienation, frustration, the sense of aloneness—these, as we have seen, are major states of mind in Western society at the present time. The image of man is decidedly different from what it was in the day of Mill. It is ludicrous to hold up the asserted charms of individual release and emancipation to populations whose most burning problems are those arising, today, from moral and social release. To do so is but to make the way of the Grand Inquisitor the easier. For this is the appeal, as we have seen, of the totalitarian prophet—to "rescue" masses of atomized individuals from their intolerable individualism. Once partially in the communal State, men will not leave it to walk into a moral and social vacuum.

The longing for community which now exists as perhaps the most menacing fact of the Western world will not be exorcised by incantations drawn from the writings of Bentham, Mill, and Spencer. No theory of freedom in our age will be either effective or relevant that does not recognize the present centrality of the quest for community.

Seven

It would be calamitous, however, if the creative, liberal *purposes* of individualism were to be lost because their social contexts and psychological requirements are incapable of renewal. The individualist has been right in his insistence that genuine freedom has nothing to do with the nervous exhilaration that comes from participation in the crusading mass, nothing to do with acquiescence before a General Will. He has been right in his contention that real freedom is bound up with the existence of autonomies of personal choice among clear cultural alternatives. Above all, the individualist has been right in his stress upon human *privacy*.

"All freedom," wrote Lord Acton, "consists *in radice* in the preservation of an inner sphere exempt from State power." The political mystic may boggle at this, but the proposition is, when amended to include any type of power, political or other, irrefutable. Both freedom and the desire for freedom are nourished within the realization of spiritual privacy and among privileges of personal decision. Apart from these, any structure of authority becomes almost limitless in its scope.

But to recognize the role of privacy and the importance of autonomies of choice is to be forced to recognize also the crucial problem of the *contexts* of privacy and personal choice. For man does not, cannot, live alone. His freedom is a social, not biologically derived, process. We are forced to consider, as I have argued in this chapter, the indispensable role of the small social groups in society. It is the intimacy and security of each of these groups that provide the psychological context of individuality and the reinforcement of personal integrity. And it is the *diversity* of such groups that creates the possibility of the numerous cultural alternatives in a society.

In dealing, however, with the role of the small social group in society, we are inevitably brought face to face with the problem of the distribution of *power* in society. For, in the same way that the social group forms the context of the development of personality, the larger structure of authority in society forms the context of the greater or lesser significance possessed by the small social groups. Social groups, I have argued, thrive only when they possess significant functions and authorities in the lives of their members. When all functions and authorities are consolidated in the State, as is true in totalitarian Russia and was true in Germany under Hitler, the role of the autonomous social group is destroyed. We cannot deal adequately with the social group, in short, without taking into consideration the system of political power within which it exists. Here we must turn our attention to the political framework of democracy.

Definitions of democracy are as varied as the interests of persons and generations. Democracy is made identical with intellectual freedom, with economic justice, with social welfare, with tolerance, with piety, moral integrity, the dignity of man, and general civilized decency. As a word, democracy has come to be a kind of terminological catch-all for the historic virtues of civilization even as the word totalitarianism has become a catch-all for its evils. But the understanding of political democracy, its excellences and capacities, is served no better by this indiscriminating approach than is the understanding of totalitarianism.

Democracy may be associated with any and all of the virtues listed above, but it is, fundamentally, a theory and structure of *political power*. The historical root of democracy, as distinguished from liberalism which is historically a theory of *immunity* from power, is the proposition that the legitimacy of all political power arises from, and only from, the consent of the governed, the *people*. Lincoln's famous definition of democracy as government of, by, and for the people cannot be improved upon either as a moral ideal or as a historical description. And it is as right and as institutionally relevant today as it was in Lincoln's day.

But with respect to the "people," as with the "individual," everything depends upon the practical, cultural contexts in which we choose to regard the people. The "people," no less than the "individual," is an abstraction, subject not merely to varying verbal usages but also to historically changing political demands and moral imperatives.

We may regard the people as simply a numerical aggregate of individuals regarded for political and administrative purposes as discrete and socially separated, an aggregate given form and meaning only by the nature of the State and its laws. Or, alternatively, we may regard the people as indistinguishable from a culture, its members as inseparable from the families, unions, churches, professions, and traditions that actually compose a culture.

The difference between the two ways of considering the people is vast, and it is decisive in any political theory of democracy. The "will of the people is one thing, substantively, when it is conceived in purely political terms as arising from a vast aggregate of socially separated, politically integrated *individuals*. It is something very different when it is conceived in terms of the social unities and cultural traditions in which political, like all other, judgments are actually formed and reinforced.

In the first view of the people, a conception of political democracy must inevitably rest heavily upon the State and its formal agencies of function and control. Units of administration become, necessarily, atomistic individuals, conceived abstractly and divorced from the cultural contexts. When the people are regarded in this way, the principal problem of democratic theory and administration becomes not the larger problem of distribution of function and authority in *society* but, rather, the discovery of means by which the human being is brought ever closer to the people *in their political wholeness* and, in practical terms, to the formal administrative structure of the State. By omitting reference to the other authority-wielding and need-gratifying associations in society, by focusing on the abstract political mass, this view of the people becomes administratively committed at the outset to a potentially totalitarian view of the State.

But if we take the second view of the people, the State emerges as but *one* of the associations of man's existence. Equally important to a democratic theory founded on this perspective is the whole plurality of other associations in society. The intermediary associations and the spontaneous social groups which compose society, rather than atomized political particles, become the prime units of theoretical and practical consideration. The major objective of political democracy becomes that of making harmonious and effective the varied group allegiances which exist in society, not sterilizing them in the interest of a monistic political community.

Historically, we find both conceptions of the people in the writings of democratic philosophers and statesmen. But it is the second, the pluralist, conception that is more relevant to the actual history of democracy, especially in the United States, England, the Scandinavian countries, and Switzerland. And, as I shall emphasize in this chapter, it is the reaffirmation of this conception that seems to me absolutely indispensable to the success of liberal democracy at the present time.

It would be naive, however, to fail to see the powerful influence that is now exerted everywhere by the first, the unitary, view of the people and democracy. It is highly important that we examine this unitary tradition of democracy, for the difference between it and the pluralist tradition may well determine our effort to maintain liberal democracy under the pressure of the powerful quest for community in the present age.

Two

The unitary view of democracy, like the ideology of the political community with which it is so closely allied, arose in France during the latter part of the eighteenth century. As a theory it was constructed in light of prevailing rationalist conceptions of man and society, and as an attack upon the still largely feudal social structure. It was based foremost upon the premise that the authorities and responsibilities wielded historically by kings, nobles, and churchmen belonged by nature to the people and should, as a matter of practical policy, be transferred to the people. But the French rationalists used the term people in a way that was remarkably abstract and as divorced from circumstance as some of their other terms.

The image of the people that governed the minds of men like Rousseau and Condorcet and was to spread in revolutionary fashion throughout the world in the nineteenth century was an image derived not from history or experience but from the same kind of conceptualization that had produced the fateful conception of the General Will. Just as the "real" will of the people was distinguished by Rousseau and his disciples from the attitudes and beliefs actually held at any given time by the people, so, in this rationalist view, the "people" had to be distinguished from the actual plurality of persons which experience revealed. If right government was to be made a reality by the rationalists, the "people" had to be separated from existing institutions and beliefs and brought into the single association of the people's State.

Just as the rationalist made the realization of individuality contingent upon the individual's release from his primary contexts of association, so he made the realization of the "people's will" dependent on the release of the whole people—abstractly regarded—from traditional institutions and authorities. And just as the rationalist conceptually endowed the individual with social instincts and drives independent of any social organization, so he endowed the people itself with a natural harmony and stability that would give it all the necessary requisites of persistence and continuity. What we may notice in the case of the rationalist's construct of the people, as in his construct of the individual, is the unconscious transfer of virtues, stabilities, and motivations from a *historical social organization* to an entity regarded as naturally independent of all historical change and social pressure.

Here, of course, the philosophy of Progress was marvelously comforting. For the very essence of the idea of secular progress was its premise that history is inherently organizational in direction, leading always, and without the need of man's guiding hand, to ever higher conditions of civilization. The consequences of institutional dislocation, of the ruthless separating of the people from cherished values and memberships, could be disregarded. History would supply its own correctives. It was only necessary to be certain that the *obstacles* to progress—classes, religious institutions, family solidarities, gilds, and so forth—were removed.

Inevitably the principal strategy of unitary democracy came to be fixed, like the strategies of nationalism and military socialism, in terms of the sterilization of old social loyalties, the emancipation of the people from local and regional authorities, and the construction of a scene in which the individual would be the sole unit, and the State the sole association, of society. Hence, the rising stress on large-scale bureaucracy: to provide new agencies representative of the *whole* people for the discharge of powers and responsibilities formerly resident in classes, parishes, and families. Hence, the increasing administrative centralization of society: to reduce in number and influence the intermediate social authorities. Hence the growing stress upon standardization: to increase the number of cultural qualities shared by the people as a whole and to diminish those shared only by fractions of the population. Hence, also, the drive toward political collectivism: to bring into full light that pre-existent harmony which the rationalists never doubted made a natural unity of the people.

State and individual were the two elements of the unitary theory of democracy. The abstract individual was conceived as the sole bearer of rights and responsibilities. The State, conceived in the image of people who lay incorruptible beneath the superstructure of society, would be the area of fraternity and secular rehabilitation. All that lay between these two elements—gilds, churches, professions, classes, unions of all kinds—were suspect for their fettering influence upon the individual and their divisive consequences to the people's State.

This, in its essentials, is the unitary tradition of democracy. It is, despite its exalted motives, almost indistinguishable from the ideology of the absolute political community. This is the tradition that provides so much of the historic relation between democracy and nationalism, between democracy and collectivism, between democracy and that whole tendency toward cultural standardization which has periodically alienated some of the most liberal of minds. This is the tradition that offers so many of the catchwords and deceptive slogans of contemporary Communism in its typical forms of the "People's States." This is the tradition that led Proudhon to define democracy, bitterly, as the State magnified to the nth power, and Tocqueville to see in it, for all his reluctant admiration for democracy, the seeds of despotism greater than anything before provided by history.

In its most impressive form, this tradition of unitary, collectivist democracy was largely confined, in the nineteenth century, to France and Germany, and to areas that came under their political and cultural influence. The long tradition of Roman law, with its unitary legal premises, the profound influence of the French Revolution, and the growing attraction of the centralized Napoleonic Code provided in these countries a highly propitious set of circumstances for the development of the unitary conception of democracy.

From the Continent, however, the ideas of unitary democracy and centralized administration have spread widely during the past half-century. Beginning in the last part of the nineteenth century these ideas took root in the United States and England, fed by the soil of nationalism which, in the

United States, had been enriched by the Civil War, and given increasing relevance by the social callousness of the new business class. Given the mounting evils of the new industrialism, the appearance of new structures of economic power beyond anything seen before, and the widening incidence of economic insecurity, the techniques of administrative centralization were tempting indeed to men of good will. As against the possibilities of redress and security inherent in voluntary association, in the church, and in the local community, those of the State seemed not merely greater but infinitely more swift in possible attainment. Increasingly, American liberalism became committed to the State as the major area of social rehabilitation and to administrative centralization as the means. Imperceptibly the historic emphasis upon localism was succeeded by nationalism, pluralism by monism, and decentralization by centralization.

Today, it is the widening appeal of the collectivist, unitary ideal of democracy, set in conditions of social dislocation and moral alienation, stimulated by the demands of mass warfare, that makes the problem of power so ominous in the Western democracies.

Three

We may see in the administrative techniques of unitary democracy certain justifications of a historical nature. Given a society overpowered by inherited traditions, traditions manifestly inimical to both technical advancement and human rights; given a society that is nearly stationary from the hold of ecclesiastical, class, or kinship ties, and overrich to the point of chaos in local and regional diversity, the techniques of administrative uniformity and centralization can have a pragmatic value that is unquestionable. Such, in considerable degree, was the European society of the eighteenth century. Such, in even larger degree, is the society of, say, contemporary India.

Plainly, however, we are not, in the United States, living in that kind of society. Ours is a society characterized increasingly, as we have seen, by the sterilization of group differences—local, class, regional, and associative—which lie outside the administrative framework of the State. And ours is a State characterized by ever-rising centralization of function and authority. Both characteristics—social atomization and political centralization—are the unmistakable attributes of the beginnings of mass society. And because of these social and political realities the requirements of liberal democracy are profoundly different from what they were a century or two ago.

The principal problems of liberal democracy today arise from what Philip Selznick has so aptly called the "institutional vulnerability" of our society.[1] This is a vulnerability reflected in the diminished moral appeal of those primary centers of cultural allegiance within which the larger ends of liberal society take on binding meaning. It is reflected in the relative ease with which totalitarian strategies penetrate the normal cultural enclosures of institutional life.

"The decay of parliaments," G. D. H. Cole has written, "has accompanied the democratization of electorates not because democracy is wrong, but because we have allowed the growth of huge political organizations to be accompanied by the atrophy of smaller ones, on which alone they can be securely built."[2] While we seek constantly to make democracy more secure in the world by diplomatic agreements and national security legislation, we do not often remind ourselves that the most powerful resources of democracy lie in the cultural allegiances of citizens, and that these *allegiances* are nourished psychologically in the smaller, internal areas of family, local community, and association.

These are the areas that contain the images of the larger society, the areas within which human beings are able to define, and render meaningful, democratic values. When the small areas of association become sterile psychologically, as the result of loss of institutional significance, we find ourselves resorting to ever-increasing dosages of indoctrination from above, an indoctrination that often becomes totalitarian in significance. We find ourselves with a society that suffers increasingly from, to use the expressive words of Lamennais, apoplexy at the center and anemia at the extremities. To be sure, liberals strive earnestly to maintain the rights and equalities of individuals before the rising structure of legislative and executive political power. They appeal to the courts, but not even the American judicial system can remain for very long untouched by the drive toward political uniformity and centralization. They appeal to the rights of man but, except in a religious sense which few liberals take seriously, there are no rights of man that do not proceed from the society in which human beings live. In any event, it is the liberal concentration of interest upon the *individual,* rather than upon the associations in which the individual exists, that serves, paradoxical as it may seem, to intensify the processes that lead straight to increased governmental power.

"More and more is it clear," wrote J. N. Figgis in 1911, "that the mere individual's freedom against an omnipotent State may be no better than slavery; more and more is it evident that the real question of freedom in our day is the freedom of the smaller unions to live within the whole."[3] The prophetic quality of these words will not be lost upon even the most insensitive observer of our period. It has surely become obvious that the greatest single internal problem that liberal democracy faces is the preservation of a culture rich in diversity, in clear alternatives—and this is a cultural problem that cannot be separated from the preservation of the social groups and associations within which all culture is nourished and developed.

Individual *versus* State is as false an antithesis today as it ever was. The State grows on what it gives to the individual as it does on what it takes from competing social relationships—family, labor union, profession, local community, and church.

And the individual cannot but find a kind of vicarious strength in what is granted to the State. For is he not himself a part of the State? Is he not a fraction of the sovereign? And is he not but adding to his political status as citizen what he subtracts from his economic, religious, and cultural statuses in society?

He is; and in this fractional political majesty the individual finds not only compensation for the frustrations and insecurities to which he is heir in mass society but also the intoxicating sense of collective freedom.

To find the essence of freedom in the fact of the ultimate political sovereignty of the people, in the existence of mass electorates, in the individual's constitutionally guaranteed participation every two or four years in the election of his public servants, is tempting in the modern world. For it is supported by the premise, so alluring to the reformer and the disinherited alike, that political power, however great and far-reaching it may be, if it is but continuously and sensitively in touch with mass wish and acquiescence, ceases to be power in the ordinary sense. It becomes collective self-determination, collective freedom. Power becomes, in this view, marvelously neutralized and immaterialized.

"Our contemporaries," Tocqueville observed a century ago, "are constantly excited by two conflicting passions: they want to be led and they wish to remain free. As they cannot destroy either the one or the other of these contrary propensities, they strive to satisfy them both at once. They devise a sole, tutelary, and all-powerful form of government elected by the people. They combine the principle of centralization and that of popular sovereignty; this gives them respite: they console themselves for being in tutelage by the reflection that they have chosen their own guardians. Every man allows himself to be in leading strings, because he sees that it is not a person or class of persons, but the people at large who hold the end of the chain. . . .

"I admit that by this means room is left for the intervention of individuals in the more important affairs: but it is not the less suppressed in the smaller and more private ones. It must not be forgotten that it is especially dangerous to enslave men in the minor details of life. For my own part, I should be inclined to think freedom less necessary in the great things than in the little ones, if it were possible to be secure of the one without possessing the other."[4]

It is especially dangerous to enslave men in the minor details of life. Could any insight be more relevant to the contemporary problem of power in Western society? Too often in our intellectual defenses of freedom, in our sermons and manifestoes for democracy, we have fixed attention only on the more obvious historical threats to popular freedom: kings, military dictators, popes, and financial titans. We have tended to miss the subtler but infinitely more potent threats bound up with diminution of authorities and allegiances in the smaller areas of association and with the centralization and standardization of power that takes place in the name of, and on behalf of, the *people.*

Here, of course, it is always persuasive to argue that modern increases in the administrative authority of the State have been generally associated with the enhancement of mass welfare. But this is no answer to the problem of power. As Jefferson shrewdly pointed out, the State with the power to do things *for* people has the power to do things *to* them. In plain fact the latter power increases almost geometrically in proportion to the former.

Nor is it an answer to the problem of power to argue that political power in the democracies is achieved in the name of the people and through actions of representatives of the people. For we have learned from European experience that it is not primarily the source of power that is at issue but the nature of the power and the degree of unity and unconditionality which it holds over human beings.

The collective political power of the people has increased enormously during the past century. So have available means of political participation by the common man: the referendum, the direct primary, the recall, the continuous abolition of restrictions on voting, and other even more direct means of participation. Yet, along with these increases in popular democracy, it must be observed that there has been a general leveling of local, regional, and associative differences, a nationalization of culture and taste, a collectivization of mind, and a continuous increase in the real powers of government over management, labor, education, religion, and social welfare. Democracy, far from heightening human autonomy and cultural freedom, seems rather to have aided in the process of mechanization that has weakened them. It must be repeated again, however, that this is not the inevitable consequence of the democratic ideal of power vested residually in the people. It is the consequence of the systems of public administration which we have grafted onto the democratic ideal.

Four

In this development of unitary democracy, of bureaucratic centralization, contemporary mass warfare has, of course, a profoundly contributory significance. "War is the health of the State," Randolph Bourne once declared. It is the health of the State as it is the disease, or rather the starvation, of other areas of social function and authority. Everything we observed earlier in this book with respect to the community-making properties of mass warfare in the contemporary world is, deeply relevant to the administrative problem of liberal democracy. Even Tocqueville, with all his fear of centralization, was moved to write: "I do not deny that a centralized social power may be able to execute great undertakings with facility in a given time and on a particular point. This is especially true of war, in which success depends much more on the means of transferring all the resources of a nation to one single point than on the extent of those resources. Hence it is chiefly in war that nations desire, and frequently need, to increase the powers of the central government. All men of military genius are fond of centralization, which increases their strength; and all men of centralizing genius are fond of war which compels nations to combine all their powers in the hands of the government."[5]

It is precisely this military imperative of governmental centralization that makes continued warfare, or preparation for war, have so deadly an effect on all other institutions in society. For it is difficult to perform the administrative measures necessary to political and military centralization without drawing in drastic fashion from the functions, the authorities, and the allegiances that normally fall to such institutions as religion, profession, labor union, school, and local community. Quite apart from direct administrative action, the sheer brilliance of the fires of war has the effect of making dim all of the other lights of culture. The normal incentives of family, occupation, education, and recreation—already so weakened as the result of processes embedded in modern history—become singularly unattractive and irrelevant compared with the intoxicating incentives that arise from war and its now unlimited psychological demands. Given the quickening effects of war on social dislocation and cultural sterilization, it is not strange that the State should become, in time of war, the major refuge of men. Democracy cannot but become ever more unitary, omnicompetent, centralized.

To the imperatives of modern war must be added two other supports of the unitary, collectivist view of democracy. These are two intellectual perspectives, idols of the mind, as Francis Bacon might have called them. The first is the veneration, nurtured by countless centuries of discord, for *unity*. The second is the seemingly ineradicable faith, derived from ancient, medieval, and modern ideas of change, in *historical necessity*.

With respect to the first, it is hard to avoid the fact that unity has had, historically, a symbolic appeal greater than any possessed by the values of plurality and diversity. From the earliest Greek metaphysicians down to the present, the greatest single objective of philosophy has been that of converting plurality into unity, "chaos" into intellectual order. Mind itself has been interpreted in terms that suggest monistic sovereignty by so many philosophers. The deep religious appeal of unity in experience, the craving of all human beings for an inner sense of order, and the age-old rationalist desire to transmute the flux and diversity of experience into symmetrical schemes of meaning have all, in one way or another, contributed to the modern veneration for unity and uniformity in society.

The worship of unity offers no problems so long as it is confined to areas of aesthetics, religion, and metaphysics. But when transferred, under the stress of social dislocations, to the area of politics, it frequently becomes sinister. For then it tends to become absorbed, as an ideal, by existent structures of administrative power. The philosophical quest for unity and certainty becomes, as it were, a kind of apologetics for political standardization and centralization. It is assumed that the spiritual unity which every human being inwardly prizes can be achieved only by an environment made ever more uniform institutionally. In the present age, certainly, he who cries Unity will inevitably have more listeners than he who cries, so irrelevantly it must seem, Plurality and Diversity.

The second intellectual perspective reinforcing the unitary view of democracy is that of historical necessity. The tendency of the human mind to convert the empirical order of changes and events in history into a logical, *necessary* order gives strong support to the view that centralization and political collectivism are somehow in the ordained direction of the future even as they have been the apparent logical development of the past.

The greatest intellectual and moral offense the modern intellectual can be found guilty of is that of seeming to think or act outside what is commonly held to be the linear progress of civilization. It is not the deviation from opinions of others that is censured. Nor is it deviation from established morality, religious or secular. Among modern intellectuals the cardinal sin is that of failing to remain on the locomotive of history, to use Lenin's expressive phrase. This is the most damnable of all offenses in the modern rational mentality. Ordinary heresies, defections, and moral obliquities may be excused, but not the offense of being willfully outside the presumed course of historical realization. In practical terms, we are dealing with a habit of mind that seizes selectively upon *certain* aspects of the present age, e.g. political omnicompetence and administrative centralization, and invests these not just with the ordinary attributes of goodness or rightness, but with that far greater virtue of *necessity.*

We tend thus to subordinate our planning to an imaginary course of evolution in society. In the perspective of Progress the data of the past are necessarily ruled out of practical consideration for present planning purposes simply because, within this perspective, the past can only be likened to the infancy or youth of an organism that is now in maturity and looking toward endless intensification of maturity. History is conceived as a continuous movement, a flow, a unified process, a development, with a beginning, a middle, and a logical, ethical end. This process is regarded as inherently *selective,* always pushing what is good to the chronological front. The evil in an age is held to be no more than persistences or outcroppings of the past. Social philosophy and social planning that do not accept the "necessity" of modern changes are consequently damned as utopian or nostalgic.

The supremacy of Marxism in the modern history of socialism comes in large part from the tactical success Marx and Engels had in investing the ethical ideal of socialism with historical necessity. Other socialists had held up their ideal as something to be described in detail, planned for, and worked for. When Marx scorned such efforts as being utopian and unhistorical and insisted that the future must develop inexorably out of the present, he not only prevented any further consideration of what he contemptuously called "kitchen recipes" but also placed the ideal of socialism firmly in the context of existent trends toward national collectivism and administrative centralization. For Marx, socialism was a stage of society that must develop dialectically out of the *significant* present. Pluralism, localism, voluntary association—all of these to Marx were mere survivals of medievalism. What was *real* in the present was industrialism, collectivism, and administrative centralization.

What is true of Marxian socialism has been true of a great deal of modern political and economic philosophy. As Martin Buber[6] has recently reminded us, the intellectual's dread of utopianism and his pious desire to be historically "realistic" have led him generally to an all too willing subordination of moral categories to the presumed "direction" of history.

The modern facts of political mechanism, centralization, and collectivism are seen in the perspective of inevitable development in modern history. They seem to be the very direction of history itself. Present differences of political opinion hence usually resolve themselves into differences about who shall guide this developing reality and how little or how much should be administered it in the way of fuel. Any sharp alternative has the disadvantage of running up against the widely flung facts of uniformity and centralization, and the additional disadvantage of seeming to be filiated with historical conditions of the past which give it a manifestly "unprogressive" character.

The imperatives of war, the veneration of unity and uniformity, and the faith in historical necessity, with its corollary of irreversible historical processes—these, then, are the most powerful supports for the unitary perspective of democracy at the present time. Given these, together with the constant diminution in the significance of the nonpolitical areas of kinship, religion, and other forms of association, the task of centralization and omnicompetence is not too difficult even in the presence of liberal values. Given these conditions and perspectives, the transition from liberal democracy to totalitarianism will not seem too arduous or unpleasant. It will indeed be scarcely noticed, save by the "utopians," the "reactionaries," and similar eccentrics.

Five

Admittedly, there is a degree of unity without which any culture, like any musical composition, would become chaotic. And there is indeed a degree of centralization of authority apart from which no structure—political government, church, or labor union—could operate. So much is true. Yet, given the society in which we now live, it is difficult not to conclude that the requirements of liberal democracy are very different from those which seemed so necessary to men of good will a century ago.

The problem of freedom and authority can no longer be given even the semblance of solution by appeals to the talisman of popular sovereignty. For, despite the unquestioned moral rightness of the proposition that all legitimate political power must flow from the people, we are living in an age in which *all* forms of government, totalitarianism as well as liberal democracy, seek to root their authority in the soil of popular acquiescence. The greatest discovery in nineteenth-century politics, as we have seen, was the principle that the real power of a State may actually be enhanced, not diminished, by widening its base to include the whole of a population. The exploitation of this revolutionary principle of power reaches its highest development in the total State where no effort is spared to drive the functions and symbols of political authority as deeply as possible into the minds and wills of all the people, thus making State power a part of human personality, a projection of the self.

Popular sovereignty, then, is not enough. As a moral principle it must remain our point of departure, but if democracy is to remain liberal democracy, if it is not to become transmuted into the State of the masses, with its power converted into a monolith, we must face the crucial problems of the relation of political authority to all the other forms of authority in society. The reinforcement of these and their constitutional relationship to the political authority of the State become, in the present century, the major problem of democracy. Because of our single-minded concentration upon the individual as the sole unit of society and upon the State as the sole source of legitimate power, we have tended to overlook the fact that freedom thrives in cultural diversity, in local and regional differentiation, in associative pluralism, and above all, in the *diversification of power.*[7]

Basically, all of these are reducible, I believe, to the single massive problem of the relation of political government to the plurality of cultural associations which form the intermediate authorities of society. These are many: religious, economic, professional, local, recreational, academic, and so forth. Each of them is a structure, often large, of authorities and functions. Each of them is an organization of human purposes and allegiances related to some distinctive institutional end. Each of them is, apart from the checks provided by the existence of other and competing forms of association, potentially omnicompetent in its relation to its members. And whether it is the economic corporation, the hugh labor union, or the profession, each offers, in its own way, innumerable problems of freedom and control in society. There is no unalterable guarantee of freedom in any one of them.

Nevertheless, it is the continued existence of this array of intermediate powers in society, of this plurality of "private sovereignties," that constitutes, above anything else, the greatest single barrier to the conversion of democracy from its liberal form to its totalitarian form. It is the fact of *diversity* of appeal that is foremost in this social constitution. Apart from its setting in a competitive framework, any one of these large-scale intermediate authorities is capable of expanding its own control over members to a point that exceeds the requirements of freedom. But the most notable characteristic of this whole array of social authorities in European history has been the ceaseless competition for human allegiance that goes on among them.

Six

Historically, there are to be seen in Western society recurrent waves of intermediate association.[8] In the eleventh and twelfth centuries arose the gilds, the communes, the universities, and all the other fellowships of interest and belief which, taken together, provided so much of man's protection from the vicissitudes of fortune and the despotism of kings, popes, and feudal lords. The rise of the sovereign national State, as we have seen, weakened or destroyed many of these. Doctrines of political monism and legal individualism became dominant. But these notwithstanding, we are struck by a renewed efflorescence of social and cultural associations in Western society in the seventeenth century, particularly in England—new organized professions, learned societies, and scientific associations. These have proved among the most powerful supports of cultural diversity and freedom in modern Western Europe. They were weakened in France by the Revolution, as were almost all forms of autonomous association, but in England they proved resistant to administrative centralization and Utilitarian individualism alike.

In the nineteenth century we see another great wave of association rolling over large areas of the Western world. Trade unions, benevolent societies, cooperatives, and mutual aid associations of all kinds arose spontaneously, in Europe and the United States, to meet the problems of individual security and freedom that had been created by the spread of national centralization and by the burgeoning factory system. In these associations, lying intermediate to man and the State, to the worker and market society, lay the promise of both security and freedom—security within the solidarity of associations founded in response to genuine needs; freedom arising from the very diversity of association and from the relative autonomy these associations had with respect to central systems of law and administration. These were the associations that Tocqueville saw, during his visit to the United States, as the real protections of personal liberty, the actual supports of parliamentary or representative government, and the major barriers to the peculiar and oppressive despotism he found latent in the democratic State.

Modern liberalism unfortunately has tended on the whole to step from the cherished individual of the nineteenth century to the myth of the all-benign State in the twentieth. While it has seldom been intolerant of intermediate associations, it has made little effort to formulate a theory of liberal democracy that includes them, that makes them indispensable to free, representative government. In general, modern democratic thought has settled single-mindedly upon the same elements that are crucial to the political community: the abstract individual and the State.

Yet, any careful historical examination reveals the roots political democracy has had in practice in social groups and cultural communities. Man does not live merely as one of a vast aggregate of arithmetically equal, socially undifferentiated, individuals. He does not live his life merely in terms of the procedures and techniques of the administrative State—not, at least, in a free society. As a concrete *person* he is inseparable from the plurality of social allegiances and memberships which characterize his social organization and from the diversities of belief and habit which form a culture.

Most of the tendencies in contemporary society toward the erosion of cultural differences and the standardization of cultural tastes, beliefs, and activities, which are so often charged, mistakenly, against technology and science, are the product, actually, of a centralization of authority and function and a desiccation of local and cultural associations.

The great cultural ages of the past were, almost invariably, ages of social diversity, of small, independent communities and towns, of distinct regions, of small associations which jealously guarded their unique identities and roles. In the competition and rivalry of these, as Bertrand Russell has pointed out,[9] lay the conditions of cultural energy and diversity which gave imperishable works to the world. Culturally, there is little to hope for from a world based increasingly upon mass relationships and upon the sterilization of intermediate associations.

Nor is there much to hope for in the way of freedom. "Who says liberty, says association," declared Lamennais in the early nineteenth century, and he was echoed a generation later by Proudhon: "Multiply your associations and be free."

Only through its intermediate relationships and authorities has any State ever achieved the balance between organization and personal freedom that is the condition of a creative and enduring culture. These relationships begin with the family and with the small informal social groups which spring up around common interests and cultural needs. Their number extends to the larger associations of society, to the churches, business associations, labor unions, universities, and professions. They are the real sources of liberal democracy.

The weakening of these groups reflects not only growing spiritual isolation but increasing State power. To feel alone—does this not breed a desire for association in Leviathan? The individual who has been by one force or another wrenched from social belonging is thrown back upon himself; he becomes the willing prey of those who would manipulate him as the atom citizen in the political and economic realms. Given nothing but his own resources to stand on, what can be his defenses against the powerful propaganda of those who control the principal means of communication in society? The recent history of Western Europe should remind us that a sense of the past, even more than a hope of the future, is the basis of the will to resist; and a sense of the past presupposes cultural continuities within associations which have deep moral appeal.

Only in their social interdependences are men given to resist the tyranny that always threatens to arise out of any political government, democratic or other. Where the individual stands alone in the face of the State he is helpless. "Despotism," wrote Tocqueville, "is never more secure of continuance than when it can keep men asunder; and all its influence is commonly exerted for that purpose." The desire for freedom arises only out of men's reverence for exterior and competing values. Genuine freedom is not based upon the negative psychology of release. Its roots are in positive acts of dedication to ends and values. Freedom presupposes the autonomous existence of values that men wish to be free to follow and live up to. Such values are social in the precise sense that they arise out of, and are nurtured by, the voluntary associations which men form.

Seven

But neither social values nor autonomous social relationships can thrive apart from their possession of meaningful functions and authorities. We end this chapter on the theme with which it began: the centrality of the problem of power, its distribution in society, and its control. Man may be a social animal, but he does not devote himself in any serious way to groups and associations that are no longer clearly related to the larger structure of function and authority in society.

What has been so apparent in the modern history of the family will be no less apparent in the future histories of profession, university, labor union, and all other forms of association in our culture. Deprive these entities of their distinctive functions through increasing nationalization of service and welfare, divest them of the authorities over their members through increasing centralization of political power in society, and these associations, like the extended family, the church, and the local community, must shrink immeasurably in their potential contributions to culture.

Modern philosophies of freedom have tended to emphasize, as we have seen, either the individual's *release* from power of every kind—generally, through an appeal to natural rights—or the individual's *participation* in some single structure of authority like the General Will, which replaces all other structures.

But from the point of view of the real, the historical roots of liberal democracy, freedom has rested neither upon release nor upon collectivization but upon the *diversification* and the decentralization of power in society. In the division of authority and the multiplication of its sources lie the most enduring conditions of freedom. "The only safeguard against power," warned Montesquieu, "is rival power." He was echoed by Lord Acton more than a century later, who declared that "Liberty depends upon the division of power."

Freedom, it has been well said, lies in the interstices of authority. This is indeed, I believe, the real reconciliation of the demands of order and the demands of freedom. Authority, any society, any association, must have. It is simply the structure of the association. But the sole possibility of personal freedom and cultural autonomy lies in the maintenance of a plurality of authorities in any society. Each of these may be tight enough as an individual system to provide a context of security for its members. So long as there are other and competing authorities, so long as man has even the theoretical possibility of removing himself from any that for him has grown oppressive and of placing himself within the framework of some other associative authority, it cannot be said that his freedom has suffered.

It is in these terms, I think, that the role of political government becomes clear in the democracies. Not to sterilize the normal authorities of associations, as does the total State through a pre-emption of function, a deprivation of authority, and a monopolization of allegiance, but to reinforce these associations, to provide, administratively, a means whereby the normal competition of group differences is held within bounds and an environment of law within which no single authority, religious or economic, shall attain a repressive and monopolistic influence—this is the role of government in a democracy.

In what Frank Tannenbaum has well termed "the balance of institutional power" lie the possibilities for a harmonization of personal freedom and associative authority. "The road to social peace," Mr. Tannenbaum writes, "is the balance of the social institutions, and a wise statesman would strengthen those institutions that seemed to be losing ground, even if he were not addicted to them; for the only way to peace in this world of fallible human nature is to keep all human institutions strong, but none too strong; relatively weak, but not so weak as to despair of their survival. *It is only thus that peaceful irritation and strife, so essential to social and individual sanity, can be maintained.*"[10]

How can the power of the State or that of any large-scale association be limited if there do not exist authorities that are always in competition? No one can doubt that there are by now many areas of function which must come under the exclusive jurisdiction of the State. No longer can one doubt that, in modern society, mundane power over human beings will lie in the State itself. And it has become obvious that a politically planned society is, in one degree or another, absolutely essential. These points are not in question.

What is crucially important is not the residual location of power in society. Rather it is the formal administration of that power and the relation between formal public administration of political power and the administrations of the various other forms of power in society—religious, economic, educational, and the like. The philosophy of administrative centralization had its origin at a time when the extrication of the State's power from other powers in society—mostly feudal in nature—was a matter of burning importance. But this problem now belongs in the dustbin of history. There is no other institution that can seriously challenge the sovereignty of the State in the contemporary world.

Unfortunately, our philosophy of administration has not, on the whole, kept pace with the history of sovereignty. We have at the present time only the beginnings of a theory of administration to do justice to the psychological complexities of personality and culture which contemporary social science has discovered. Modern public administration has been too generally dominated by the nineteenth-century rationalist's conception of society as a vast aggregate of unconnected political particles.

It is easy—too easy—to plan for abstract aggregates of *individuals,* regarded for planning purposes as so many arithmetically equal units composed of identical drives and needs. It is far more difficult to plan for, to legislate for, *persons* who live not in simple economic or political perspectives but in complex associative and normative systems that are the product of tradition and custom. But planning blind to the autonomous groups and traditional values of a society is a planning likely to be effectuated by an administration that seeks to obliterate, for purposes of rational simplicity, these groups and values.

A distinction has grown up in the literature of applied anthropology relevant to the needs of public administration in contemporary democracies. It is the distinction between direct and indirect rule. In indirect administration every effort is made by colonial administrators to work with and through traditional relationships and lines of authority in native cultures. In direct administration, on the other hand, such relationships and authorities are disregarded, supplanted by new and more "rational" administrative relationships and powers. Not a few of the tragedies connected with Western administration of native cultures in so many areas of the world have come from the well-meaning efforts of administrators, steeped in the intellectual resources of Western political rationalism, to minister directly to the supposed life needs of natives.

Similar tragedies of "direct" administration fill the social histories of Western nations themselves. Under the spur of unitary democracy and through rationalist techniques of administrative centralization, planners and reformers have systematically disregarded local and regional cultures and the traditional social relationships and values of ethnic minorities, and have planned instead from abstract values and assumed "needs," and through channels created by fiat.

It has been one of the deficiencies of much public administration in Western democracies that little distinction has been made between the demands of sovereignty and the possibilities of governmental administration. Sovereignty, we may agree with every major political philosopher since Bodin, is unitary, absolute, and imprescriptible. This is as true in democracy as in any other type of government. No other conception of State authority has been feasible since the breakup of the medieval synthesis. In power the contemporary State is, and must be, *sui generis*. Not all the semantic analyses of misguided pluralists or the adjurations of moralists will change this fact.

But the centrality of sovereignty does not lead logically to the centralization of administration in public affairs. Because the theory and practice of modern administration arose at a time when sovereignty itself was struggling for supremacy against inherited structures of feudal power, it was perhaps inevitable that early conceptions of governmental administration should have been based upon the example of military government. But the residual power of the State is today no longer seriously questioned. The political relationship is as central as was the relationship of the Church in the thirteenth century. Decentralization of administration is not merely feasible technically; it is a prime necessity of free culture.

David Lilienthal is an eloquent public servant who has discovered from practical experience that administrative decentralization is absolutely indispensable to modern democracies if they are not to become victims of the creeping totalitarianism inherent in administrative monopoly and centralization. The Tennessee Valley Authority is itself a magnificent illustration of the basic compatibility between democratic government and administrative decentralization. With all allowance for its errors and for the impatience of certain disciples of centralization, TVA demonstrates that central planning is not inconsistent with local and associative autonomies. We readily admit that planning in terms of aggregates of abstract individuals, conceived in the image of Economic Man, is much easier than planning in terms of existent families, professional associations, labor unions, churches, and regions. But such planning is the surest avenue to an eventual sterilization of the moral appeal of these unities. And from the decline of these and similar associations can come only the cultural atomization that leads to irresistible Power.

Planning that dispenses with the autonomous, traditional values of a population can be effectuated only by a system of administration that is eventually forced to liquidate these values. For these will then constitute forces of distraction, even of subversion, to the abstract ends of planning.

The assumption that centralized power must carry with it centralized administration was tenable only in a day when the range of governmental activities was limited. It is no longer tenable. As government, in its expanding range of functions, comes ever closer to the primary spheres of man's existence, the need is intensified for a theory of public administration alive to the fact that the necessary roots of democracy are in the decisions and responsibilities of the people diversified in regions, communities, and associations.

"Centralization in administration," David Lilienthal has written, "promotes remote and absentee control, and thereby increasingly denies to the individual the opportunity to make decisions and to carry those responsibilities by which human personality is nourished and developed. I find it impossible to comprehend how democracy can be a living reality if people are remote from their government and in their daily lives are not made a part of it, or if the control and direction of making a living—in industry, farming, the distribution of goods—is far removed from the stream of life and from the local community. 'Centralization' is no mere technical matter of 'management,' of 'bigness versus smallness.' We are dealing here with those deep urgencies of the human spirit which are embodied in the faith we call 'democracy.'"[11]

Eight

We cannot be reminded too often that the stifling effects of centralization upon society are as evident in large-scale private industry as they are in political government. Big government and big business have developed together in Western society, and each has depended on the other. To these two has been added more recently a third force in society—big labor. In all three spheres, and, for that matter in our universities, charities, and various other activities, there is a strong tendency to organize administration in terms of the ideas of power inherited from the seventeenth and eighteenth centuries.

But there is a point beyond which centralized administration cannot go if the meaning and urgency of the ends of any association are to be kept alive in the minds of the individuals who comprise the association. Bertrand Russell has recently written: "In a highly organized world, personal initiative connected with a group must be confined to a few unless the group is small. If you are a member of a small committee you may reasonably hope to influence its decisions. In national politics, where you are one of some twenty million voters, your influence is infinitesimal unless you are exceptional or occupy an exceptional position. You have, it is true, a twenty-millionth share in the government of others, but only a twenty-millionth share in the government of yourself. You are therefore much more conscious of being governed than of governing. The government becomes in your thoughts a remote and largely malevolent 'they,' not a set of men whom you, in concert with others who share your opinions, have chosen to carry out your wishes. Your individual feeling about politics, in these circumstances, is not that intended to be brought about by democracy, but much more nearly what it would be under a dictatorship."[12]

It will be recognized at once that planning and administration in terms of decentralization, localism, and associative autonomy is far more difficult than administration carried on under the myth of territorial masses of discrete individual atoms. Not only does it go against the tendency of the whole history of modern economic, educational, and political administration, but, on its own terms, it raises problems of organization that are immense. "It is obvious," Karl Mannheim wrote, "that the modern nature of social techniques puts a premium on centralization, but this is only true if our sole criterion is to be technical efficiency. If, for various reasons, chiefly those concerned with the maintenance of personality, we deliberately wish to decentralize certain activities within certain limits, we can do so."[13]

What Lewis Mumford has written in *The Culture of Cities* is eloquent and irrefutable. "We need, in every part of the city, units in which intelligent and cooperative behavior can take the place of mass regulations, mass decisions, mass actions, imposed by ever remoter leaders and administrators. Small groups: small classes: small communities: institutions framed to the human scale, are essential to purposive behavior in modern society. Very stupidly we have overlooked the way in which large units limit opportunity all along the line: not merely by physical friction of space, or the burden of a vast mechanical and administrative overhead, but also by diminishing opportunities for people with special capacities. Thus Sir Raymond Unwin has pointed out that twenty communities with a population of fifty thousand people would not merely be more adequately governed, probably, than one city that contained a million: it would, for example, give an opportunity for twenty mayors or city managers, against one in the big center. This rule holds true in every other part of society. We demand the impossible in the way of direction and specialized service from a few people, and we fail to demand the possible from those who are better equipped to handle adequately a smaller job. With our overgrown institutions, overgrown colleges, overgrown corporations, overgrown cities, is it any wonder that we easily become the victims of propaganda machines, routineers, and dictators?"[14]

The passage from Mr. Mumford's book makes it plain that the necessity of decentralization is by no means confined to the structure of the political State, great as the need there may be. Decentralization is just as necessary in the operation of the other great associations of modern society—the industrial corporation, the labor union, the large church, the profession, and the great university. More than a little of the diminution in the psychological and cultural influence of these associations in recent times results from their failure to remain responsive to the small areas of association within them. This is the consequence of the same kind of centralization and collectivization we see in politics. The fault lies in the common failure to unite the broad purposes of the larger associations with the small, informal relationships composing them.

The labor union, the legal or medical association, or the church will become as centralized and as remote as the national State itself unless these great organizations are rooted in the smaller relationships which give meaning to the ends of the large associations. To conceive of a great labor union, industrial enterprise, or church as an association of *individual* members is but to intensify the processes of atomization which such associations can and should counteract. No large association will remain an object of personal allegiance, no matter how crucial its goals may be, unless it is constantly sensitive to the existence of the informal but potent relationships of which it is really composed. It has surely become evident by this time that the most successful and allegiance-evoking business enterprises and cultural associations in modern life are those that regard themselves as associations of *groups,* not of raw individuals. To recognize the existence of informal social relationships, to keep central purposes constantly alive in these small groups, and to work toward the increased spontaneity and autonomy of these groups is, I believe, the cardinal responsibility of the great private association.

Only thus will the large formal associations remain important agencies of order and freedom in democracy. Only thus will they succeed in arresting and banishing the augmenting processes of insecurity and moral isolation which now paralyze individual wills and strike at the roots of stable culture.

There is a vast difference between the type of planning—whether in the large State, industry, or the school—that seeks to enmesh the individual in a custodial network of detailed rules for his security and society's stability, and the type of planning that is concerned with the creation of a political and economic *context* within which the spontaneous associations of men are the primary sources of freedom and order. The latter type of planning is compatible with competition, diversity, rivalry, and the normative conflicts that are necessary to cultural creativity. The former type is not.

Nine

I cannot help thinking that what we need above all else in this age is a new philosophy of *laissez faire.* The old *laissez faire* failed because it was based on erroneous premises regarding human behavior. As a theory it failed because it mistook for ineradicable characteristics of individuals qualities that were in fact inseparable from social groups. As a policy it failed because its atomistic propositions were inevitably unavailing against the reality of enlarging masses of insecure individuals. Far from proving a check upon the growth of the omnicompetent State, the old *laissez faire* actually accelerated this growth. Its indifference to every form of community and association left the State as the sole area of reform and security.

We need a *laissez faire* that will hold fast to the ends of autonomy and freedom of choice; one that will begin not with the imaginary, abstract individual but with the personalities of human beings as they are actually given to us in association. "What we actually see in the world is not on the one hand the State, and on the other, a mass of unrelated individuals; but a vast complex of gathered unions, in which alone we find individuals, families, clubs, trade unions, colleges, professions, and so forth."[15]

To create the conditions within which autonomous *individuals* could prosper, could be emancipated from the binding ties of kinship, class, and community, was the objective of the older *laissez faire*. To create conditions within which *autonomous groups* may prosper must be, I believe, the prime objective of the new *laissez faire*.

I use the word create advisedly. We should not suppose that the *laissez-faire* individualism of the middle nineteenth century was the simple heritage of nature, the mere untrammeled emergence of drives and motivations with which man is naturally endowed. *Laissez faire*, as the economic historian, Polanyi, among others, has emphasized, was *brought* into existence.[16] It was brought into existence by the planned destruction of old customs, associations, villages, and other securities; by the force of the State throwing the weight of its fast-developing administrative system in favor of new economic elements of the population. And it was brought into existence, hardly less, by reigning systems of economic, political, and psychological thought, systems which neglected altogether the social and cultural unities and settled single-mindedly on the abstract individual as the proper unit of speculation and planning. What we need at the present time is the knowledge and administrative skill to create a *laissez faire* in which the basic unit will be the social group.

The liberal values of autonomy and freedom of personal choice are indispensable to a genuinely free society, but we shall achieve and maintain these only by vesting them in the conditions in which liberal democracy will thrive—diversity of culture, plurality of association, and division of authority.

CONCLUSION

At the present time we are suspended, so to speak, between two worlds of allegiance and association. On the one hand, and partly behind us, is the historic world in which loyalties to family, church, profession, local community, and interest association exert, however ineffectively, persuasion and guidance. On the other is the world of values identical with the absolute political community—the community in which all symbolism, allegiance, responsibility, and sense of purpose have become indistinguishable from the operation of centralized political power. In the Western democracies we have moved partly into the second, but not wholly out of the first. In this suspended position lie both our danger and our hope—our hope because we have not yet become separated wholly, as have many European populations, from the social sources of freedom, and because our wills have not yet become anesthetized into moral passivity; our danger because manifestly these sources have become weakened and the spell of the political community has become ever more intense.

We are dealing with a problem that demands a new classification of States, one that is relevant to the actual conditions of order and freedom in the contemporary world. Traditional labels—democratic, republican, capitalist, socialist, et cetera—have by now become nearly as archaic as older classifications of monarchy and aristocracy.

Of what value now are differentiations in extent of electorates, in frequency of elections, in mass participation in politics? Government of, by, and for the people, for all its verity as an abstract proposition, becomes nearly irrelevant in a world where all despotisms rest upon foundations of mass acquiescence and where all the arts of political propaganda are employed to sink the roots of government deeply in popular consciousness and participation.

Equally illusory and irrelevant is socialism. When Sir William Harcourt declared, at the end of the nineteenth century, "We are all Socialists now," his words had a prophetic quality that he did not quite intend. For most of the cherished goals of nineteenth-century socialism have become accepted procedures of democratic and totalitarian governments alike. We must conclude that all States in the future will be able to demonstrate, and will *have* to demonstrate, attributes of socialism. But, by themselves, these will promise nothing in the way of freedom.

What are the terms by which free and unfree societies in the contemporary world may be distinguished? Merely to ask the question is to reveal the poverty of present political vocabulary in this respect. We are still operating with words and phrases drawn from a day when the lexicon of freedom bore meaningful relation to the rise of the people in politics and to the emancipation of individuals from inherited social structures. In plain fact we have no set of evocative terms at the present time that correspond to our realities in the same way the words "people," "individual," and "change" corresponded to the realities and aspirations of the eighteenth and nineteenth centuries.

There is the kind of State that seeks always to extend its administrative powers and functions into all realms of society, always seeking a higher degree of centralization in the conduct of its operations, always tending toward a wider measure of politicization of social, economic, and cultural life. It does not do this in the name of power but of freedom—freedom from want, insecurity, and minority tyranny. It parades the symbols of progress, people, justice, welfare, and devotion to the common man. It strives unceasingly to make its ends and purposes acceptable—through radio, newspaper, and document—to even the lowliest of citizens. It builds up a sense of the absolute identity of State and society—nothing outside the State, everything in the State.

Increasingly, in this type of State, the basic needs for education, recreation, welfare, economic production, distribution, and consumption, health, spiritual and physical, and all other services of society are made aspects of the administrative structure of political government. This process of transfer comes to be accepted by almost everyone—by businessmen in search of guaranteed production and profit, by educators in need of funds, by labor in the interests of guaranteed jobs and living wages, and by liberal reformers in the interests of housing programs or other projects. Autonomous areas of economy, education, and other spheres of culture shrink constantly. Invasions of minority rights are defended, as are invasions of social authority and responsibility, and limitations upon right of association in the name of the people, of social justice, of preparedness for war against poverty, ignorance, disease, and external national enemies.

Such a State may well call itself democratic and humanitarian. All contemporary totalitarian States so refer to themselves. Such a State may found itself upon the highest principle of virtue, even as did the Republic of Plato. There can be such a thing as democratic totalitarianism even as there can be, as we have learned in disillusion, socialist totalitarianism. The design of totalitarianism, as Dostoevsky's Grand Inquisitor has taught us, can be infinitely varied and in human hands can proceed from the formal veneration of God as easily as from the hatred of God. The impersonal despotism of virtue, as someone has said, is not the less despotic because it is virtuous.

But there is also the kind of State that seeks, without sacrificing its legitimate sovereignty grounded in the will of the people, to maintain a pluralism of functions and loyalties in the lives of its people. It is a State that knows that the political absorption of the institutional functions of an association, be it family, local community, or trade union, must soon be followed by the loss or weakening of psychological devotions to that association. It is a State that seeks to diversify and decentralize its own administrative operations and to relate these as closely as possible to the forms of spontaneous association which are the outgrowth of human needs and desires and which have relevance to the economic, educational, and religious ends of a culture. It seeks cultural diversity, not uniformity. It does not make a fetish of either social order or personal adjustment, but it recognizes that the claims of freedom and cultural autonomy will never have recognition until the great majority of individuals in society have a sense of cultural membership in the significant and meaningful relationships of kinship, religion, occupation, profession, and locality. It will not spurn the demands of human security but it will seek means by which such demands can be met through spontaneous association and creation rather than through bureaucratic rigidities of formal law and administration.

Either type of State may be labeled democratic and humanitarian. But the difference between the two types is infinitely greater than the differences between capitalism and socialism, or between monarchy and republic. The first type of State is inherently monolithic and absorptive and, however broad its base in the electorate and however nobly inspired its rulers, must always border upon despotism.

The second type of State is inherently pluralist and, whatever the intentions of its formal political rulers, its power will be limited by associations whose plurality of claims upon their members is the measure of their members' freedom from any monopoly of power in society.

References and Notes

Chapter One

1. *Democracy and the Organization of Political Parties* (London, 1902), vol. i, p. 50.

2. "Can the anonymity, mobility, impersonality, specialization, and sophistication of the city become the attributes of a stable society, or will society fall apart?" asks one of America's foremost sociologists, Kingsley Davis, in his *Human Society* (New York, 1949), p. 342. Questions of this sort form the moral perspective of a great deal of theoretical and empirical work in the contemporary sciences of human behavior.

3. See, for example, such recent studies as Philip Rahv, *Image and Idea* (New York, 1949), Newton Arvin, *Hawthorne's Short Stories* (New York, 1947), and the superb appraisal of Dostoevsky and his critics, "The Insufficient Man," *Times Literary Supplement,* 20 September 1947.

4. *The Protestant Era* (University of Chicago, 1948), p. 245–6.

5. *The Nature and Destiny of Man* (London, 1941), vol. i, p. 59.

6. *Christian Polity* (London, 1936), p. 87.

7. See Durkheim's *Suicide* (Paris, 1897), especially the final chapters. The writings of Durkheim's German contemporary, Georg Simmel, have had something of the same influence upon modern thought.

8. *The Social Problems of an Industrial Civilization* (Harvard University, 1945), p. 7, 56.

9. National Resources Committee, *Our Cities* (Washington, D.C., 1937), p. 53.

10. S. M. Molema, *The Bantu, Past and Present* (Edinburgh, 1920), p. 308.

11. *The Neurotic Personality of Our Time* (New York, 1937), p. 117.
12. *A Study of History* (London, 1946), vol. 5, p. 63.

Chapter Two

1. Elsewhere, I have dealt briefly with certain aspects of nineteenth century conservatism. See my article on de Bonald in the *Journal of the History of Ideas* (June 1944), on Lamennais in the *Journal of Politics* (November 1948), and on the origins of sociology in France in *The American Journal of Sociology* (September 1952).

2. It was to the Middle Ages that most of the nineteenth-century conservatives looked for inspiration in their revolt against revolutionary secularism, power, and individualism. The conservatism of our own day has deep roots in the medieval view of man and society.

3. The conservatives bequeathed three important ideas to modern thought: the conception of the atomized masses; the idea of personal alienation; and the vision of omnipotent political power arising from the disorganization of social institutions.

4. See the fascinating symposium on modern criticism in *The American Scholar* (Winter 1950–51 and Spring 1951).

5. Op. cit. p. 34. The reference to Niebuhr is primarily to his article, "The Impact of Protestantism Today," in the *Atlantic Monthly* (February 1948).

6. My remarks refer essentially to sociology, social anthropology, and social psychology, but they have relevance to the other social sciences.

7. *Time and Tide* (26 November 1949).

8. In his *Burge Lecture,* 1947.

9. "The Hungry Sheep," *Times Literary Supplement* (30 March 1951).

10. Ibid.

11. In *The God That Failed,* edited by R. H. Crossman (New York, 1949), p. 99.

12. Some of these paragraphs are taken from an article I wrote while serving in the Army in the Pacific in 1944. See "The Coming Problem of Assimilation," *The American Journal of Sociology* (January 1945).

Chapter Three

1. This approach is, happily, less common now than a generation ago. The writings of such men as R. M. MacIver, Talcott Parsons, Kingsley Davis, and Howard Becker, among others, have done much to place the study of the family in a more coherent perspective.

2. *Colonial Policy and Practice* (Cambridge University Press, 1948), p. 3.

3. There is a kind of historical awareness implicit in this focusing upon the family, for the overwhelming majority of communal or sacred areas of society reflect the transfer, historically, of kinship symbols and nomenclature to non-kinship spheres. We see this in the histories of religion, gilds, village communities, and labor unions. Kinship has ever been the archetype of man's communal aspirations.

4. Margaret Redfield has pointed out that "Mother's Day, originally promoted by the florists, and still a source of profit to them, has its whole point in an organization of society in which parents and children lose touch with one another." "The American Family: Consensus and Freedom," *The American Journal of Sociology* (November 1946).

5. *Capitalism, Socialism, and Democracy* (New York, 1942), p. 160.

6. E. H. Norman, in his *Japan's Emergence as a Modern State* (Institute of Pacific Relations, 1940), p. 153, has pointed out the value of the extended family in Japan in making possible a relatively low-wage structure and, derivatively, greater profits and capital expansion.

7. *Knowledge For What?* (Princeton University Press, 1939), p. 83.

8. Throughout modern economic society the problem of incentives has become explicit. Both business and governmental planners find themselves with difficulties which, although economic in nature, begin in a structure of motivations that is non-economic. The almost total absence in earlier economic thought, socialist as well as orthodox, of concern for the problem of incentives is some indication of the changes that have taken place in the institutional framework and psychological substructure of capitalism.

9. This paragraph is a paraphrase of Mirra Komarovsky's penetrating study, "The Voluntary Associations of Urban Dwellers," *American Sociological Review* (December 1946).

10. *White Collar: The American Middle Classes* (New York, 1951), p. xvi.

11. Op. cit. p. 145.

Chapter Four

1. *Adventures in Ideas* (Cambridge University Press, 1933), p. 55.

2. *Ancient Law*, Everyman's Library edition (London, 1861), p. 99.

3. *Communist Manifesto*, section 1.

4. *Gemeinschaft und Gesellschaft* (Berlin, 1887).

5. *The Sociology of Georg Simmel*, translated, and edited by Kurt Wolff (The Free Press, Glencoe, Ill., 1950), p. 293, 414f.

6. See *From Max Weber: Essays in Sociology*, edited and translated by H. H. Gerth and C. Wright Mills (New York, 1946), especially p. 199f. and 216f.

7. *Le Suicide* (Paris, 1897), p. 446.

8. *The Civilization of the Renaissance in Italy*, new edition (Phaidon Press, London, 1950), p. 81.

9. *Political Theories of the Middle Ages*, translated by F. W. Maitland (Cambridge University Press, 1900), p. 37.

10. *Villainage in England* (Oxford, 1892), p. 400.

11. *English Villagers of the Thirteenth Century* (Harvard University Press, 1942), p. 106.

12. See especially Henri Pirenne, *Medieval Cities* (Princeton University Press, 1925).

13. *The Universities of Europe in the Middle Ages*, edited by F. M. Powicke (Oxford, 1936). Of all specialized institutional studies of the medieval period this seems to me most illuminating of the culture as a whole.

14. "Medieval Political Thought" in *The Social and Political Ideas of Some Great Medieval Thinkers*, edited by F. J. C. Hearnshaw (London, 1923), p. 28.

15. See the brilliant essay of Frank Tannenbaum, "The Balance of Power in Society," *Political Science Quarterly* (December 1946).

16. *Puritan and Anglican* (London, 1901), p. 234.

17. *Religion and the Rise of Capitalism* (New York, 1926), p. 97.

18. *The State*, translated by J. Gitterman (Indianapolis, 1914).

19. J. L. and Barbara Hammond; see especially their *The Town Laborer* (London, 1917).

20. *Democracy and the Organization of Political Parties*, vol. 1, p. 47.

Chapter Five

1. *Law and Politics in the Middle Ages* (New York, 1898), p. 308.

2. *A Preface to Morals* (New York, 1929), p. 80.

3. The most penetrating of all studies of this influence of the State is that of Jenks, referred to above. See especially chapters 4–7.

4. Miriam Beard, *A History of the Business Man* (New York, 1938), p. 327. This role of the State has also been stressed by such historians as Sombart, Hecksher, and Karl Polanyi. There is indeed much to be said for regarding capitalism as simply the forced adjustment of economic life to the needs of the sovereign State in the various national areas.

5. On the political aspects of Protestantism, see especially the works of J. N. Figgis, *Studies of Political Thought from Gerson to Grotius*, second edition (Cambridge, 1923) and "Political Thought in the Sixteenth Century" in *Cambridge Modern History*, vol. 3 (1904), ch. 22.

6. Although Protestantism, capitalism, and modern science have been extensively dealt with as contexts of the rise of modern individualism, the role of the State has been comparatively neglected. This is the result of a narrow concentration upon the State as mere power.

7. See Tocqueville's *The Old Régime and the Revolution* for the most illuminating account of the affinity of political power and equality. In his *The Growth of Philosophical Radicalism*, p. 506, Halevy wrote: "Conservative parties know that law is a leveller, and that is why they plead the cause of tradition and custom as against legislative uniformity."

8. It was with a kind of unwonted historical wisdom that leaders of the Revolution in Paris in 1790 made the term *citizen* the highest of address. It connoted freedom from old authorities *and* absolute subjection to France *une et indivisible*.

9. See the illuminating discussion by A. N. Whitehead of medieval and modern referents of the term "liberty." *Adventures in Ideas* (Cambridge University Press, 1933), p. 74f.

10. *Wolsey* (London, 1928), p. 218.

11. "The first and fundamental principle . . . is the supremacy of the law or custom of the community over all its members from the humblest free man to the King." A. J. and R. W. Carlyle, *A History of Medieval Political Theory in the West* (London, 1903–36), vol. 3, p. 11. This is the finest of all general studies of medieval social thought.

12. C. H. McIlwain, *The High Court of Parliament* (New Haven, 1910) is the classic study of this momentous fact.

13. Op. cit. vol. 1, p. 301–2.

14. Eli Hecksher, in his study of mercantilism, has pointed out how much more resistant to monarchical centralization the particularism of the Middle Ages was than the oft-cited universalism.

15. A. J. and R. W. Carlyle, op. cit. vol. 3, p. 74.

16. *The History of Freedom and Other Essays* (London, 1909), p. 151.

17. *Fundamental Principles of the Sociology of Law,* translated by W. L. Moll (Cambridge, 1936), p. 235.

18. *Collected Papers* (Cambridge University Press, 1911), vol. 3, p. 309.

19. On this, see Herbert A. Smith, *The Law of Associations* (Oxford, 1914), especially Appendix 1.

20. *The Greek Commonwealth* (Oxford, 1911), p. 76.

21. For an excellent account of this aspect of Cleisthenean legislation, see Gustave Glotz, *The Greek City,* translated by N. Mallinson (New York, 1930), p. 106f.

22. The solution to the problem that is offered by Plato is unmistakably totalitarian in design. But the efforts of Karl Popper, in his *The Open Society and Its Enemies,* volume 1, to support this indictment by dubious ascription of base motives and by labeling Plato a "reactionary" seem to me highly questionable. As I shall argue in chapter 8, there can be a totalitarianism of virtue as well as vice. Popper's whole approach is based upon the modern liberal's seemingly ineradicable suspicion that all authoritarianism is simply a reversion to the past.

23. *Greek Political Theory* (London, 1918), p. 234. See also the fine discussion along these lines by John Linton Myres, *The Political Ideas of the Greeks* (New York, 1927), p. 108f. Both Barker and Myres show a far more perceptive insight into Plato's totalitarianism than Popper does.

24. *The Social and Economic History of the Roman Empire* (Oxford, 1926), p. 41.

25. J. Declareuil, *Rome the Lawgiver,* translated by E. H. Parker (New York, 1926), p. 314.

26. *Historical Introduction to the Private Law of Rome* (London, 1916), p. 387, 390.

27. J. Ernest Renan, *Histoire des Origines du Christianisme,* cited by Alfred Zimmern, op. cit. p. 146.

28. *Decline and Fall of the Roman Empire,* Modern Library edition (New York, 1932), vol. 1, p. 451.

29. See the eloquent passage along this line by Krishnalal Shridharani, *My India, My America* (New York, 1941), p. 131.

Chapter Six

1. The bulk of this chapter is taken up with the political writings of Bodin, Hobbes, and Rousseau—specifically with respect to their ideas on the role of intermediate social groups. It is well, at this point, to express my great indebtedness for relevant insights on these matters to such students of political thought as Otto von Gierke, especially as translated and made available through the brilliant interpretative comments of F. W. Maitland and Ernest Barker; and also to the historical writings of J. N. Figgis, G. H. Sabine, C. E. Vaughan, and the early work of Harold Laski. There are others, but the studies of these historians have done the most, I believe, to bring to my attention the matters discussed in this chapter.

2. All quotations are from Bodin's *Six Books of a Commonweals,* translated by Richard Knolles (London, 1606).

3. All quotations are from the Oxford edition of Hobbes's *Leviathan* (Oxford, 1909), a reprint of the first folio edition of 1651.

4. This section on Rousseau is a slightly revised version of an article I wrote in 1943: "Rousseau and Totalitarianism," *Journal of Politics* (May 1943). Quotations are mainly from the Everyman edition of Rousseau's political writings edited by G. D. H. Cole. This contains not only the *Social Contract* but also the three *Discourses,* a reading of which is so basic to an understand-

ing of the *Social Contract.* The quotation from C. E. Vaughan is taken from his penetrating essay on Rousseau, which forms the Preface to his edition of *Du Contrat Social* (Manchester, 1918). Of all English interpreters of Rousseau, Professor Vaughan is, I believe, the most clarifying and convincing. See also his two-volume edition of the *Political Writings of Jean J. Rousseau* (Cambridge University Press, 1915) with its valuable comments.

Chapter Seven

1. Quoted by C. E. Vaughan in his Preface to his edition of *Du Contrat Social* (Manchester, 1918).

2. Cited by C. J. H. Hayes, *Historical Evolution of Modern Nationalism* (New York, 1931), p. 68.

3. On this aspect of the Revolution, the destruction or weakening of intermediate associations, I am indebted chiefly to the following works: Etienne Martin Saint-Leon, *Histoire des corporations de métiers* (Paris, 1898), Philippe Sagnac, *La Législation civile de la Révolution francaise* (Paris, 1898), and Marcel Rouquet, *Evolution du droit de famille vers l'individualisme* (Paris, 1909). I have profited also from accounts of the Revolution in the writings of Geoffrey Bruun, Crane Brinton, Bertrand de Jouvenel, A. D. Lindsay, and C. J. H. Hayes.

4. See the discussion of this aspect of the Revolution in F. W. Maitland, *Collected Papers* (Cambridge University Press, 1911), vol. 3, p. 310f.

5. Cited by Bertrand de Jouvenel, *On Power,* translated by J. F. Huntington (New York, 1949), p. 258.

6. Cited by John Morley in his biography of Rousseau (London, 1915), vol. 2, p. 132.

7. Op. cit. vol. 2, p. 627.

8. *The Modern Democratic State* (London, 1943), vol. 1, p. 151.

9. Hans Kohn in his *Idea of Nationalism* (New York, 1944) has made emphatic this relation of nationalism to earlier forms of social unity. See his comments in the Introduction.

10. *Addresses to the German Nation,* translated by R. Jones and G. Turnbull (Chicago, 1922), p. 10, 11, and 190.

11. Culture and Anarchy, edited by J. Dover Wilson (Cambridge University Press, 1935), p. 76, 94, and 96. "We have not the notion," Arnold laments, "so familiar on the continent and to antiquity, of *the State*—the nation in its collective and corporate character, entrusted with stringent powers for the general advantage, and controlling individual wills in the name of an interest wider than that of individuals."

12. Karl Polanyi, *The Great Transformation* (New York, 1944), p. 139ff.

13. See the discussion by W. A. Phillips in *Great Events in History,* edited by G. S. Taylor (London, 1934).

14. In his *Discourse on Political Economy,* Rousseau writes: "But how, I shall be asked, can the General Will be known in cases in which it has not expressed itself? Must the whole nation be assembled together at every unforeseen event? Certainly not. It ought the less to be assembled, because it is by no means certain that its decision would be the General Will; besides, the method would be impracticable in a great people, and is hardly ever necessary where the government is well-intentioned: for the rulers well know that the General Will is always on the side which is the most favorable to the public interest, that is to say, most equitable; so that it is needful only to act justly, to be certain of following the General Will." In his *Social Contract* Rousseau qualifies this manner of interpreting the General Will, but the revolutionary significance of the passage above to apostles of the political community in the nineteenth century need not be elaborated.

15. *Political Parties,* translated by Eden and Cedar Paul (reprinted by the Free Press, 1949), p. 218–19.

16. The dependence of my treatment of Bentham upon Halévy's *The Growth of Philosophical Radicalism* will be apparent to all who have read that great work. In addition I must express my appreciation to the anonymous writer in the *Times Literary Supplement* (21 February 1948) for his keen analysis of Bentham.

17. Ostrogorski has discussed the significance of these changes in a most illuminating manner; op. cit. vol. 1, p. 50ff.

18. This section on Marx owes much to A. D. Lindsay's essay, *Karl Marx's Capital* (Oxford University Press, 1925), to the recent work by Martin Buber, *Paths in Utopia* (London, 1949), and to some of the writings of the nineteenth-century anarchists.

Chapter Eight

1. *Democracy in America,* Reeve translation edited by Phillips Bradley (New York, 1945), vol. 2, p. 318–19.

2. *The Origins of Totalitarianism* (New York, 1951), p. 301. This is by all odds the most penetrating study of the nature of the totalitarian State even if its account of the historical origins of totalitarianism is debatable. It owes much of course to the earlier works of Peter Drucker, Herman Rauschning, and especially Emil Lederer.

3. Op. cit. p. 305.

4. *The End of Economic Man* (New York, 1939), p. 67.

5. On the Stalinist creation of the masses in Russia, see Arendt, op. cit. p. 312f.

6. The most preposterous of all interpretations of German Nazism current in the nineteen-thirties was that which took Nazi propaganda at its word and declared Nazism to be simply a recrudescence of German familism.

Chapter Nine

1. Christopher Dawson, *Religion and Culture,* Gifford Lectures for 1947 (London, 1948), p. 217.

2. Robert Sherwood, in his masterful study of Roosevelt and Hopkins, makes this emendation of Acton's aphorism. It is an important one. Over and over in history we have exemplified, it seems to me, the principle that the men who inherit, or easily gain, their power are less likely to intensify it at the expense of society than those men who have struggled for it in the service of a burning ideal.

3. *Symbolism, Its Meaning and Effect* (New York, 1927), p. 73.

4. *Philosophy in a New Key, A Study in the Symbolism of Reason, Rite, and Art,* Penguin edition (London and New York, 1948), p. 235, 237–8.

Chapter Ten

1. *Idealism and the Modern Age* (New Haven, 1919), p. 35.

2. *Human Society* (New York, 1949), p. 53.

3. *Journal of Social Issues*, vol. 1 (1945), p. 55.

4. See Elton Mayo, *The Human Problems of an Industrial Civilization* (New York, 1933), and George Homans, *The Human Group* (New York, 1950).

5. Evidences of this were repeatedly brought to my attention while I was engaged in personnel work with combat soldiers in the Pacific during the Second World War.

6. *Individualism Old and New* (New York, 1930), p. 81–2.

7. *Road to Xanadu* (Boston, 1930), p. 428–30.

8. John Dewey has made this point illuminatingly in his *Art as Experience* (New York, 1934). See the discussion beginning on p. 326.

9. Writers as philosophically far apart as Bertrand Russell and T. S. Eliot have emphasized the close relation between individual creative achievement and the small community. See Russell's *Authority and the Individual* (London, 1949) and Eliot's *Notes Toward the Definition of Culture* (New York, 1949).

10. This point has been stressed recently by Wilhelm Röpke in his *The Social Crisis of Our Time* (University of Chicago Press, 1950).

11. Op. cit. p. 162.

12. Ibid. p. 142.

13. Such historians as Kenneth Scott Latourette, Edwyn Bevan, and Gilbert Murray have stressed the immense appeal that lay in early Christianity's organization in small, compact, social communities. For the Roman masses Christianity offered not merely heavenly redemption but social identity and protection in this world.

14. "The Impact of Protestantism Today" in the *Atlantic Monthly* (February 1948).

15. Walter Lippmann has written brilliantly on this point. "When Luther, for example, rebelled against the authority of the Church, he did not suppose the way of life for the ordinary man would be radically altered. Luther supposed that men would continue to behave much as they had learned to behave under the Catholic discipline. The individual for whom he claimed the right of private judgment was one whose prejudgments had been well fixed in a Catholic society. . . . For what he believed in was Protestantism for good Catholics." *Preface to Morals* (New York, 1929), p. 14.

Chapter Eleven

1. "Institutional Vulnerability in Mass Society," *The American Journal of Sociology* (January 1951).

2. "Leviathan and Little Groups," *The Aryan Path* (October 1941).

3. *Churches in the Modern State* (London, 1913), p. 51–2.

4. Op. cit. vol. 2, p. 319–20.

5. Op. cit. vol. 2, p. 300–301.

6. *Paths in Utopia* (London, 1949).

7. Works that have stressed the crucial role of associative pluralism and diversification of social power in the structure of liberal democracy are, unhappily, not numerous. It is a pleasure however to mention the writings of such men as Ernest Barker, A. D. Lindsay, John Dewey, R. M. MacIver, Lewis Mumford, Sidney Hook, and Frank Tannenbaum.

8. It is unfortunate that no single, systematic historical study of inter-mediate associations exists. The nearest approximation is the massive study done by Otto von Gierke three-quarters of a century ago in Germany, but, except for the fragments translated by F. W. Maitland and Ernest Barker, this work is virtually inaccessible and, in any event, it was written from a point of view that killed much of the work's substance.

9. Op. cit. p. 59.

10. "The Balance of Power in Society," loc. cit. p. 501. Italics mine.

11. *T.V.A.: Democracy on the March* (New York, 1944), p. 139.

12. Op. cit. p. 98.

13. *Man and Society in an Age of Reconstruction* (New York, 1940), p. 319.

14. The Culture of Cities (New York, 1938), p. 475–6.

15. J. N. Figgis, op. cit. p. 70.

16. Op. cit. *passim.*

INDEX

THE QUEST FOR COMMUNITY

INDEX

A NOTE ON THE BOOK

This book was designed by David Peattie of ICS Press using Ventura Publisher software on a Mitsubishi MP386 personal computer. The type is Adobe Garamond designed by Robert Slimbach and based on the original type design by Claude Garamond and the italics of Robert Granjon. Pinnacle Type of San Francisco provided linotronic camera-ready copy, and R. R. Donnelley & Sons printed and bound the book in Harrisonburg, Virginia.